The

STRESSED

YEARS *of*

THEIR LIVES

The

STRESSED

YEARS *of*

THEIR LIVES

Helping Your Kid
Survive and Thrive
During Their College Years

B. JANET HIBBS, Ph.D., M.F.T. &
ANTHONY ROSTAIN, M.D., M.A.

St. Martin's Press ⚏ New York

Note: With the exception of "Jensen" and his family, all of
the individuals discussed reflect composites designed to illustrate
a variety of experiences, problems, and solutions in which no real
names are used, and identifying details have been changed for
both those discussed and their treating providers. In the case of
Jensen, all names have been changed.

www.stmartins.com

Library of Congress Cataloging-in-Publication Data

Names: Hibbs, B. Janet, author. | Rostain, Anthony L., author.
Title: The stressed years of their lives : helping your kid survive and
    thrive during their college years / B. Janet Hibbs, Ph.D., and Anthony
    Rostain, M.D.
Description: First edition. | New York : St. Martin's Press, 2019. |
    Includes bibliographical references and index.
Identifiers: LCCN 2018041166 | ISBN 9781250113139 (hardcover) |
    ISBN 9781250113160 (ebook)
Subjects: LCSH: College students—Mental health. | College students—
    Psychology. | Education, Higher—Parent participation.
Classification: LCC RC451.4.S7 H53 2019 | DDC 616.8900835—dc23
LC record available at https://lccn.loc.gov/2018041166

Our books may be purchased in bulk for promotional,
educational, or business use. Please contact your local bookseller
or the Macmillan Corporate and Premium Sales Department at
1-800-221-7945, extension 5442, or by email at
MacmillanSpecialMarkets@macmillan.com.

First Edition: April 2019

10 9 8 7 6 5 4 3 2 1

In memory of my mother, Jeannette J. Hibbs, who embodied hope, advocacy, and perseverance.

And in honor of my caring and courageous sons, Jared and William, who taught me what I didn't know and who I needed to become.

—B. HIBBS

I dedicate this book to the memory of my mother, Gita Alfandary, whose love of life and whose generosity of spirit were a continuous source of inspiration to me. And with deep appreciation to my life partner, Michele, and to my children, Isabelle, Julian, Sam, and Genevieve, who've taught me the meaning of family.

—A. ROSTAIN

Contents

Acknowledgments   ix

PART ONE
✖

OF STRESS *and* RESILIENCE

1. Fault Lines in the World of Today's Youth   3

2. Before You Go: Social-Emotional PREP   31

3. Welcome to Campus: Overcoming Mindset
    Barriers to Success   52

4. What to Expect When Johnny's Got Issues   72

5. How to Plan—and How to Follow Through   103

PART TWO
✖

OF CRISIS *and* RECOVERY

6. Risky Business: The Adolescent Brain   119

7. Anxiety and Depression   149

8. Crisis Care   178

9. Adjusting to the Boomerang Kid   208

10. From Recovery to Relaunch   233

11. Recasting the Safety Net   262

Appendix   285

Notes   297

Index   315

Acknowledgments

This book had many lives. Its first incarnation, as a memoir, brought author Libby Mosier, B.'s Bryn Mawr alum and soon friend, into the project. Libby's insightful guidance was deeply encouraging. Next, award-winning journalist and author, Brigid Schulte, generously and enthusiastically recommended her discerning agent, Gail Ross. Gail immediately "got the book," and envisioned and wisely guided its conceptual evolution, offering many important ideas to strengthen its relevance to future readers. Gail's talented team of Anna Sproul-Latimer and Dara Kaye presented keen comments in the proposal stage. Later, Gail introduced us to fellow writer Allan Fallow, intelligent, earnest, and charming in equal measure, who expertly converted many a phrase, sentence, and paragraph from academic to lay speak. Gwenn Hibbs, B.'s sister, was an invaluable and reliable research assistant, critical reader, and copy editor throughout the entire writing process.

The book found a welcome home at St. Martin's Press. We are enormously grateful to executive editor Jennifer Weis, whose unwavering belief in the book buoyed us over the duration of our journey as co-authors. Ms. Weiss' incisive, wise, and candid refinements were joined in their excellence by editor Sylvan Creekmore, who shepherded us through crucial and thoughtful revisions. Sylvan was also a fantastic heart line of the St. Martins' team, graciously responding to our many questions and requests. We also extend our thanks to other members of the remarkable team at St. Martin's, including Sallie Lotz, Laura Clark, Brant Janeway, Eric C. Meyer, Scottie Bowditch, Chloe Volkwein, and Karen Masnica. David Rotstein artfully created the book jacket, which perfectly captured the zeitgeist of the college years.

We are also especially grateful to those colleagues who heard about the idea for this project and strongly encouraged us to pursue it. Dr. Victor Schwartz, chief medical officer of the Jed Foundation, and Alison Malmon, founder and director of Active Minds, were very enthusiastic about the direct approach we were taking to educate parents and families of college students with mental health issues. They generously offered honest feedback about our vision and our message, and they provided important technical resources from which we have extensively borrowed. Steve Pilch, head of the Shipley School; Maureen Rush, vice president for public securty at Penn; Bill Alexander, former director of Penn's counseling and psychological services; and Eric Furda, dean of admissions at Penn, were reliable sources of great insights into the realities of the college experience and were kind enough to be interviewed and quoted for the book.

A special thanks to the students, parents, principals, and post-secondary educators whose experiences and interviews personally illuminate the disparate stressors and needed resilience of the college years. To SLA principal Chris Lehmann, whose visionary leadership inspires many deserving youth; to the students and parents at SPEAKUP! whose founder, Martie Gillin, and president, Martie Bernicker, have done so much to teach parents and youth to speak openly and listen with acceptance. Martie Gillin's enthusiastic conviction in the book's mission included an introduction to national mental health advocate Patrick J. Kennedy, who gave a key endorsement of the book. Dr. Glenda Wrenn, director of the Kennedy Center for Mental Health Policy and Research, contributed an important and timely read and recommendation of the book. Lisa Joy Tuttle assisted with thoughtful suggestions during the final editing.

Jessica and Joanna Berwind welcomed the book's emphasis on social emotional learning, which dovetailed with their foundation's mission of youth development. They provided a warm embrace to launch the book's ideas and reception. Many thanks to the dedicated, enthusiastic members of the Berwind team. Catherine Murphy offered unconditional support for the shared hopes and vision of this book. Her colleagues, Simran Sidhu, Laura McHugh, and Sydney Battle, graciously hosted us at the hive at Spring Point Partners and fostered rich dialogues about the challenges of transitioning to college.

We especially want to thank our patients and families over the years, from whom we have learned so much and without whom this entire body of work would not have been possible.

A final note of thanks from each of the authors.

My deepest appreciation goes to B. Hibbs, who entrusted me with

Jared's care and who participated fully in the family sessions we held to foster his recovery. B.'s devotion to her sons is inspiring, as is her dedication to the project of getting Jared's story into print. I am forever grateful for her unflagging pursuit of this goal and for her warm and generous invitation to join her in this writing project. In more ways than one, she has been the moving force bringing *The Stressed Years of Their Lives* to fruition. It's been a wonderful journey of co-creation.

Among my colleagues in the Department of Psychiatry at the University of Pennsylvania Perelman School of Medicine, I'm especially grateful to Dr. J. Russell Ramsay, my partner for almost twenty years in the adult ADHD treatment and research program. Our collaboration has been a constant source of energy, creativity, discovery, fulfillment, and fun. I also am thankful for the mentorship and friendship of Dr. Aaron Beck, who has always been a role model and a genuine tutor—not unlike the role Merlin played for young King Arthur. Last but not least, I want to thank Dr. Richard F. Summers for his steadfast encouragement and sage advice as I embarked on this writing project during the time we served together as co-directors of psychiatry training for the department.

I gained a tremendous amount of knowledge and insight about the systems aspects of college mental health from my role as co-chair of the president's and provost's task force on student psychological health and welfare. I thank President Amy Gutmann and then-Provost Vincent Price for their faith in my leadership and Professor Rebecca Bushnell for her wisdom and savvy guidance as co-chair. Vice Chair Joann Mitchell; the task force members Jody Foster, Eric Furda, Charles Howard, Valerie Swain-Cade McCoullum, Maureen Rush, Wendy White, and Beth Winkelstein; and staffers Rob Nelson and Leah Popowich were invaluable contributors to our work, as was William Alexander, head of counseling and psychological services, and Myrna Cohen, director of the Weingarten Learning Center. I owe each of them a debt of thanks for helping me to learn about how college administrators understand and deal with the mental health challenges of college students on a daily basis.

I want to recognize and profoundly thank Dr. Eugene Beresin, Dr. John Sargent, and Dr. Adrian Sondheimer, all remarkable child and adolescent psychiatrists, for their constant friendship and support over my entire professional career and for their invaluable insights into the thorny clinical issues facing college students and their families.

I also want to thank Drs. Adele Martel, Vivien Chen, and Jennifer Derren for welcoming me on to the TAY/College Mental Health Committee of the American Academy of Child and Adolescent Psychiatry, which has become an important focus of my academic work in recent years.

Going back to my undergraduate years, I'm most grateful to Dr. Seymour Lustman, the late master of Davenport College at Yale, who saw me at my worst and offered me a life preserver with which to swim out of the turbulent waters in which I was drowning. I'm also thankful to the late dean Horace Taft for helping me to return to school when I was ready to resume my studies.

Last but not least, I'm forever grateful for the love, friendship, and unquestioning acceptance of my amazing wife and partner, Michele Goldfarb. We re-met twenty-one years ago on a task force at the University of Pennsylvania investigating alcohol and other substance abuse on campus. From then on, we have been constant companions on life's winding path. I am truly fortunate to have had her steady support and warm encouragement during the long process of turning the ideas behind this book into a reality.

—Anthony Rostain,
June 12, 2018

For many reasons, I am deeply indebted to my co-author, Tony Rostain, whose remarkable professional accomplishments are, if possible, exceeded by his warmth and his lively and caring spirit. Thank you, Tony, for "being there" both professionally and personally. You are irreplaceable. It has been a true privilege to share the experience of writing this book with you.

In my stressed years, and long before they assumed printed form, my late mother, Jeannette J. Hibbs, remained ever hopeful and gave the great comfort of unwavering support. My mother-in-law, Ruth, whose memory is enduring, and Papa Earl were wonderfully loving and ever-present grandparents. In addition to her exceptional insights as primary reader, which threatened to become a lifetime job, my sister Gwenn was a remarkable wellspring of medical and mental health resources for the family. Far-flung siblings Kelcie, Kendall, and Gayle, offered ongoing, loving support.

Heartfelt thanks to loyal friends and family therapists Jane Buhl and Susan and Tony LaDuca, who lived and breathed these times. Their compassion and good company were always a balm. Heaps of gratitude to my dear college-era friends, Claire and Michael Robinson, whose decades'-long friendship has endured across time and space. They hosted me in New York for publishing meetings and generously participated in interviews. Over two rainy spring days, Michael expertly and graciously persevered to capture the perfect author's photo. More thanks to my longtime colleagues Drs. Arlene Houldin, Steve Levick, Suzanne Brennan, Andrea Bloomgarden, Debi Ettinger, Peter Doris, and Jessica DeGroot, who patiently accepted my years of book excuses. Each of these family, friends, and colleagues cared deeply, commiserated when needed, and celebrated each milestone of child, adult, and book alike. Thank you—you were indispensable.

To my architect, my dearest husband Earl, who created a room with a view for my writing, and supported me in myriad ways. Earl was top chef and lovingly prepared many delicious meals for the family. At the end of his tiring day, he imaginatively assumed many tasks, unasked, so that I could resume my solitary immersion. He indulged my fretting and expounding; then, finally, celebrated the metamorphosis from idea to book. For your generosity of spirit, devoted kindness, and whole-hearted blessings, I treasure you and am eternally thankful.

I am grateful beyond words to my best teachers, my sons, Jared and William, who have deepened my humility and humanity and allowed me to share experiences of their college years to benefit other students and families. You are my heroes.

—B. Hibbs,
June 12, 2018

PART ONE

———✖———

OF STRESS
and RESILIENCE

1

Fault Lines in the
World of Today's Youth

*Academic intelligence offers virtually no preparation for
the turmoil—or opportunity—life's vicissitudes bring.*
—DANIEL GOLEMAN, *EMOTIONAL INTELLIGENCE*

Carson was the salutatorian of his large public high school, earning the school's English award and a partial merit scholarship to a top-rated college. He felt proud and enormously relieved. His hard work had paid off. Without that scholarship, the commuter branch of the state university would have been his destination. And his parents had generously offered to help repay his student loans from the prestigious institution that had accepted him.

Their hopes, his dreams, mocked him as he sat in Freshman English, staring at his paper, marked with a large red "D". The class hour passed in a blur, and Carson next found himself on the eighth floor of the University Library overlooking the Great Hall below. He observed himself, contemplating what he would hit if he jumped. The glassed-in archive displays? The long polished table profiling the many recent faculty publications? A fellow student wafted through his thoughts. A girl in his French class had committed suicide only a month into the semester. She'd had a wonderfully droll sense of humor. Carson hadn't understood why she'd killed herself. It seemed she had everything going for her. So sad, so strange. But now, panicked and believing his scholarship jeopardized, his future ruined, he grasped her desperation.

A wave of vertigo forced him back from the library's overhang. He sat down and numbly hit the speed dial for the college hotline. Another student answered and kept Carson on the phone long enough for him to calm down and agree to go to the walk-in campus counseling service. And so, Carson resisted his terrible and momentary impulse. Very fortunately for him, his crisis of confidence was not superimposed upon major depression or bipolar disease. His momentary panic eventually led to therapy, which promoted a greater resilience and better ability to tolerate setbacks and distress.

In addition to vertigo and the absence of mental illness, the serendipity of many emotional skills came to Carson's aid that afternoon. A strong connection to his family and friends and a willingness to seek help also enabled him to step back from the balcony and make that call. His family environment had fostered the noncognitive skills that empowered him to ask for help when needed. His parents consistently praised his effort more than the outcome; they quietly noticed and supported his interests. When Carson made mistakes, they joked, "pobody's nerfect." His family talked through problems but didn't solve them for him. His emotional preparation broke through his fleeting despair. As his thinking cleared, he recalled how he had coped with another D—on a high school calculus test. At first he had freaked out—"my high school ranking will drop"—then he told his parents, who encouraged him to talk with the teacher. It was this emotional resilience and preparation for adversity that saved him when his academics failed him. Whether coming early or late to these skills, we firmly believe that all students can learn them.

Yet the sad truth is that many students are not so fortunate or so well-prepared when caught in the epidemic of college-age mental health problems. The current and incoming generations of college students need to be better equipped with the maturity boost that social-emotional intelligence provides. Being better prepared for the roller coaster of college life will reduce the chances of their coming off the rails.

And what about the parents on the other side of these frightening experiences? Instead of the nostalgic truism that college will be "the best years of your life," we hear from countless parents concerned about how their children's lives are falling apart. Despite all they've done to educate and support their talented child, they see signs of wobbling begin to appear in the form of poor coping, anxiety, depression, or emotional upheaval.

As two well-established experts on late adolescent psychiatry and family psychology, we've coached families through such times, giving parents tools to help their once-confident students preserve or regain their ability to organize time, work, and even the basics of sleeping and eating. Yet, many students are unprepared for the removal of home's invisibly embedded emotional and cognitive scaffolding.

In his role as Professor of Psychiatry and Pediatrics at the University of Pennsylvania Perelman School of Medicine and co-chair of the President's and Provost's Task Force on Student Psychological Health and Well Being, Dr. Rostain has closely watched the dramatic rise in campus mental-illness rates with deep concern. Colleges and universities across the country are reporting an explosion of mental health problems verging on an epidemic, with a skyrocketing number of students seeking help. Rostain is very familiar with the risks, challenges, and complex systems issues facing young people, and has made it his mission to find solutions for these students and parents alike. As a family psychologist, faculty member, and clinical supervisor, Dr. Hibbs has had decades of experience helping parents and students cope in challenging and crisis-laden times.

As parents ourselves, we know all too intimately the gnawing anxiety that can be fed by pervasive media coverage of such campus hazards as hazing, binge drinking, drug use, and sexual assault, as well as the quieter desperations of "not fitting in" or feeling that you're "not making it." When these all-too-common risks give rise to emotional disorders or psychiatric illnesses, students and parents alike can be overwhelmed.

That was Dr. Hibbs's experience when her son Jensen suffered a depression that required a medical leave from college. Despite her professional expertise, Jensen's harrowing crisis left Hibbs humbled and scrambling for answers, while more deeply informing her of the preparation, knowledge, and skills that parents and students need. Following Jensen's treatment by Dr. Rostain—and his subsequent recovery—we resolved to coauthor *The Stressed Years of Their Lives,* a book that provides solutions, strategies, and solidarity for parents who want to help their students avoid, resolve, or recover from a mental health problem or crisis. It is also a book to give hope and support to students, through the stories of their peers. We thank Jensen, as well as the many students, parents, and educators who so generously lent their stories to this book.[1]

However rapid the recent and ongoing shifts in our culture, we're optimistic that today's parents have better tools at their disposal than ever before to build a sturdy and enduring emotional scaffold for their children. To help you assess its stability, we'll show you how to strengthen some key skills—namely resilience, executive functioning, and healthy habits of independent living—that can reinforce a young person's ability to cope with the coming challenges. Though individual lives are complicated, we are convinced that both parents and students alike can benefit through the thoughtful discussions, skills, and lessons described in this book. We hope that our experiences and insights will help many generations to come.

When the Best Are Stressed

Beyond panic and resilience, Carson's story acquaints us with a generational truth. Like Carson, everyone will experience a crushing disappointment at some point in time, yet in the college of a generation past, a single bad grade didn't portend doom. Nor was life success so inextricably linked with a linear trajectory from high school through the perfect college and on to a high-paying career, without allowing for a single stumble.

Increasingly, however, it can often seem as if this is the case. Contemplating adulthood, today's youth confront a gloomy forecast of increased competition and narrowing possibilities. "The college degree is becoming the new high school diploma," *The New York Times* recently intoned, "the new minimum requirement, albeit an expensive one, for getting even the lowest-level job."[2]

Given the pressure to succeed, it's no wonder that today's adolescents vie with adults for the dubious title of "America's Most Stressed."[3] The younger group may even be pulling ahead: According to a recent survey by the American Psychological Association, teens experience higher stress than adults, even in summer. That pressure, the APA survey revealed, leaves a third of teens feeling overwhelmed, depressed, and fatigued.[4] Nor does it show any sign of letting up soon: 34 percent of the teen survey respondents expected their stress levels to rise even higher in the year ahead.[5]

And how are both groups handling the pressure? Not well: neither the teens nor the adults reported doing enough to manage their stress. Most were indulging in unhealthy behaviors: skipping meals or "stress eating" and getting nowhere near enough exercise or sleep.[6] By college, stress combusts with mental health diagnoses and an increased risk of self-harm.

Parents sound confused and alarmed: *What's the deal with kids' stress levels today? And how long does it take for a kid to grow up?* We often hear parents voice variations of a standard lament: "We're at our wits' end. We've struggled to give him every chance to succeed—more than we had at his age, certainly—so what's gone wrong?"

Beginning with the Millennials and continuing in Generation Z (also known as iGen),[7] students experience the very real burdens of constant striving on behalf of uncertain futures, amidst swiftly changing political and economic landscapes. They're also stressed by the 24/7 availability of the Internet, by social media pressures, and by the resulting metrics of constant comparisons, whether social or academic. GPAs, the dream college, scholarships, prestigious summer internships, and later, starting salaries, are all insubstantial proxies for meaning and purpose, as one MIT professor observed.[8] Today's pressures can overwhelm brains already struggling with developmental tasks and insecurities, among them: forming an identity, developing friendships, exploring romantic relationships, and germinating the seeds of a career.

Parents are stressed too. The parental urge to protect their young can result in over-parenting, which paradoxically hinders the emotional skills needed for a successful launch. These multiple forces often come to a head in the crucible of college life and immediately thereafter, when many stress-induced emotional problems first appear. These two phenomena—college stressors and the emergence of mental health problems—feed into one another in a closed loop, increasing the pressure of both.

Let's crunch the numbers on college mental health, then take a look at the uniquely stressful climate in which young people are coming of age today. With this understanding, we'll see how parents can teach—and students can learn—what's truly necessary to thrive in college and beyond.

Crunching the Numbers

In recent years there has been no shortage of reports about students' stress responses to the academic pressure cooker of college, with antidepressant use, mental health problems, and prescription-medication misuse all on the rise. "Rates of anxiety and depression have soared in the last decade," notes *The Chronicle of Higher Education.*[9] The rise in the rate of college students seeking counseling is five times higher than the average rate of enrollment growth.

According to the American College Health Association's recent annual survey, 1 in 4 college students was either diagnosed or treated for anxiety in the prior year.[10] This is approximately the same number as those reporting that a cold or flu hurt their academics in the prior 12 months.[11] Untold millions went undiagnosed and untreated. Another large student survey reveals a glimpse of the magnitude of the campus problem: *more than half* reported the experience of overwhelming anxiety during the prior school year, while *about a third* reported that depression had significantly affected their academic performance.[12] The numbers only go up from there, with even more feeling "hopeless" and "overwhelmed." Yet only about one-fourth of the affected students received counseling for these conditions,[13] and many of those in counseling often dropped out of treatment prematurely.[14]

The following lists summarize this alarming trend:

Mental Health–Related College Problems[15]
- Anxiety is the most common student mental health problem.
- Almost one-third of all college students report having felt so depressed that they had trouble functioning in the last twelve months.
- Mental health issues in the college student population, such as depression, anxiety, and eating disorders, are associated with lower GPA and higher probability of dropping out of college.
- More than 80 percent of college students felt overwhelmed by all they had to do in the past year, and 45 percent have felt things were hopeless.
- Minority students are less likely to seek treatment.

Mental Health Issues Can Be Deadly
- Suicide is the second leading cause of death among college students, claiming the lives of 1,100 students each year.
- 67 percent of college students tell a friend they are feeling suicidal before telling anyone else.
- More than half of college students have had suicidal thoughts and 1 in 10 students seriously consider attempting suicide. Half of the students who have suicidal thoughts never seek counseling or treatment.
- 80 to 90 percent of college students who die by suicide were not receiving help from their college counseling centers.

Why are these numbers so high? A key contributor is the fact that most psychiatric disorders show up from ages 14 to 26[16]—possibly the most tumultuous decade in a person's life. The academic and social demands of college can readily magnify emotional and learning problems that were mild enough to be overlooked or successfully handled in childhood or later dismissed as just a "passing teenage phase."

Certain disorders typically emerge right before and during the college years. Eating disorders reach their peak among young women, while binge drinking and substance abuse hit their crest among young men. Also common to many are anxiety, depression, and what psychologists call "problems of executive functioning"—that is, the capacity for unsupervised self-management that underlies good judgment, organization, and self-control. Combine the psychological and social vulnerabilities of college-age kids with the heightened stress of leaving home and learning to swim in an academic shark tank, and it's easy to see why the core symptoms of so many mental health disorders appear at this vulnerable time in their lives.

Emelia's story puts a face on these statistics. The distress call came from Mrs. Carr, who left an urgent message on Dr. Rostain's voicemail. Uncharacteristically, Emelia hadn't answered her mother's phone calls or texts for almost twenty-four hours.

When Dr. Rostain reached Mrs. Carr, she was less panicked but still very concerned. She had just spoken to Emelia and learned that her roommate had moved out of their dorm room. Emelia sounded annoyed with her mother for "checking up" on her, but insisted that she was "basically fine."

Two weeks later, the college called Mrs. Carr and told her to pick up Emelia and bring her home. She was failing every class and wouldn't be able to salvage the semester.

Emelia's college experience is common to many unsuccessful launches: she lacked the necessary executive functioning skills to independently organize the many academic, social, and emotional demands of being away from home. Until college, Emelia had never done a trial run of managing independently, even if that meant missing assignments or failing a subject. Mrs. Carr had helped her daughter to succeed at all costs; the stakes seemed too high to let her flounder. Once at college, Emelia was too embarrassed, ashamed, anxious, and overwhelmed to ask for help. We'll return to the dilemma many parents share: When is help unhelpful? Where is the fine line between parenting and over-parenting? But what Mrs. Carr first wanted to know was: What were colleges doing to help? She was furious with Emelia's school for not alerting her "until it was too late to do anything about it."

The Stressed Years:
What Are Colleges Doing?

Beginning in the late 1990s, colleges observed a sudden rise in student mental health problems. By the early 2000s, mental health task forces were springing up on campuses across the country. Colleges were pressed to furnish additional services—including academic support and psychological counseling—that many of them were not prepared to provide. Over the past six years, there has been a 30 percent national increase in the number of students seeking counseling on campus.[17] By some estimates, approximately one-half of current college students will seek mental health services at least once during their college career. "I don't know if [this trend is] related to the way we parent," says Marvin Krislov, formerly president of Oberlin college, now president of Pace University. "I don't know if it's related to the media or the pervasive role of technology. What I can tell you is that every campus I know is investing more resources in mental health."[18] In response to the startling rise in students seeking help, colleges have beefed up their support. The good news: the rise reflects a few positive trends:

1. Admissions policies have widened to include talented young people who might have been denied a college education in an earlier era. Among them, students of lower income, first-generation students, and youth with preexisting psychiatric conditions, as well as those needing accommodations for social, emotional, and learning challenges.
2. Awareness of campus mental health needs and services is rising.
3. The stigma of mental illness is receding.

Over the past decade, colleges have spent millions to augment counseling staff and to focus on suicide prevention, risk reduction, threat assessment, and the identification and treatment of troubled students. In addition to traditional, individual, and face-to-face therapy, colleges have expanded services to include telepsychology/telepsychiatry, group therapy, and mental health apps.

These trends have converged to trigger a welcoming campus outreach. Students are repeatedly advised of the wide range of student support and mental health services that can quickly come to their aid. Thanks largely to counseling-outreach efforts, more faculty members are referring students for treatment, and more students are seeking treatment of their own accord. Many colleges, especially those with a ratio of one full-time counselor to every 1,000 to 1,500 students, are on target to meet the accrediting standards recommended by the International Association of Counseling Services.

Yet challenges remain. Many counseling offices and mental health centers have been unprepared for this unprecedented demand for services. One-third of colleges have long waiting lists for therapy, and half of all college dropouts have never availed themselves of mental health services.[19] That was true for Emelia. She needed help, but never sought it. Nor did Emelia sign HIPAA and FERPA confidentiality waivers to allow the administration to alert Mrs. Carr. We'll return to this issue in depth in an upcoming chapter.

For all their efforts, schools can't staff their way out of the growing demand. Colleges are increasingly looking to parents to help prepare their students for the challenges ahead. Preparation relies first on an understanding of the component parts of "stress and distress," and next on what parents and students can do to promote the social-emotional maturity that true independence requires.

Mental Health and Stress

Although the word "stress" has become something of a throwaway term, the phenomenon itself has long been understood to be a potent precursor to mental health disorders. It's normal for individuals to respond to the potential threat or intense emotions of stress for short periods of time. Yet new findings from neuroscience and social science point to toxic long-term consequences of chronic stress. When the brain's "alert system" stays on too long, it creates anxious and maladaptive responses that contribute to psychiatric disorders.

Nowadays, mental health problems are as prevalent as the common cold. And, like a cold, an emotional problem or mental disorder can vary by severity and length. By young adulthood, almost everyone will experience an emotional upheaval.[20] At any one time, only about 20 percent of the population is experiencing a mental health disturbance, though it may be invisible to others. An episode for some will be so transient that the individual won't seek treatment. Similarly, parents may chalk up the "cold" symptom of moodiness to adolescent angst or miss the stealth flyover of an anxiety disorder or a bout of depression. When a depressive episode or anxiety disorder is unrecognized, we "let it pass," just as we do with a cold. Sometimes that's okay, but more often it isn't. Undiagnosed and untreated, a mental health problem may worsen into an illness episode that amplifies the effect of the next occurrence. For example, half of all individuals with alcohol use disorder at age 19 will still suffer from it by age 25.[21]

And, despite its prevalence—its utter ordinariness—a bout of such an emotional illness typically takes both students and parents by surprise.[22] The frequency of undiagnosed and undertreated mental illness helps explain why having a mental health problem is the number-one cause of college dropouts.

Unlike an indiscriminate cold, there's a gender split for just what kind of mental health problems will occur for young women and men and what the prevailing symptoms will be. Because brain networks operate differently, women may be more vulnerable to stress-related conditions.[23] The chart below summarizes some recent studies of such disorders in U.S. adolescents and young adults.

LIFETIME OCCURRENCE OF
STRESS-RELATED DISORDERS, BY SEX

Disorder	Female %	Male %
Panic	6.2	3.1
Generalized anxiety	7.1	4.2
Any anxiety disorder	36.4	25.4
PTSD	9.7	3.6
Major depression	20.2	13.2
Any affective disorder	24.4	17.5
Alcohol abuse	7.5	19.6
Drug abuse	4.8	11.6
Migraine	18.2	6.5
Insomnia	12.9	6.2
Irritable bowel syndrome	14.5	7.7

Source: D. A. Bangasser and R. J. Valentino, 2014[24]

Clinicians pinpoint many contributing stressors: economic worries, tuition inflation, the continuous self-metrics of academic and social comparisons, stiffer competition, even "helicopter" or over-parenting tendencies that prevent adolescents from learning from failure. But what has gone into creating this uniquely challenging time?

Some of This Isn't New

Fretting over "the wreck of American childhood," historian Steven Mintz reassures us, is habitual to periods of economic stress and rapid social change. Indeed, the parental influence on anxiety-driven change goes back to our country's earliest days.[25] The religious freedom sought by the Puritans in the New World was an outgrowth of their fretful moral imperative to save "posterity [who] would be in danger to degenerate and be corrupted" in the Old World.[26] In today's New World of social and economic disruptions, with the omnipresent Internet, social media pressures, and heightened global competition, anxious parents endeavor to "save" their children from screen time, the disappearance of secure jobs, or even an imagined robotic and jobless future.

Whether colonial or contemporary, parenting seesaws between protective control and the promotion of childhood independence. Autonomy and self-reliance in childhood and adolescence are embraced during periods of necessity—the American frontier, for example—but also in times of political and economic stability. In the post–World War II era in American family life, parents experienced decades of stable jobs, rising incomes, and more predictable family structures. In this relatively safe domestic era, children were allowed to exercise more freedom. By contrast, parental protection and increased control asserts itself most during epochs of great social change—incidentally, a characteristic of the past forty years.[27]

The 1980s unfurled four decades of precipitous social and economic change and resulted in a renewed panic over children's safety and well-being.[28] The free-range youth of Boomers and Gen-Xers has disappeared, first with milk carton warnings of child abductions, followed by the Columbine era of school shootings, the 9/11 attacks in 2001, and the global Great Recession of 2008. Parents reacted with heightened control and by adapting a more rigid definition of success that has exalted protection over childhood autonomy and self-reliance. Protection now includes arranged playdates, no peanut butter in school, and trigger warnings in classrooms. Successful parenting today means a "well-managed child," honed to a fine edge from an early age.

Mintz suggests that the recurrent worries about young people actually reflect the unmooring of *adult* lives and the concomitant stressors on parents. Viewed through the filter of history, parents may be reassured to learn that their periodic panics over the well-being of their children are commonplace. Let's face it: the troubled essence of growing up long predates the anxieties of American parents. "Youth are heated by nature," wrote Aristotle, "as drunken men by wine." Two millennia later, Shakespeare arranged for an unnamed shepherd to lament in *The Winter's Tale*, "I would there were no age between sixteen and three-and-twenty, or that youth would sleep out the rest."

More recently, parents influenced by time's nostalgic effect of selective amnesia may idealize their own college years as carefree and wonder why their children aren't experiencing a similarly halcyon time. Yet, the very nature of generational change, Mintz reminds us, is that parents can neither replicate their past nor predict the future. The future uncertain, the present unprecedented, leaves today's youth uniquely stressed.

But Some of It Is Unprecedented

> "I must be a soldier so my son can be a farmer and his son a poet."
>
> —JOHN ADAMS

That classically American parental aspiration—a better life for his children and successive generations—appeared in a 1780 letter to his wife, Abigail, from future U.S. president John Adams.[29] Today, parents with the same aspirations often behave as if their children still face only three choices: college, the military, or a minimum-wage job (i.e. failure).

When—and why—did this blinkered view occur?

In the post–World War II period, the path to a good life wasn't nearly so narrow. It neither mandated attendance at a brand-name college nor even required a college degree. The cultural narrative said it was okay to go to work after high school, then go to college if your job or aspirations warranted it. Not until the 1980s did the expectation of attending a four-year college become a national imperative.

The gradual shift to "College for All" began decades earlier, with the

1944 introduction of the G.I. Bill. The number of degrees awarded by U.S. colleges and universities more than doubled from 1940 to 1950, while the percentage of Americans with a bachelor's degree or higher rose from 4.6 percent in 1945 to 25 percent half a century later.[30] As more and more mid-century adults obtained college degrees, they transferred their aspirations for the same—or better—to their children.

The College for All movement was further propelled by the civil rights movement, with its emphasis on equal educational opportunity, and by the 1983 presidential report, "A Nation at Risk: The Imperative for Educational Reform,"[31] which sparked the federal and state dismantling of vocational tracks. The unintended consequences: unrealistic expectations for a linear academic path, lengthier post-secondary education, marginalization of skilled trades, prolonged parental financial dependence, and—importantly—a deferral of full adulthood.[32]

Simultaneously, automation and globalization spurred the decline of well-paid but low-skill jobs in trade and U.S. manufacturing. As these and other viable paths to the middle class shrank, graduating from a four-year college became the benchmark for successful "launching" into adulthood. Recently, education has become synonymous with institutional stress and its narrow and intense focus on academic metrics that ratchet up the pressure on teens from middle school through college.[33]

Institutional Stress

It used to be enough to think that your child was learning, broadening his experiences, or finding a purpose. Yet, as parents grew more anxious about the stiffer competition their children faced, striving became the norm. Stress became the parental badge of honor and the test for providing the "good enough" preparation for college admissions. You may well be acquainted with this pressure: Did you ever feel you hadn't done enough in comparison with other parents? Fretted that you were a slacker upon learning that the playmate of your five-year-old was taking Chinese as a second language? Or that your child's résumé wasn't packed with extracurriculars?

In parallel, high school students were encouraged to shoulder a heavy load of Advanced Placement (AP) courses that fuel sleep deprivation, anxiety, and depression.[34] This premium on success, in turn, seduced many students into equating mistakes with disaster. We are now recognizing that our widely accepted education benchmarks—standardized tests, honors in high school, the increasing necessity of a degree from a name-brand college—all intended to prepare children for adult success, are often toxic to emotional development. Professor and pediatrician Stuart Slavin asserts:

> *My personal feeling is that we are conducting an enormous and unprecedented social experiment on an entire generation of American children, and the evidence of a negative impact on adolescent mental health is overwhelming. This is particularly disturbing given the fact that having mental health problems in the teen years predisposes to mental health problems in adulthood. It is even more profoundly disturbing when one considers that there is absolutely no evidence that this educational approach actually leads to better educational outcomes.*[35]

Educators, guidance counselors, and admissions officers nationwide are taking note. In pressure-cooker high schools across the country, midterm and final exams are being abolished. Weekend homework is being phased out. The number of AP courses is being capped, and classes are starting later in the morning. (Though many sleep deficits can be traced to late-night online activities, later class start times acknowledge the correlation between sleep deprivation and adolescent depression.)[36] High schools and colleges are likewise implementing creative solutions to alter their achievement metrics, combating the culture of over-achieving perfectionism that can destroy students' psychological health.

With these trends under scrutiny, it's easy to see how a myopic focus on academic success feeds an intense fear of failure and a profound sense of shame that can result from real or even imagined underachievement. This *destructive perfectionism* distorts self-worth, making it nearly impossible for young people to tolerate personal flaws, take reasonable risks, or face the failures they will inevitably encounter on the road to maturity. Of far graver import, it undermines students' willingness to seek help when needed.

Branding the Self

Our branding culture has also promoted striving at younger and younger ages. In certain circles, there are feeder preschools for the "right" K–12 school, whose glossy brochures announce their graduates' acceptances to the "right" colleges, defined in turn by real or engineered admissions scarcity. An army of test tutors and résumé and essay advisers stand in the wings, ready to correct any deficit, provide any advantage. As college branding has come to mean "this way to a good life," the competition has stiffened. Sadly, we even brand ourselves, through social persona management.

Teens feel intense pressure to construct and present an acceptable media pseudo-self. At a time in life when everyone seeks "likes" on Instagram and Facebook and views on Snapchat, many young people feel that to fit in, they must project endless confidence and popularity. These popular social media sites stoke the contagion of conforming "Be happy" posts and propagate FOMO (Fear of Missing Out).[37]

The cheerful Facebook posts of one college sophomore we counseled, for example, flummoxed her parents, who were simultaneously fielding her high-volume anxious texts. Asked to decipher this stark contrast, she texted them: "Don't want my friends to think I'm a downer." Like many students, she was engaged in *impression management*—strategically filtering information to shape her friends' (and others') perceptions of her. The experience of emotional challenges or of mental disorders in this era of media immersion can lead many to feel incompetent and isolated, lowering their sense of self-worth—and worsening their feelings of hopelessness. The bifurcation between inner life and self-exposure grows wider and deeper.

This phenomenon has been tragically noted in certain college suicides. The split screen of inner turmoil, in sharp contrast with the projected happiness of online posts, was recently observed in the highly publicized suicide of a University of Pennsylvania freshman. "Over the course of the semester before she died, Madison posted uplifting pictures on Instagram with captions implying that she was having a great time at Penn, but she was not."[38]

Persona management is among the many stressors fanning the rise in adolescent mental health problems. The emergence of smartphone connectedness has profoundly changed the lifestyles, sleep patterns, and learning environments of young people. The online world floods youth with endless sources of stimulation, distraction, pleasure, obsession, compulsion, and even addiction. We know that social media's power to link kids day and night also exacerbates the experience of feeling left out and, more often than not, leaves its users feeling unhappier.[39] The parallel pressures of endless striving, academically and socially, extract a high price, as reflected in the greater numbers of stress-related illnesses in adolescents and young adults.

The Yin and Yang of Youth

Accompanying these stressors, a new developmental period of delayed adulthood has been accepted as normal in industrialized nations. Just as childhood wasn't recognized as a distinct developmental stage until the late nineteenth century (and adolescence not until the 1940s), deferred adulthood has required a new terminology for this new stage of life. Backed by extensive international research, psychologist Jeffrey Arnett has proposed *emerging adulthood* as the stage from late adolescence through one's twenties. It is a period of growing independence from parents but delayed arrival of fully adult roles. Recognizing this new developmental stage is vital because traditional adult markers—the financial independence of a steady job, stable housing, marriage and parenthood—may no longer reliably occur in one's twenties.[40] By the turn of the twenty-first century, the experiences of our youth are vastly different in industrialized countries than they have ever been.[41]

Millennials and their younger counterparts in Gen Z are taking longer and struggling harder to reach adulthood than any previous generation. "30 is the new 20," Arnett alerts parents.[42] Prior to the Great Recession of 2008, many parents encouraged their college-bound students to search for a personally meaningful career. Students imbued with this noble ambition often unknowingly prolonged their financial dependence—and instilled a vague unease in parents now witnessing what can feel like an eternal launch. For this reason, the Millennial generation often gets a bad rap as selfish, lazy, or dilatory. That caricature is harsh and undeserved.

Since the 2008 recession, parents and teens have been awash in media reports about income inequality, economic uncertainty, and job market stagnation. Today's longer path to full adulthood simply reflects certain new realities, chief among them: salaries and wages have not increased alongside the cost of living. This makes it stressful or impossible for emerging adults to live independently or attain those "traditional adult markers," all of which are based on financial independence. *College is a scam,* according to many young skeptics. *Why pay all this money for a credential that doesn't even get you a job with a decent liv-*

ing wage? they challenge. *You can't buy a house, let alone furnish your one room and go to the dentist, if you're spending 60 to 75 percent of your income on rent and student loans.*

Emerging adults know they will have to compete for good jobs of *any* kind, never mind top jobs and professional careers. It is often the pressure to make good money from your career, and the feeling that if you fail even once in college your entire future is over, that pushes students over the edge. Or perilously close to the edge, as we saw with Carson.

In this brave new world, where extended parental protection exists alongside exposure to adult pressures at ever-younger ages,[43] it's not surprising that the standard milestones to full independence are taking longer to reach. Not only do today's college students take longer to graduate—six is the new four—but they more frequently change majors, transfer from one institution to another, drop out, or re-enroll.

This generational shift also gives rise to the boomerang kids. Today, more young adults aged 18 to 34 live at home with a parent than ever in recorded history (U.S. census data goes back only to 1880).[44] With wage stagnation and towering student loans, parental support often includes financial assistance. Consequently, the yin and yang of youth experience, as Arnett notes, includes the feeling of *in-betweenness*, as neither adolescent nor adult.

The upside? Remember the Generation Gap? Boomers who embraced its mantra ("Never trust anyone over thirty") and Generation X (the latchkey kids, turned cynical on authority) are both startled and delighted to discover they've become best friends with their teenage and adult children.[45] This closer relationship allows today's parents to provide genuine emotional support and connectedness well beyond the launch from home.[46] Yet, the new developmental era for the emerging adult presents dangers for parents.

The Dangers of Parental Investment

Heightening parents' sense of competitive threat is the tremendous investment made in raising a child. We're not sea turtles, after all: we don't lay eggs on the beach, then swim away and hope that a few survive. Instead, we spend long years nurturing a child, long past what was once regarded as late adolescence—and, as just discussed, this period is steadily lengthening.

The modern parent assumes the burdens of a child's physical and psychological well-being, socialization, and an extensive and expensive education, all to ensure future success, backstopped by a boomerang-ready home. The good news is that the stigma of returning home is going away. Parents are often glad to facilitate the next step toward full independence. No matter the age, we're strongly attached, deeply dedicated, and emotionally driven to exert whatever effort we can summon to protect our young, sometimes well beyond college.

However, when parental concern leads to over-investment, dangers emerge. The reality is that not only the youth have become more stressed—parents agree the feeling is entirely mutual. Parents are juggling too many demands, with too little time and too few resources. Many have a family constellation far different from the one in which they were raised. According to the Pew Research Center, the twenty-first-century U.S. family is no longer "one dominant family form."[47] Two-parent families have been decreasing and single-parent families have been increasing, as have step-families. Many parents are dual-wage earners, as more mothers (64 percent) with preschool-aged children work.[48]

Parents who are overworked, stretched thin, or anxious that their kids deserve a better life than they had (remember John Adams?) can unintentionally pass this pressure on, as parenting today has also become a stressful, striver's job. We feel the same pressures our children do, to do everything right, to make sure they succeed, to take on their failures as our failures. We forget that until the seventies came along, the word "parenting" was neither in common use nor a tyrannical verb instructing parents what they "should do." Just listen to Pulitzer Prize winner Marilynne Robinson describe her 1950s childhood:

> ... they were the adults and we were the kids, you know what I mean? Sort of like two species. But if they noticed me doing something—drawing a painting or whatever we were doing—then they would get us what we needed to do that, and silently go on with it. One of the things that I think is very liberating is that if I had lived any honest life, my parents would have been equally happy. I was under no pressure.[49]

Robinson's parents were attuned to her needs. They noticed and quietly supported her interests with no special outcome in mind. Developmental psychologists today would define this orientation as *flourishing,* as opposed to the narrower, outcome-driven model of success. Educational experts say that certain key developmental changes from ages fifteen to twenty-two rely on the parents' promotion of autonomy, self-regulation, a reflective mindset, and the ability to navigate the larger world of healthy relationships and community engagement.[50] Flourishing encompasses these developmental goals and allows a child to pursue his own needs, pastimes, and even quirky interests.

In healthy parent–child relationships, parents maintain age-appropriate expectations and promote a child's assumption of increasing responsibilities for herself and others, best served up with warmth and loving support. The fundamentals of good parenting haven't changed, but times have.

Instead of quirky interests and self-directed play, there is screen time, scheduled sports, and extracurriculars to fill a résumé. All accompanied by decreasing expectations for age-appropriate help—old-fashioned chores. Parents may hesitate to assign family responsibilities that seem too time-consuming and unimportant to youth, who are too busy studying or playing violin or performing community service. When these parental shifts promote the competitive child, they risk eroding traditional parental authority, making it harder for parents to set limits and enforce demands.[51]

This pressured emphasis on achievement can contribute to students who carry a distorted view of what it takes to become self-sufficient. There's a harmful feedback loop when the pressure on youth to achieve academically is not being offset by the inherent balance of everyday, non-stimulating, non-goal-directed activity. It was a part of childhood past, alongside an ordinary parental role that's gone AWOL for many.

We forget that chores are good for kids and so are interests that aren't geared to the brag sheet. Stressed kids and parents today tend to overvalue striving and underestimate just how much simple grunt work and tedium go into success. The underlying message? A youth's dismissal of humdrum tasks as boring or somehow beneath them. Yet if children into adolescence never learn to manage their frustration at the necessity of performing unpleasant household tasks, or later, work a boring job, how will they develop the "grit" to accept a bad grade rather than drop a course, the discipline to try again rather than give up, and the insight to recognize that perfect is the enemy of the completed? How will they learn to turn off the Internet . . . opt for healing sleep . . . say no to friends who want to party?

For both generations, this means the sources of distress are not just around us, but within us and between us. It's therefore worth the time it takes to become aware of this mutually reinforcing dynamic. Parents will be better able to help their children balance the stressors in their lives if they bear in mind that independent living demands many small sacrifices—and parents must impose exposure to these tradeoffs. As role models, parents can both free their children from incessant striving and simultaneously gird their children for the anxieties, tedium, and disappointments that inevitably lie ahead, whether in a college career or in life itself.

Yes, today's world may be a more competitive and less forgiving place, but when that assessment yields a constricted definition of personal success—one that magnifies unnecessary tensions and undermines a balanced approach to pursuing one's goals—then it fans the flames of destructive perfectionism. The all-or-nothing thinking of success versus failure can also rob youth of creativity and diminish the value of caring for others. It's vital to recall how varied the pathways are to a happy and successful life. When parents can separate their own anxieties from their children's personal choices, they promote autonomy and well-being.

A Parent's Job in the Age of Anxiety

"Your job is to be there to be left."

—ANNA FREUD

A parent's fundamental goal of providing safety and security earlier in childhood is precisely to allow adolescents and young adults *to take risks*—that is, to meet the challenges of the new world that each generation inherits. We provide safety and security early on, first for a child's survival, and then "to be there to be left."

The monkey wrench thrown into this eloquent generational sequence occurs when parents perceive any sort of threat in their children's environment. Then they instinctively try to exert more control over their fledglings. And this protective urge is hardwired, with three factors that may trigger it:[52]

1. The perception of a danger that threatens a child's well-being or survival

2. Activation of parental fight-or-flight response
3. Degree of parental investment

Today's first-world "dangers" are no longer the survival threats of centuries past; yet eons of human evolution amid predatory animals, tribal warfare, pestilence, and famine have conditioned us to perceive and react to potential as well as actual risks to our children's future. Those physical threats have receded, replaced by changes in modern complex societies, globalized economies, and fast-paced telecommunications. The result? Our brains still have trouble discerning a true survival threat from an imagined one, and we exist in a default state of near-constant fight-or-flight readiness. These factors reflect the stark reality that we are parenting in a state of chronic anxiety.

The college years see students undergo remarkable developmental tasks and changes in their final ramp-up to adulthood. During this critical period—just before and after students head off to college—parents understandably want to hold on ever more tightly. Yet this is precisely the time when a youth's normal psychological development compels him to pull away.

Help Not Helicopter

Recognizing this dilemma, college administrators have taken to sponsoring "parent bouncer" events at new-student orientations to facilitate goodbyes and calm jittery parents about letting go.[53] Given the headlines about campus life, of course, and all the stressors we just discussed, such reassurances may ring hollow. Within one recent four-week span in August–September, reports *Inside Higher Ed,* at least eight freshmen died on U.S. university campuses. Several fatalities were from alcohol poisoning or other party-related accidents, the leading cause of college deaths; others were due to suicide, the second-leading cause.[54]

Out of a pure nurturing instinct, many parents react to these perils by attempting to eliminate them altogether. They may even go so far as to immerse themselves in the day-to-day management of their child's high school and college experience. Indeed, it's probably not too much of a stretch for any fretful parent to imagine being in the shoes of one concerned mother of an incoming freshman who heard about the heavy partying that typically goes on during new-student orientation week. In response, she rented an apartment just two blocks from campus to keep a watchful eye on her daughter's comings and goings. It was just one more case of a well-meaning parent who transformed her fears into the belief that her child was in actual danger.

It is crucial for parents to remember that despite the headlines, only rarely is a student in bona fide jeopardy. Yes, college *does* present young people with high-risk situations aplenty—and bounteous opportunities to make bad decisions. But doesn't the rest of adult life too? So long as a teen's family life affords a sturdy platform for the transition, the college years will not be inherently dangerous. As colleges turn to parents to better prepare students, parents are left to discern, "What is the difference between help and helicopter?"

Recall Mrs. Carr, who had dedicated herself to Emelia's high school success? She had over-dedicated herself, over-parented her daughter. Worried that her daughter's problems with organization would sink her college chances, Mrs. Carr was afraid to let Emelia learn from her mistakes. During her daughter's high school years, Mrs. Carr functioned as the morning alarm clock, the external memory drive, and reminder prompt. Mrs. Carr's efforts left Emelia ill-equipped to manage these necessary life skills, which resulted in a failed semester and boomerang from college.

Propelled by critiques of helicopter parenting, and general dismay at a younger generation of "excellent sheep,"[55] the pendulum today is swinging back toward the promotion of childhood independence. Parents can play a part in this groundswell, and cushion the body blows of destructive perfectionism by avoiding three common pitfalls:[56]

1. *Over-preparation.* It's easy to overemphasize a child's academic preparation. But do you really want to wind up with regrets like: Did we push too hard, requiring five years of Spanish? Does our young person care more about grades than about learning?

2. *Over-parenting.* This arises from the quandary between protecting and hovering. Yes, "protection" generally carries positive associations, yet its impact on a child's psychosocial development isn't always beneficial. If you've ever "helped" with a teen's report or lent a heavy hand on a school project, you're familiar with over-parenting.

3. *Over-investment.* This third peril is the backfire that results when "wanting the best" makes you lose sight of your underlying mo-

tivations. A child presents a seductively vicarious chance to become the ballerina or pro athlete you always longed to be. Or, thanks to the sacrifices you've made, your child can pursue the scientific career you couldn't, or become the painter or musician you are not. Or perhaps there's simply the academic degree you missed out on, and still regret. Isn't this all just wanting the best for your child? Won't they thank you later that you pushed them so hard to excel?[57]

But how do you avoid these mistakes and build a platform of support that serves as a springboard for launch?

Readiness

Let's face it: a brave new world awaits adolescents in their launch from home. As discussed above, the youth scene has been forever transformed by the globalization of the economy, sweeping cultural and lifestyle changes ushered in by the Internet, the widespread use of smartphones and other mobile technologies, and the amplifications and distortions of social media. In our current era, it makes perfect sense that parents are likely to favor control and protection—that is, "holding tight"— over independence and letting go. Yet "holding tight" constricts an individual's readiness, at just the time that colleges are asking parents to better prepare incoming students for the high-risk situations and mental health demands of this phase of life.

What can parents do? They can promote mature autonomy through readiness, both cognitive and noncognitive. The ultimate goal of cognitive readiness (as reflected in grades, etc.) is academic success—that's a given. Yet, we often over-focus on cognitive skills, and disregard the noncognitive ones, even though the best predictors of college (and life) success are actually *social and emotional readiness,* or old-fashioned life skills and maturity.

Social readiness
Rather than pushing a narrow definition of success, parents can promote flexible pathways toward the true goal of a mentally healthy adulthood: developing the skills to overcome obstacles, handle stress, and flourish. Parents can resist the urge to run social interference (and hinder social competence). Without practice in social skills, a college student may wind up like Sal.

As a college sophomore, Sal complained to his mother that his room-mate, Joey, was smoking pot in the privacy of his bedroom in their off-campus apartment. Sal objected to marijuana use, though not to under-age drinking, for which he had a fake ID. Sal's mother emailed Joey's mother twice, then called and asked her to intervene. Joey's mother politely but firmly refused, suggesting the roommates solve the problem themselves. Eventually, of course, they did. The takeaway? By learning to recognize how it hamstrings autonomy, parents can conquer the fear-based impulse to resolve social tensions on behalf of teens.

Emotional readiness

The linear view of preparation concentrates overwhelmingly on intellectual skills and academic achievement. Parents can fall into the trap of vicariously memorizing and—be honest, now—sometimes even crowing about our children's AP grades or standardized test scores. Yet, equating success to align self-worth with achievement yields a predictably hollow identity for the student. Such self-regard can crater as demands and stress rise and performance drops below the high-water mark: *How can I face my life when I'm no longer a 4.0 high school student, but a 2.75 college student?*

A young person is truly prepared for college or life only when success is a by-product of life interests, sustained effort, or valued personality traits ("I'm a hard worker; I'm a team player; I'm a caring and worthwhile person—even when I screw up"), not when defined by the ephemeral outcome of grades or "likes." That is when they are *emotionally* ready.

If noncognitive skills have been largely overlooked until now, it's because they are so hard to quantify: What parent can say precisely what percentages of "resilience," or "grit," or "life-management skills" are present in their student's character? While chores and family responsibilities teach competence, endurance, and self-sufficiency, more and more, experts are embracing the need to teach students skills in self-awareness.[58] These include the ability to recognize emotions in one's self and others, which builds compassion and tolerance for the inevitable mistakes and failures everyone encounters. It also includes the ability to self-regulate one's emotions and behavior. Self-regulation promotes better coping and allows an individual to thoughtfully respond rather than impulsively react, and to make better choices in the face of powerful urges. Increasingly, these noncognitive skills are regarded as critical to college readiness—an essential ingredient in any recipe for coping well as pressures increase and problems arise. These skills equip young people to face life's inevitable disappointments and failures with equanimity and resolve, becoming resilient enough to seek help for themselves when it is needed.

Parents can steep their kids in emotional intelligence by giving them the courage to own up to being lonely or depressed and to face these difficult feelings. Make them aware that masking psychic pain is a double-edged sword: not only does it suppress the motivation to seek treatment, it can also spur a cultural contagion of interrelated phenomena, including drinking, substance misuse/abuse, eating disorders, sexual risk-taking, and suicide attempts. With a combined sixty years of clinical practice, we've come to believe that a college student stands the best chance of success when his parents make him aware of—and prepare him to overcome—the emotional obstacles ahead.

Emotional-preparedness training is also a handy way to quell parental anxiety, whose levels tend to spike at this time. Preparing yourself—and your student—to deal effectively with any mental health concerns that emerge down the road is not just prudent but empowering. Even highly resilient youth encounter situations that can stress and sometimes overwhelm them, whether it's a major loss, such as a death or divorce in the family, an anguished romantic breakup, the trauma of sexual assault, or the more mundane torments of blowing an important exam, nagging fears of not fitting in, or just not making it. Knowing that you and your child have prepared for inevitable ups and downs will go a long way toward calming that anxiety.

Help Is Here

That's where *The Stressed Years of Their Lives* comes in: this book is designed to backstop parents as they impart the social, emotional, and life-management skills their kids will need to thrive in college and beyond. With the increasing occurrence of college mental health challenges, the book is both a cautionary tale and a survival guide. It alerts you to what we deem to be the likelihood of a mental illness surfacing during the college years, but in the same breath it presents resources

and ideas to help both generations handle that scenario, should it occur. We share the stories of many others—both university students and
their parents, frequently in their own voices—who have weathered a
mental health challenge together.

As practitioners of family systems therapy (a clinical framework that
views the individual through the social-emotional context of the family),
we see parents as crucial partners to emerging adult development. We
prize active listening, honest communication, a willingness to resolve
family conflicts in a face-the-facts way, and a high degree of mental
health awareness.

That latter attribute in particular can stave off the social stigma that
can make teens reluctant to seek counseling. Mental health prejudices
remain both prevalent and persistent. This sort of blinkered thinking
associates seeking help with feeling "weak, crazy, or broken." In the
absence of such stigma, the mental health profession's holy triad—
prevention, early identification, and effective intervention—can spell the
difference between sustained illness and recovery.

The Stressed Years of Their Lives organizes this triad into two parts.
Part One focuses on readiness and the early identification of barriers to success. There's no test for readiness, but there are key conversations we'll provide to help parent and student discern strengths and
vulnerabilities. We'll show how to shed mindset barriers, gain self-
acceptance, and build resilience. Parents can help reduce stigma and
learn what to expect when problems arise.

Part Two takes you behind the scenes and into the lives of college
students and their families as they encounter both normative and
difficult mental health concerns. Parents and students alike need insight to distinguish normal mood swings from full-blown clinical
disorders.

Drawing on three different wells of knowledge—the scientific literature; our interviews with students, parents, high school principals,
and college mental health student-support personnel; and our decades of clinical experience helping young people make the "jump to
hyperspace"—we'll help you differentiate worrisome problems of the
college era from true mental health crises. We'll discuss and review
the signs of poor coping, the symptoms of emotional turmoil, and the
markers of a true mental health or substance-use disorder. And if a
mental health crisis does emerge, we'll show exactly how your direct
involvement can accelerate your student's recovery.

Many students will experience relatively smooth sailing, though all will face challenges. Demanding circumstances, lack of emotional preparation, immaturity, an undiagnosed or untreated disorder, or an unwillingness to seek help will create a stutter start for some, while a few may crash and return home to regroup and relaunch. We'll look at the necessary supports that allow a student to overcome obstacles and remain in college, as well as the stories of those who temporarily fall out of the expected trajectory and require more intensive mental health treatment. Part Two concludes with an overview of the baton pass from home to college, as college administrators join parents' collaborative efforts to keep students safe and emotionally healthy and help them succeed.

With these insights, *The Stressed Years of Their Lives* offers a road map that steers you along a middle path between intense parental involvement on one hand and unfettered student freedom on the other. Older adolescents and young adults yearn to pilot their own course through life, so we don't stint on the "route details" of what this will mean for parents: You must let this age group make their own choices—*even the questionable ones!* You must realize that they are going to do things you aren't comfortable with or of which you don't approve. And you must accept that they will make mistakes and suffer the consequences. Despite the current vogue for vicarious and virtual sensations, it remains vitally important to allow young adults to learn life's lessons through direct experience.

Because true independence is a multi-year project, both parent and child must be prepared for stumbles along the circuitous path to adulthood. Both must gather the courage to ask for and receive help when needed.

Finally, we issue both a challenge and an invitation to parents and students to evaluate any misconceptions they may still harbor about mental health; bias is the enemy of treatment. Our hard-won insight on the matter is that many seemingly insurmountable difficulties of the college years are in fact common, predictable, and solvable. It's therefore crucial that parents and students start thinking about mental health as an integral part of college planning and experience.

You've spent years raising your child, preparing them for the exciting launch to independence. Whether your student is about to lift off, needs a course correction, or has returned home to refuel, we're confident that parents and youth can work together to minimize the risks of a mental health crisis in the years ahead. The stressed years, it turns out, can also be the best years of both of your lives. We are eager to share our guidance for getting through them. In short, you are not alone. Help is here.

2

Before You Go:
Social-Emotional PREP

Join student clubs. Go to your professor's office hours. If you're feeling down, talk with someone about it. And please, don't drink too much.

—JONATHAN ZIMMERMAN[1]

Welcome to your typical freshman orientation: those thirty-minute musicals on the dos and don'ts of college life may be amusing, but they only scratch the surface of the realities of the years ahead. Far more useful would be to start some ongoing conversations about the concept of *readiness*.

Before college, much of readiness centers upon academic preparation for college admission. As previously discussed, it's only one small (and very specific) indicator of a student's overall collegiate readiness. Apart from easily accessed metrics (GPA, SAT, ACT) and the carefully curated portfolio of extracurricular activities, however, what are the best predictors of college success? They're the same as those of life success: social-emotional readiness and resilience. The very notion of leaving home is predicated on the assumption of self-discipline and emotional and financial readiness. Yes, that elusive quality of "maturity" is hard to measure, but it's one of the surest predictors that a student will successfully adjust to college life.

In this chapter we'll look at eight key components of social-emotional maturity, imagining some essential conversations that will better prepare high school students for the complex demands of college life—or ease the burden of college students struggling with them already. Parents today strive to be in touch with the many new developments in youth culture, especially those brought about by the digital revolution. Yet, it can be difficult for worried parents to talk *with* rather than talk *at* their teens. And kids, in turn, may tune out. Here, we share insights about how to encourage the trickier conversations regarding the emotional responsibilities that autonomous life demands.

You might wonder, "How well is my college-bound student able to demonstrate the skills that underlie maturity?" To help you answer that question, we suggest that the junior year of high school offers a natural opportunity for conversations to flow out of that most basic question of all: "Where do you want to go to college?" They can also emerge from a more deliberate effort to get to know your teenager as a person—and to figure out what makes him happy and what hopes and dreams he has for the future.

We imagine these conversations as ongoing dialogues that may continue over the long launch to adulthood. And though we have framed them as preparatory to college, any one of them may be prompted by a college student's problematic experience. (New demands and situations often teach us the most about our abilities and limits.) So don't fret if your student leaves for college with some resistance to these discussions— the long path to adulthood will present many opportunities for the two of you to have one of these better-late-than-never talks.

To make the most of these conversations, try to explore each issue as openly and honestly as possible, with as much dialogue and conflict-free communication as possible. Make sure you are up-front about where you are coming from but respect fundamentally your teen's perspective and his unique life experiences. Whatever differences of opinion emerge can be used to engage the young person in looking more closely at himself: What unexpected challenges to his coping abilities might the college experience present? How might he or she begin to prepare for these challenges in concrete and practical ways?

Handled effectively, these conversations can drive home a priceless lesson: We never stop learning social and emotional skills. The better a young person masters these skills, the more prepared he will likely be on the day of his departure from home. And in situations where the young person is *not* ready, alternative pathways for post–high school education can be identified; we review some of these in Chapter 4. The list on the next page summarizes the key components of social-emotional maturity that we will discuss in this chapter.

Key Components of Social-Emotional Maturity

1. **Conscientiousness**: Are you ready to take responsibility for the consequences of your actions?

2. **Self-management**: Are you ready to take over the routine tasks of everyday life in the relatively unstructured environment of college?

3. **Interpersonal skills**: Are you ready to make friends, deal with roommates, and find suitable social activities?

4. **Self-control**: Can you resist temptations? Are you ready to set limits on the time spent watching TV or interacting on the Internet, whether through virtual reality games, social media, or web surfing, that can lead to insufficient sleep and disruptions in self-care and studying, among others? Can you avoid overeating or consuming too much junk food?

5. **Grit**: Are you ready to cope with frustration, disappointment, and failure, and persist in the face of setbacks and obstacles?

6. **Risk management**: Are you ready to have fun without taking too many risks, or too many substances?

7. **Self-acceptance**: Can you accept your faults, tolerate your mistakes, and deal with your problems without feeling too guilty or ashamed?

8. **Open mindset/Help-seeking**: Are you ready to ask for help when things aren't going well for you?

1. Conscientiousness: Owning one's actions

Taking ownership of one's actions—and, critically, of their consequences—is all about conscientiousness. Conscientious people say what they mean, do what they say, and own up to their mistakes. Reliability, predictability, trustworthiness—what counts most here is that the individual holds himself accountable for his actions. When mistakes are made, or when unexpected negative consequences ensue, the person readily acknowledges these and seeks to rectify the situation in a straightforward fashion.

Take Alan: a bright, hardworking high school junior who was juggling extracurricular activities, AP courses, and an active social life. He was president of his class, captain of the debate team, and co-editor of the school newspaper. In the weeks leading up to the drama club's winter show—in which he had a lead role, of course—Alan was clearly burning the candle at both ends.

Because their son seemed stressed out and sleep-deprived, Alan's constant "overdrive" started to worry his parents, but they accepted it as a side effect of his achievement orientation. Shortly after the show's conclusion, however, they were called into school to discuss a serious matter: in a meeting with their son and the dean of the junior class, his parents learned that Alan had recently plagiarized an English term paper. Lacking time to prepare for the assignment and under pressure to maintain his GPA, Alan tearfully explained he had purchased an essay from a "paper mill" website (for more information on these see the following website: http://www.mga.edu/student-success-center /plagiarism/paper-mill.aspx). He admitted his mistake and took full responsibility for it, stating that he knew it was wrong.

After extensive discussions in the dean's office, Alan was given a disciplinary notation in his school record rather than being suspended. And if no further instances of cheating occurred, the dean explained, his record would be expunged. Though devastated by their son's wrongdoing, Alan's parents recognized that his ability to take responsibility for his actions—and his willingness to admit his error in judgment—had led to a more favorable outcome.

A model student had found himself in a bind and tried to wriggle out of it by breaking the rules. Rather than denying, minimizing, or avoiding the consequences of his actions, however, Alan bit the bullet and owned up when he was caught. This act of taking ownership and accepting the consequences for cheating demonstrated his authentic conscientiousness; Alan was moving in the right direction.

To what extent has your own young adult taken charge of his life? Your admiring acknowledgment of his progress in this arena can be a great way to kick off a conversation about conscientiousness. It can also be instructive for you to reflect, out loud, on your own degree of conscientiousness: there are likely to be areas in which you measure up, and others in which you fall short; no one's perfect, after all. The primary objective of this conversation is to identify areas where your student demonstrates a high degree of responsibility and any others where there may be room for improvement. This could mean recommitting to obligations that aren't particularly rewarding (such as household chores) or owning up to behaviors that aren't exactly ennobling (such as being too self-centered). But giving your teen a chance to practice the *skill* of taking ownership is never a bad parental move.

2. Self-management

In today's pressured society, high school students' lives are so tightly scheduled that many have little free time at their disposal. "Programmed" by their families and schools to move through the day in more or less lockstep fashion, many adolescents are kept on track by well-meaning parents from the moment they wake up until the time they fall asleep. This over-parenting may stem from a sense of duty— "Isn't it our moral obligation to ensure our children's success?"—but the excessive scaffolding has left many young people unable to manage themselves.

Self-management is the ability to take care of day-to-day activities on one's own. This encompasses waking up on time, preparing for the day, remembering all the appointments and tasks that need to be accomplished and following through on most of them, making adjustments in the day's schedule as needed, taking care of one's basic needs, and developing a routine for winding down and going to sleep at a reasonable hour. Self-management also includes mundane chores such as preparing meals, washing up, doing the laundry, paying bills, and straightening up before things get too messy.

This sounds pretty straightforward, doesn't it? It's a familiar and timeless truth that many teens see these humdrum jobs as "too boring," "too time-consuming," or "not important enough to take seriously." The difference today is the increased and intensified premium that households place upon high achievement; anything that undermines the completion of schoolwork or extracurricular activities is seen as a waste of time. Small wonder, then, that parents encounter pushback from their teens when the latter are asked to manage on their own.

According to Eric Furda, dean of undergraduate admissions at the University of Pennsylvania, the real test of college readiness is whether a student can rise to the challenge of managing life on their own: "We see lots of prospective students whose academic credentials are impeccable and whose extracurricular activities are impressive," says Furda. "What we look for are indicators that the applicant has taken charge of his or her life and has formulated a vision for how they see themselves in the college environment. It's not enough to have a high GPA or great test scores. They need to be self-starters and self-managers."

Yet, to the applicant (and parents) "self-starters and self-managers" translates as the super student who does it all, holds leadership positions, and balances their well-rounded curricular and extracurricular interests without apparent difficulty—an interpretation that's proved every year when admissions decisions arrive. We encourage parents to dismantle the scaffolding of excessive parental management well before college.

Like conscientiousness, self-management is not an all-or-nothing phenomenon. People are capable of managing their affairs in certain domains more than in others, and almost everyone gets better with practice. Predictably, parents and students often encounter conflict around which management skills are important and must be practiced.

When Anne and her parents visited Dr. Rostain's office, she was a rising high school senior with ADHD and recurring depression. She had spent the summer working two jobs and taking care of several pets at home, including a snake, two rabbits, a cockatiel, and her dog. From Anne's point of view, it had been a successful summer: she had made a lot of money and found the time to do things with friends.

Her parents, by contrast, reported a summer's worth of conflict and frustration. For all their nagging, Anne refused to make her bed or pick her clothes up off the floor. She didn't shower or brush her teeth regularly. She didn't do her own laundry—and when her mother did it for her, Anne refused to fold the clean clothes. She made no effort to stay on top of her ADHD medication schedule. Topping it all off, her parents fretted that Anne was going to bed too late, eating too much junk food, and breaking her promise to hit the gym on a regular basis.

"Stop micromanaging me!" Anne countered. "I know what I need to do to stay on top of my personal things, and I'm not concerned about cleaning my room to your liking!" Not showering every day was "just fine," said Anne, adding that the more her parents insisted she do the "stupid stuff" they thought she needed to do, the less likely she would be to do it.

At this point her parents appealed to Dr. Rostain. In holding down two jobs and managing her pets, he observed, Anne had demonstrated a great deal of initiative, diligence, and maturity. At the same time, she had shown little interest in tackling the self-care duties her parents were most concerned about, and she was rebuffing her parents' pressure to do them. Dr. Rostain also pointed out that Anne's parents were appropriately concerned about their daughter's self-management skills, but hadn't yet found a suitable way to make their case.

He reframed their conflict as an important developmental transition between Anne and her parents. Anne needed to take on certain unwanted tasks—showering, brushing her teeth, going to the gym—while her parents needed to let go of their role as "naggers and critics." And senior year—when older adolescents must practice taking responsibility for themselves—was the perfect time to have this intergenerational conversation. At Dr. Rostain's suggestion, Anne and her parents entered a negotiation process and came up with a "change contract": Anne agreed to assume progressively greater ownership of her self-care and family responsibilities, while her parents agreed to limit their comments about her conduct. The three of them agreed to periodically review the evidence that she was mastering these skills. In return for her steady progress, Anne's parents agreed to let her apply to faraway colleges and not just a commuter school.

This was the ultimate motivator for Anne, who longed to attend a certain out-of-state college with an excellent International Relations program. Individual and family sessions continued that year, allowing the parents to step back—and enabling Anne to step up. It was a step-by-step process with gradual acquisition of self-management skills. Initially, she needed assistance from her parents to complete tasks like cleaning her room and doing her laundry. Next, she was doing these on her own but she needed frequent reminding, which at times resembled nagging but was part of the change contract they had drawn up. In the final months of her senior year, Anne was admitted to her first-choice school. While she and her parents were very happy about this, they pointed out that until she was regularly completing all her chores on her own (without any reminding), they were not convinced that she would be ready to leave in August. That summer, she not only took charge of her chores, but also went out of her way to help her parents with other household tasks. By demonstrating and exercising her capacity to manage her daily tasks, Anne convinced her parents to let her attend the out-of-state college.

3. Interpersonal skills

For most high-school students, college holds the promise of unbounded time in the company of peers with little or no supervision by adults. The chance to hang out until the early-morning hours chatting with roommates, playing video games, watching sports, or going to parties is among the greatest attractions of university life.

For the vast majority, the reality lives up to their expectations. Parents need only look back on their own "bright college years" to recall how important this time is: Lifelong friendships are forged. Romantic relationships are explored. Vital social skills are acquired and refined.

Of course, there are bumps and bruises along the way. It's common for roommates to argue, for friends to fall out, for intimate relationships to end badly. The critical question for parents is the extent to which their child is prepared to face these social opportunities and challenges. Indeed, according to many surveys, making friends, keeping friends, losing friends, and finding a suitable niche of social relationships are among the most stressful aspects of college life.

The complex social ecology of college life is even more difficult for young people with learning disorders and/or social-interactional difficulties, among them autism spectrum disorder (including Asperger's syndrome), attention deficit hyperactivity disorder (ADHD), communication disorders, nonverbal learning disorder, and social anxiety disorder. These youths are particularly stressed out by situations that require a skillful reading of social cues (especially nonverbal ones) and the rapid selection of an appropriate behavioral response. Unawareness of social norms; difficulty carrying on everyday chitchat; awkward speech, clothing, or behavioral quirks; or even just a tendency to be very quiet in the company of others—any of these can have profoundly negative effects on a person's efforts to navigate the whitewater rapids of modern college social life.

As difficult as these concerns have always been for people in this age group, the explosion of social media in everyday life has complicated the process of social adaptation even more. Facebook, Snapchat, Instagram, and Twitter, among others, have drastically changed the ways in which young people form peer relationships. Not only are such relationships reported and commented on in myriad public forums, but the infiltration of once-personal spaces by video-capable smartphones has transformed the very notion of intimacy. It has become commonplace for youth to keep (and share) nude photos of themselves and others on a mobile device. (See the tips on the following page for taming a smartphone.)

SEVEN WAYS TO OVERHAUL YOUR SMARTPHONE USE

1. **Make choices.** Make conscious choices about what you really need your phone for and what's optional: lists, clock, etc. Otherwise, join the crowd who texts sixty times a day and becomes anxious when their phone is off.
2. **Retrain yourself.** Notifications are addictive. Reduce your "connection anxiety" by gradually checking less and less often.
3. **Set expectations.** Remember, you are not on call 24/7. Let friends and family know what to expect.
4. **Silence notifications.** Turn off the default settings to reduce distractions and stress.
5. **Protect sleep.** Avoid using your phone late at night. Turn it off or place it in another room. You'll sleep better.
6. **Be active.** Active posting of ideas, photos, and other content feels better than just looking at the posts of others.
7. **Don't text/email/call and drive.** In the United States in 2016, close thirty-five hundred people were killed in distracted driving incidents.

The first step in assessing your teen's interpersonal maturity is to inventory his social skills. Use these reflective questions as a starting point:

- How easily does your teen make friends? Where does he fit in the social hierarchy? Is that an issue for him?
- What are his greatest social strengths (extroversion, assertiveness, humor, intelligence)?
- What are his most obvious vulnerabilities (shyness, awkwardness, introversion, passivity)?
- Who is in your teen's friendship circle? Do you know them? What do you think of the way they treat your teen? How does your teen talk about them when you ask?

- What level of trust does your teen have in his friends? What conflicts does your teen tend to have with peers? What do you make of the way your teen handles disagreements with their friends?
- What about romantic involvements? How much do you know about what is going on with your teen's sexuality? Do you have concerns about the way he forms intimate attachments?
- Is your teen dating someone? What do you think of that person? If you have concerns, have you raised them with your teen?

Once you've weighed these questions on your own, open up a dialogue with your young person. Peer relationships are essentially a black box for most parents, so broach the discussion with frankness and openness as well as humility. You might begin by explaining your motives: "I want to learn more about how you view your friendships in order to make sure I'm doing my job as your parent in preparing you for college." Acknowledge that you've been wondering how to approach the topic and you're aware it might take more than one conversation. If your teen is willing to spend some time talking about his friendships, that's great. But be prepared to make several requests before a young adult agrees to share their views. Most will react defensively when queried about their social relationships, so it's best to ask your teen to guide you through this world. Admitting your ignorance and emphasizing your eagerness to learn about their social life might make it easier for your teen to open up. This is referred to as taking the "one down" position: you're not the authority on their friendships—they are. For instance, you might observe that Facebook and Instagram were *not* part of your social scene when you were their age, and that you and your peers had other ways of communicating about day-to-day issues of concern (like landlines and face-to-face conversations). As a result, you're eager to learn from them exactly how friendships are carried out in the IT age.

Once you and your teen are engaged in an open conversation, ask him to show you a few of his Instagram chats and Facebook postings; these will give you a quick glimpse into his social world. Admittedly, this request may be met with resistance, but if you ask him to show you a small sample of his postings (editing is fine), he might be willing to share. From there, it becomes easier to ask more direct questions about who he's interacting with and getting along with the most, and what kinds of discussions occupy his time. Equally important, this can lead you to consider how social media affects your teen and how he manages his online profile. It also facilitates a discussion about the persona your teen projects on the Internet: is this persona appreciated by the people with whom he's trying to forge friendships?

Once the ice is broken, you can ask a bit about each of his closest friends. What does your teen like most—and least—about them? What "issues" has he encountered with his friends, and how does he handle them? What social circles is your teen most invested in? Does your teen feel torn between his allegiances to different groups of friends? Overall, is your teen happy with his social life, and if not, why not?

The key message to convey is that you are genuinely interested in knowing who your teen's friends are, and how they treat him.

Your ability to listen without offering judgment or advice will go a long way toward creating an open dialogue about this most complex facet of human life: getting along with others. If the initial conversation is successful, it may lead to others. If not, your teen may require more time to trust you with this aspect of his personal life.

If you have serious concerns that your teen is being ignored, harassed, or bullied—or is struggling to find or maintain friendships—seek assistance from a mental health professional. Chronic conflicts with peers or a lack of close friendships are among the biggest risk factors for mental disorders in youth. Fortunately, a panoply of remedies—from individual or group therapy to social-skills classes and peer-support groups— are out there to help young people overcome their social-relationship difficulties.

4. Self-control

The human ability to delay immediate gratification in favor of longer-term goals is variously referred to as willpower, self-restraint, or self-control. Of the countless ways psychologists have studied self-control, the best known may be the Marshmallow Test.[2,3] Young children were offered a marshmallow—and a choice: they could eat it right away, but if they waited to eat it until the tester returned, they would receive a second marshmallow. For young children, this poses a very basic test of self-control: to eat or to wait—that is the question.

Some children were able to wait up to twenty minutes to receive the additional treat; others gobbled the first marshmallow as soon as the tester left the room. The difference was significant, for the ability to delay gratification turns out to be a better predictor of academic and social success than either IQ scores or socioeconomic status. When the test subjects were revisited as young adults, the marshmallow resisters were the higher achievers; they were also more socially and emotionally mature.

So what's this got to do with a university setting? The answer may depend on individual preferences, but the most common "treats" in college have to do with staying up late and hanging out with peers, playing games or watching TV, surfing the web and checking out social media sites, or indulging in hedonistic pursuits—all with virtually no adult supervision.

Parents are wise to wonder if their children are prepared to handle the innumerable temptations of college life. Unless they've had a chance to be on their own before going to school, it's difficult to assess how well your teen will use good judgment and exercise adequate self-control in the freedom of college. "College can be a very difficult place for many students," says Steve Piltch, head of the Shipley School, "because it's essentially four years of complete irresponsibility, during which they need to learn some modicum of responsibility." The achievement of real autonomy is a developmental challenge that few young people have mastered by the time they first hit campus. This is particularly true of students raised under close parental supervision, which sends an implicit message to young people: the stakes are too high for you to make any mistakes.

But what is the best way to help young people learn self-control? As Piltch observes, "In an ideal world, we're watching them just enough for them to get into trouble, make mistakes, and then figure things out on their own. Too often, we don't give them enough of a chance to make choices on their own. We need to teach them how to be independent and how to learn self-control by giving them opportunities to make decisions that matter." Experiences such as going off to a summer-college program, traveling with a teen tour group, or working in a summer camp make apt rehearsals for being independent at college.

So while your teen is still at home, give them as much freedom as possible to manage their time, to learn self-control—in short, to resist the distracting marshmallows of modern life. Make this task as practical as you can: ask what strategies they use to limit excessive Facebook and Instagram use, texting, Internet use, watching TV, playing video games, overeating, staying up too late, and other unhealthy habits that are easy to acquire and hard to change. If they don't seem to have a handle on these major time-sinks you might suggest that they need to learn and demonstrate reasonable self-control as a prerequisite for going off to college. If you're worried that they're not exercising proper self-restraint in time-wasting pursuits, online activities, and/or unhealthy habits, it's worth creating an action plan to help your teen learn how to achieve better self-control in whatever domain appears to be causing the greatest problems.

For instance, suppose your young person is having a hard time limiting computer time, especially late at night, and this is causing the loss of precious sleep and trouble waking up in the morning. Rather than hectoring him to get to sleep or threatening to limit computer access, it would be more constructive to have a focused conversation about ways to improve your teen's mastery of information technology. It should start with a discussion about IT usage and the habits developed that are the most problematic. Identifying when these habitual behaviors are occurring is also important, as is defining the line between acceptable and excessive use. The next step involves measuring the behavior by setting up a monitoring system that provides objective data on how much time and specifically what hours of the day or night are being spent on the computer, and what activities are being pursued. With that data, the two of you can begin to pinpoint occasions when "poor decisions" are being made: for example, playing games until 2:00 A.M. instead of going to bed. By closely examining these examples, your teen can observe his "behavioral scripts" (habits) and you can discuss how to modify these scripts. This modified script reduces the opportunities for poor decision-making or modifies the consequences of these decisions. Ultimately, your teen will have to learn how to self-limit in order to achieve desired goals. Yes, it's difficult to let go and watch your teen struggle at taking charge of life, but the sooner he learns self-control, the better. After all, you won't be present to teach this vital life skill once he has left the nest.

5. Grit

College life brims over with great experiences, good times—and inevitable moments when things go awry. Whether it's an argument with a roommate, a poor grade on a term paper or midterm, homesickness, or a brush-off from a love interest, there's no way to avoid disappointment and heartache. All are just part of life, and each offers an essential lesson in coping with adversity. But how successfully will your young person face these tough times? And is there a way that you can help them prepare for inevitable setbacks?

Psychology professor Angela Duckworth believes the answer may lie in the notion of "grit," which she explored in a popular 2016 book of the same name. Her research links grit—defined by Duckworth as the ability to reach long-term goals despite obstacles and setbacks[4]—with lifetime educational attainment and professional success.

Whereas self-control is the ability to regulate attention, emotion, and behavior in the face of temptation, grit refers to the capacity to maintain a high degree of motivation over an extended period of time—months or even years. It also puts a premium on persistence ("If at first you don't succeed, try, try again") and pursuing alternative pathways to goals. All of this makes grit more than a mere set of skills; it is a *mindset* that empowers individuals to keep going despite hardships or hard times. You can see why grit is a key building block of resilience—the ability of an individual to maintain personal and social stability in the face of adversity. To be sure, grit is strongly correlated with self-control, but there are many people with excellent self-control who lack grit, and others with relatively poor self-control who are very gritty—so the two are related but different concepts.

A great deal has been learned about how to foster grit in young people. The emerging field of positive psychology, for example, holds that we can help our kids develop grit by encouraging their learned optimism (an attitude that sees challenges as manageable), growth mindset (the view that one can learn from even the most difficult experiences), intrinsic motivation (a self-directed drive to achieve), and willingness to evaluate their own behavior. Many of these desirable traits have been introduced as study subjects in school curricula, such as the Social, Emotional, and Ethical Development (SEED) curriculum at the Shipley School (https://www.shipleyschool.org/page/academics/seed -service--support/seed) and, of course, in the pages of self-help books.

At the heart of grit is the ability to tolerate the distress that arises from setbacks. Distress-tolerance skills will therefore greatly benefit an individual—a college freshman, say—whenever she confronts a situation that is impossible to change. There's no easy way to learn how to tolerate distress, since most of us don't go out of our way to put ourselves into distressing situations. But there are endless teachable moments that life presents to all of us in the form of crises or "bad times" during which we have a chance to better learn how to tolerate physical or emotional pain, how to cope with the hardships that have been thrown our way, and how to keep moving on in spite of them.

To focus individuals on the wealth of concrete steps they can take to better their situation *starting right now,* therapists often invoke the acronym IMPROVE:

Use **Imagery** to visualize a safe place.
Find **Meaning** in the situation.
Use **Prayer** and **Relaxation.**
Take **One** thing at a time.
Create a **Vacation** spot in your imagination.
Encourage yourself through positive, calming self-talk.

Before assessing your teen's capacity to keep going in the face of adversity, think back on how you learned this critical life skill: What challenges did you face in your adolescence that pushed you to become grittier? How did you weather tough times? What experiences were instrumental in pushing you beyond what you thought were the limits of your endurance?

For some parents, these lessons took place on a ball field or in the wilderness. For others, a gig involving music, dance, theater, painting, photography, or poetry handed us that crucial opportunity to transcend our comfort zone. And for yet a third group of today's parents, distress tolerance came from building up the endurance required to achieve true mastery of an academic discipline or a cherished vocational skill.

Once you've had a chance to reflect on just how you learned to grin and bear it, consider one or two areas where you still struggle: will you ever remember all those jazz-guitar chords, or train enough to run that marathon, or master every in and out of Adobe Photoshop?

Having examined how you amassed your own grit, you're ready for a conversation with your teen about how he views the topic. You might start out by observing that one of the hardest things in life is to learn how to stick it out when things don't go your way. The ability to "hang in there" is one of the most important lessons you learn along the way. Through open-ended questions and a judicious amount of self-disclosure, the ensuing dialogue should emphasize that grit and distress tolerance lend themselves to lifelong learning goals and to the achievement of inner strength. There is no right or wrong approach to facing adversity, but there *is* a near-infinity of ways that people learn to cope—and some of those methods are better than others. You'll know you've succeeded when you conclude that you've presented a fair balance of advocating a growth mindset—the belief that life's obstacles are learning opportunities—and realistically acknowledging that setbacks are hard.

6. Risk management

The late-adolescent brain promotes risky decision-making and behaviors in the service of reward-seeking drives. Experiments have shown that the mere presence of peers tempts young people to take bigger risks and engage in thrill-seeking activities. This helps explain why youthful experimentation with drinking, substance use, sexuality, speeding, and extreme sports has become part of the American cultural landscape.

Just take a look at the survey research on current rates of adolescent substance use: 37 percent of U.S. twelfth graders had a drink in the last month, while 19 percent engaged in binge drinking; 36 percent smoked marijuana in the past year, and 6 percent used marijuana daily. Other surveys reveal a growing acceptance regarding the safety of marijuana use, with a corresponding rise in usage to the levels seen in the 1970s. (We will review this in greater detail in Chapter 6.)

Don't let these statistics rattle you. Most of us went through our own period of risk-taking in adolescence, and most of us managed to survive it. So before you talk about this topic with your teen, reflect on your own experiences: How much credence did you give adult warnings about the supposed evils of sex, drugs, and rock 'n' roll? (It's always instructive to recall how many activities we kept secret from our parents!) Those of us who opted not to heed these warnings should reflect on how we nonetheless learned to manage risk, while those of us who opted not to partake of the era's temptations should pause to consider the many lessons we learned from observing the behavior of our less-temperate friends.

The key is to remember that adolescent thinking differs radically from adult thinking. To understand the ways adolescents and young adults consider the risks they face, listen to them with as little judgment—with as much acceptance—as possible. Be ready to hear things you don't want to hear. Prepare to stifle the urge to come down hard when truths are revealed. And be ready to ask the simple but powerful question your adolescent will need to figure out on his own: "At what point does experimentation become a serious health hazard?"

7. Self-acceptance

Another important facet of social-emotional maturity can best be described as "liking yourself despite your flaws and imperfections"—what some might refer to as self-esteem but which we prefer to call self-acceptance. Self-esteem (or sense of self-worth) refers to a person's subjective evaluation or attitude toward himself, which is multi-determined and multi-layered. By contrast, self-acceptance is the extent to which someone is happy or satisfied with himself. Self-acceptance involves the ability to realistically look at oneself, to perceive and own up to one's strengths and weaknesses in a balanced fashion. In this respect, self-acceptance is a cornerstone of mental health—and without it, individuals are at greater risk for mental illness.

In February 2014, the president and provost of the University of Pennsylvania appointed a Task Force on Student Psychological Health and Welfare in the wake of some highly publicized suicides. The Task Force's charge: to examine the challenges confronting students that can affect their psychological health and well-being; to assess the efficacy of existing resources for helping students manage problems; and to make recommendations to improve the quality and safety of student life.

After a year of research, deliberation, and intensive discussions with key constituencies at Penn and with college mental health experts from across the country, the Task Force recommended a wide range of institutional policies and educational campaigns to enhance student wellness and facilitate access to mental health care. Despite high rates of satisfaction with their college experience and with the school's academic and social life, the Task Force noted, certain unhealthy attitudes, expectations, and social norms placed Penn students at high risk for psychological distress. Chief among these was the tendency toward "destructive perfectionism"—the belief that "one has to be perfect in every academic, co-curricular, and social endeavor." This unrealistic belief sets up students to experience feelings of being overwhelmed, inadequate, hopeless, and depressed.

Where does this belief originate? What can be done to change it? Dean Eric Furda attributes its existence to a combination of family values, economic pressures, and cultural expectations:

We see students apply to Penn with transcripts that include eight AP courses, dozens of extracurricular activities, and letters of recommendation that make the student out to be the next Steve Jobs or Bill Gates. What we wonder when we read these applications is, "Who is this teenager? And why isn't someone helping him or her slow down a little and focus some of their energy on just enjoying life?"

The problem with being achievement-oriented to this extreme is that these students begin to identify their self-worth with their accomplishments. Add to that growing concerns about the global economy, increased competition to get into "brand-name" schools along with the high cost of a college education and you begin to see how students and parents believe that nothing short of perfection is going to be acceptable for entry to a school like Penn. What they don't understand is that college admissions offices are not looking for perfect students. We're looking for students who can contribute to campus life and who are well rounded enough to benefit from being part of a diverse community.

The way out of the vicious cycle of destructive perfectionism is to confront it head-on. As a first step, identify the distorted beliefs that equate goodness and self-worth with performance and achievement. Family traditions, cultural values, and institutional practices all tend to reinforce this toxic attitude. Its "logic" leads people to grow intolerant of their very humanity, rejecting their inherent flaws, shortcomings, and failings.

Discussing this topic with your college-age child should highlight your compassion while questioning the intolerance of imperfections. Discuss how dangerous this ideology is—how much it hinders people from finding real joy and happiness. Finally, point out that the ability to laugh at—even to celebrate—our mistakes and limitations can neutralize the underlying fear and self-loathing of perfectionism.

The road to self-acceptance can be long and arduous. There are no shortcuts, no easy answers. Attaining this elusive goal is a never-ending process—one that continues throughout life, requiring constant attention, energy, and practice. Here's how clinical psychologist Tara Brach looks at the topic in her book *Radical Acceptance*:

The emotion of fear often works overtime. Even when there is no immediate threat, our body may remain tight and on guard, our mind narrowed to focus on what might go wrong. When this happens, fear is no longer functioning to secure our survival. We are caught in the trance of fear and our moment-to-moment experience becomes bound in reactivity. We spend our time and energy defending our life rather than living it fully.

Clearly recognizing what is happening inside us, and regarding what we see with an open, kind, and loving heart, is what I call Radical Acceptance. If we are holding back from any part of our experience, if our heart shuts out any part of who we are and what we feel, we are fueling the fears and feelings of separation that sustain the trance of unworthiness. Radical Acceptance directly dismantles the very foundations of this trance.[5]

8. Open mindset/Help-seeking

Parents can do their kids a favor by making it clear that openness to seeking help is a sign of maturity. Developmental transitions can be so numerous—and so head-spinning—that they often threaten to overwhelm a student. Think about it: there are academic challenges, social anxieties, romantic trepidations—any one of them momentous enough to precipitate a mental health struggle. No wonder this age group describes feeling depressed 30 percent of the time and anxious 52 percent.

One college freshman's setback illustrates how openness to accepting help in the face of setbacks can make a tremendous difference. Her name was Preeta, and as an aspiring science major she saw organic chemistry as the class where dreams go to die. Preeta's midterm exam in that course therefore created a commonly experienced but potentially devastating moment for a college student: her first failure.

Understandably, Preeta's failing score caused her to question whether she could make it in this class or, indeed, at this academically rigorous university. Well before her midterm fiasco, Preeta's semester had gotten off to a rocky start: She had little energy, she told her parents. She felt bad about herself and couldn't concentrate. At their suggestion, Preeta had begun counseling, but she was still struggling with depression by the time midterms rolled around.

And then came the devastation of that failing grade, and with it thoughts of swallowing all the pills in her cabinet. Very fortunately, Preeta's phone screen lit up just then with a text from a friend: "Let's go hang out." Her friend couldn't have known it at the time, but she had just thrown Preeta a life preserver. On the way to meeting her, Preeta threw the pills away in a dorm-hall trash bin. Being with a friend—and commiserating with her about her disastrous midterm—buoyed her spirits.

Later on, with the support of her psychiatrist, Preeta decided not to drop the course. Instead, she resolved to persist. She met with the professor, and presented this daunting assessment:

> Even if I get 100 on the final exam, I will barely pass your class. I've been struggling with depression and my concentration is pretty poor. I can bring a note from the doctor to verify what I'm telling you. But I'm here because I want to complete and pass this course.

Her professor replied: "If I see that you're improving, I'll see what I can do." Preeta rallied, using the setback as motivation to study even harder to overcome it. She earned a "B" on the final exam and passed organic chemistry.

Preeta's willingness to seek help is instructive. This type of receptive mindset is an extremely valuable noncognitive skill—one that demonstrates the maturity necessary to overcome life's inevitable stumbling blocks. Too often, young people view needing help as a sign of failure—or, even worse, of being a "loser." This is especially true of high-performing students, who may have become accustomed to succeeding with only a modicum of effort. When they suddenly find themselves in Preeta's predicament, they may be too ashamed to admit they're in trouble.

Alternatively, they may minimize the difficulty of achieving success: "I'll make up this bad grade on the next test," they tell themselves. This wishful thinking takes place in a vacuum: it exists without an examination of the reasons for the poor performance, and in the absence of any resources to face the challenge. This distorted thinking comes at the expense of objective reality; it neutralizes the anxiety associated with the bad grade. Yet that very anxiety can be a prized asset in coping with disappointments, for it mobilizes us to figure out how to deal with a problem.

So don't hold back on advising your young charge to seek help just as soon as it's needed; indeed, sending her off to college *without* this knowledge may even be thought of as irresponsible. Not only does asking for help promote academic success, but it can also save the life of a young person facing depression, suicidal thinking, or other serious problems.

Even with thoughtful preparation, many young people are unprepared for the challenges to belonging and of fitting in, atop the academic and autonomy demands of college. Others may lose steam under the pressure of financial stressors and worries about not "making it." The launch to independence, as we're about to see, involves both preparing for liftoff and making the landing "stick."

3

Welcome to Campus: Overcoming Mindset Barriers to Success

Incoming freshmen have worked hard to get where they are, and none wants to hear that "now the hard part starts." We think of college as the Junior Varsity game of life. Like actors polishing their lines in a dress rehearsal, students at traditional residential colleges practice the adult roles of living away from home, making new friends, exercising self-discipline, coping more independently, and progressively mastering more difficult challenges.

Yet, both parents and students can benefit from a better understanding of the key mindset barriers to getting a degree that many college students now experience. Although today's college dropout rates are high (roughly 50 percent),[1] it's far easier to keep a student from dropping out than it is to motivate him to return after the fact. This chapter introduces you to three primary barriers to college completion that create a dropout frame of mind:

- Not belonging socially
- Fear of not "making it"
- A negative mindset that exacerbates mental health challenges

Predictably, some young people will struggle with loneliness and feelings that they don't belong. Still other students will experience a combination of unfortunate events mixed with competitive stress, lack of experience with failure, and insufficient support, which can lead to discouragement early on. Or, despite a good freshman year, the sophomore slump appears. Parents may find themselves fielding worrisome phone calls about a myriad of problems including the feeling of not fitting in: "I couldn't find the right club. . . . I got dropped from sorority rush. . . . I hate it here!" Or perhaps you've already faced one of these scenarios:

"I'm in over my head. . . . I'll never make it. . . . I'm just wasting your money."

"I'm setting myself up to be a lifelong debt serf."

"I failed a subject in my major; should I drop out before I flunk out?"

"What's the point of staying here when I don't have a clue why I'm here?"

The first signs of trouble may create paralysis, isolation, and a deepening cycle of pessimism. These are the interior walls the human mind has an annoying tendency of erecting. To prevent dropout, we consider how students can overcome these barriers to college graduation. More than any one problem or experience, a mindset barrier entails a vulnerable and unevaluated belief system, which leads to discouragement, emotional distress, and loss of interest in classes. Whereas most students will encounter painful or distressing moments and moods, how they manage them will dictate their outcome. Will such episodes constitute mere bumps in the road or lead to a shutdown and exit home?

Knowing about these issues before college admission can be a wise safeguard, because you can screen colleges to assess the efforts they are making to reverse dropout trends. And you will almost certainly become conversant with them should a talented but vulnerable student feel disengaged, grow depressed, take a leave of absence, flunk out, or drop out.

Let's explore the three mindset barriers and introduce you to promising interventions that students, parents, and colleges are using to vault these hurdles.

Barrier 1: Belonging—
You Gotta Have Friends

The goal of college completion often focuses on individual academic abilities, the summoning of grit, and task persistence despite setbacks. College administrators bolster retention through an array of programs and practices designed to help students adjust, including (as one glossy campus brochure promises), "orientation, transition courses and first-year seminars, learning communities, intensive advising, tutoring, supplemental instruction, peer tutoring, study groups and summer bridge programs, study skills workshops, mentoring and student support groups, student-faculty research, and senior capstone projects."[2] (Whew!)

These emphases may be soundly based, yet they principally embody the perspective of parents, teachers, and college administrators. From the student's vantage point, by contrast, the one thing that makes the traditional residential-college experience an appealing one is friendships. Reflecting on her college experience, one graduate summed up the advice she gives freshmen: "Everyone's so excited and telling you what a terrific time you'll have at college; but there's nothing wrong with you if you're homesick, or worried that your social life is mostly spent inside your dorm room that first month. It takes time to belong."

Sociology professor Daniel Chambliss confirms this graduate's wisdom in *How College Works*: "First they must enter the social world of college, most importantly by finding friends. Failing that, little else matters." Indeed, Chambliss notes, "Social integration is a strong and significant predictor of graduation."[3]

His recent eleven-year study of student perspectives on college life emphatically concludes: "Satisfactory personal relationships are a *prerequisite* for learning. Only by having friends will students 'buy into' the college experience at all, and devote the time and effort to learning. Students who fail to find friends, or at least workable substitutes, are likely to drop out of college, if not officially then at least emotionally."[4,5] The power of social connection extends so far that a student's GPA often rises or falls in lockstep with that of his roommates.[6] A student's unofficial goal should therefore be to find friends early and quickly.

Proximity + Experience = Friendship

For most students, bonding occurs in a group of shared interests, or in the immediacy of dorm life. But not just any dorm. Parents and students are often wowed by the high-priced spread of the new college dorm suites, decked out with amenities. Poke your head into the community rooms, though, and no one's there. The dorm hallways are likewise empty. Everyone is cloistered in his suite, doors closed in fire-code compliance, hooked up to the screen of their choice: computer, PlayStation, iPad, smartphone. "Freshmen don't realize," writes Chambliss, "that the dorms they least prefer (long institutional hallways, shared bathrooms, multiple roommates) may in fact be the most helpful in their search for friends on campus."[7]

Shared experiences and challenges can also be pivotal in forging friendships. One student recounted a memorable bonding experience his freshman year, courtesy of the October 2012 landfall of Hurricane Sandy. Shamir's university in Lower Manhattan closed for a week. Within twelve hours of Sandy's devastating deluge of the Northeast, parents were notified that classes were canceled. Students who could do so were advised to leave campus. The dorms were operating on backup generators, with only hallway floor lighting; no hot food, heat, or hot water, and very limited Internet access. Shamir's parents, who lived ninety miles away, called to see if he could get out of the stricken neighborhood. With no subway or bus service, it would be a half-hour walk to the Amtrak station. They urged him to return home.

"I'm good," Shamir told them sheepishly. "It sounds awful to say, but I'm having a great time." He and a small group of new friends made each day an adventure: walking thirty blocks north to find hot food, taking photos of the sunset over the darkened city during the weeklong power outage, and having get-togethers unmediated by Wi-Fi or smartphones. Enduring friendships were made that autumn—and four years later, Shamir and company all graduated together.

Troubleshooting, Not Belonging

When social life fails, college fails. When students become emotionally detached, they grow less inclined to pursue their academic goals. Isolation is widely recognized as a problem afflicting older Americans, but adolescents and emerging adults are actually the ones most at risk for loneliness and depression and also run a higher risk for suicide than do prior generations. Helping students succeed should therefore begin with making ourselves aware of the obstacles to this crucial social belonging.

We typically think of vulnerable youth as those who have been discriminated against or bullied, whether physically, emotionally, or online. More recently, in addition to students whose minority status or behavioral, social, or emotional differences resulted in experiences of bullying, exclusion, or rejection, high schools and colleges have identified the risk of "intersectionality," a word coined by law professor Kimberlé Williams Crenshaw.[8] This focus explores the idea that forms of prejudice overlap. In higher education, this translates into how social identities (racial, religious affiliation, sexual orientation, disability, and class) influence educational and mental health experiences, particularly for minority and historically underserved groups.

Students from these groups may have first-person experiences of bias, racism, sexism, and related violence that increases their vulnerability to anxiety or depression. A brief glimpse of the mental health risk in college youth reflects higher suicidal ideation among Asian youth (though not suicide itself); African American college-age males have both low use of counseling services and increasing rates of suicide. Latino college-age students report some of the highest rates of depression. Muslim and international students, veterans, and LGBTQ students are also at higher risk for anxiety and depression.[9] According to surveys by the Centers for Disease Control and Prevention, LGBTQ youth report a greater risk for depression, substance use, and STDs, including HIV. Nearly one-third of LGB youth had attempted suicide at least once in the prior year compared to 6 percent of heterosexual youth.[10] These "identity" groups may of course intersect with other social and mental health vulnerabilities: the first-generation college student, the college-bound Dreamers (students lacking legal immigration status), the students from a lower socioeconomic class who feel highly responsible and pressured by their family's financial sacrifices.

Safe Spaces

Colleges increasingly understand these risks and have created "safe spaces" for students at risk due to prejudice, isolation, trauma, or feeling a burden to or in conflict with parents. These include student-led and organized clubs that promote safe spaces, such as minority-led clubs, gay–straight alliances, or gender and sexuality clubs open to all. Mental health peer support can be gained through such nationally affiliated campus groups as NAMI-Campus, JED, and Active Minds, which are fully described in Chapter 11. Additionally, counselors, faculty and staff with training, can invite students to share their own stories, or simply feel the solidarity of others.

University of Texas (UT) psychology professor David Yeager has demonstrated an effective student-led intervention. Yeager instructed small groups of students to read and write a basic message: "People can change." This long view delivers a vital message to young people who may have encountered rejection or bullying: "You will not always be a target; you can change; others can change."[11] Yeager's groups learned better coping skills from one another in a lecture-free zone where it was safe to share personal experiences.

Safe Spaces Start at Home

It's worth noting that the universal buffer against the experience of exclusion, discrimination, or stand-alone mental health problems is a warm and understanding parent–child relationship. Parents can employ the same supportive and open attitudes toward these youth, as we would generally recommend, but they may need to become more aware of their own biases or societal stigma. In the next chapter we talk about how parents can make their homes a safe space through efforts to improve effective parenting with warmer and less conflictual family relationships.

Another surefire ounce of prevention can occur in the college-search mode: Parents—trust your child's impression of whether a campus culture looks or feels right. Your student's sense of his ability to fit in is a vital clue. What may seem trivial to an adult—"The girls wear too much makeup. . . . There weren't many people in the student union. . . . The kids don't dress or look like me"—may in fact be an astute forecast of social belonging.

Post admission, the culture of an institution can be a key factor in promoting bonding. Do resident and academic "advisers" live up to their title? Are there shared classroom and extracurricular experiences?

Do campus activities foster an esprit de corps? An absence of these qualities may prove problematic.

You'll also want to fine-tune your parental radar to pick up "outlier" obstacles to social belonging: Does your student have a network of only one group? Is she involved in a romantic relationship back home? Will she face the social challenges inherent in being a transfer student? Might there be an encroaching mental illness?[12]

Let's look at how Cam got into his first-choice college—but never really gained a sense of belonging there:

> When I first visited my "reach" college, I was turned off by the vibe. I loved the big-city scene, but the college was socially disconnected. There was no real campus, just a bunch of buildings scattered over a fifteen-block radius. I should've trusted my gut, but I was so happy to get accepted—and my parents were so proud of me for getting into this competitive university—that I overrode my first impressions.
>
> I felt reassured when my new-student summer weekend went really well. But when I arrived in the fall, by the luck of the draw I didn't really make friends with anyone in my suite. The dorms were huge—like living on your own in an apartment building. No one even said "Hi" in the elevators—it was like a perpetual-loop movie shot, with everyone facing forward and not speaking.
>
> I made a couple of good friends that year, but as the year wore on the isolation became unbearable. So I transferred.
>
> That didn't solve all my social problems either.
>
> There was no dorm space for transfers, so housing was off-campus, and roommates were trial by fire. The Housing Office did very little to make sure you landed in one of the country's tightest housing markets. Once the semester started, I tried to join a fraternity to make friends, but the frat got suspended, so there went that option. I tried to join a few clubs, but only one panned out. That club is where I began to make friends—but it was a slow process.
>
> Despite it all, I graduated with honors and on time. But it wasn't the fun that had been advertised, and it sure didn't feel like the best years of my life.

TIPS FOR TRANSFERS

�֍ Transfer students often miss the early bonding of life in a freshman dorm, so they must push a little harder to meet new friends. Here are five ways they can smooth their transition:

- Find dedicated campus dorm space for transfer students. Off-campus housing typically creates barriers to belonging.
- Join a "transfer club" in addition to other campus social clubs. If one doesn't exist, start one with the help of an upperclassman designated to serve as a mentor or social support for transfer students.
- Attend orientation day when transfer students can meet one another, or become acquainted with campus and community resources.
- Have an academic adviser for transfer students assigned to you. This is especially helpful to students who must fulfill certain academic or residential requirements in order to study abroad.
- Join or start a Facebook group for transfer students. Attend their community-building activities.

Barrier 2: FONMI (Fear Of Not Making It)

The Great Recession took a heavy toll on college-graduation rates, reports Doug Shapiro, executive research director of the National Student Clearinghouse.[13] With so much recent media attention on soaring college costs, many people naturally blame the high dropout rate on financial problems. Yes, a hike in tuition or living expenses or the loss of a scholarship can force students to withdraw, but the chief instigator of dropout decisions is not financial. It is the mindset belief, precipitated by academic setbacks, that: *"I'm not cut out for this; I can't make it."* When the predictable transitional anxieties of a college freshman meet up with a disappointing grade, the result can be increased attrition. The FONMI mindset problem attacks the sense of self-efficacy for students across socioeconomic divides, yet the impact is strikingly different for students from enriched versus disadvantaged backgrounds.

FONMI and Privilege

Because the word "privilege" may connote spoiled, rich, or undeserving, and create a sense of guilt for winning the birth lottery, let's define what we mean. Related to educational achievement, a privileged background means the backing of resource-enriched familial and educational contexts. This can be embodied by a house full of print or e-books, parents or teachers that have confidence in you, being a second (rather than first) generation college student, economic security, and not being excluded for being "different" by virtue of minority or stigmatized class status.

Privilege doesn't mean that you haven't struggled or worked hard. And it certainly doesn't mean that you aren't stressed. However, privilege, with its built-in resources, does confer many invisible benefits related to the experience of "making it" in college.

Circumstances and conditioning favor the graduation rates for students from the upper socioeconomic strata (SES), 90 percent of whom will complete college within six years.[14] While these students experience intense—sometimes debilitating—pressure to succeed, they arrive at college seeing academic reverses as temporary. While half of all college freshmen will soon discover themselves in the lower 50 percent of the pack, the better resourced bring a resilient mindset that has been nurtured by their parents, their equally ambitious peers, and their secondary schools. When they flub a college exam, these students tend to believe they have the ability to improve a grade. In short, they believe—rightly or wrongly—that they *belong and can make it*. So what's their mindset problem?

Their version of not succeeding equates a less-than-stellar mark with a ruined future. They arrive in campus counseling centers freaking out over a B+ while not realizing that two-thirds of their classmates will get a B- or lower. Their problem lies in what faculty at Harvard and Stanford call "failure deprivation," or the lack of natural learning opportunities prior to college to both experience and learn from their stumbles and screwups without falling apart.[15] To combat this mindset, they need to learn to fail and to cope better with academic setbacks that attack their basic sense of self-worth. How do they learn this, when failure to them feels so dangerous to bright future prospects?

Failure Inoculation

As colleges become more transparent about their dropout rates, innovations are emerging to address this individual and societal problem. A notable development is failure inoculation. This program takes aim at the blow to self-esteem that can lead to feelings of self-defeat, isolation, and even attrition. Following the rise on campus of mental health problems such as depression and anxiety and even campus suicides, a consortium of top-notch universities has formed to share resources.[16] Certain elite colleges, where you have to look practically perfect on paper to gain acceptance, have introduced "learning to fail" teaching moments as part of freshman orientation and during exam periods. Still others have put an unofficial "failure czar" in place in residence life, a specialist whose job it is to help students learn to accept inevitable setbacks.[17] Beyond the Ivies, at the University of Texas at Austin, THRIVE is a free iPhone app developed to help students better withstand the ups and downs.[18]

And What Can Parents Do?

Prior to college, parents, counselors, and students can ask about whether a college offers failure inoculation. At home, parents can lead by example. Describe your own experiences of overcoming failure, of the non-linearity of life. Do so with a message of self-acceptance, rather than "fail upward" striving. Self-acceptance sounds like, "I did—and you will—screw up and make mistakes in relationships, regret harsh words, make poor judgments, get bad grades, and at the same time be a totally worthy human being." Whenever your child, teen, or college student shares their own disappointments and struggles, listen with compassion, don't judge, acknowledge their courage in telling you. Lending courage by example, we take a page from the life of Dr. Anthony Rostain.

Having started Yale University at age 16, he found himself academically overwhelmed and deeply alienated from the preppie culture that dominated the all-male institution. He thought about transferring schools, but the advent of co-education and the unfolding of other important political events on campus convinced him to stay on for his sophomore year. While he developed a close set of friends, became involved with a serious romantic relationship, and felt engaged in a variety of extracurricular activities (acting, radio announcing, and political activism), Dr. Rostain devoted little, if any, time to his studies. By the spring of his second year, as he was facing failures in several subjects, he decided he needed to take time away from school. With the help and support of his college dean and master, he found a job working in a day care center in Boston and took a leave of absence. This proved to be a turning point in his life, for it inspired him to dedicate his life to working with children and to pursue a college degree with a newly discovered seriousness of purpose. "The fact that I had to leave Yale and come back on my own terms really was formative for me," Dr. Rostain recalls. "I had this sense there was something I needed to do that I couldn't do at college. That 'something' was growing up."

FONMI and the Minority Experience

By contrast, minority students—whether defined by ethnicity, class, financial disadvantage, first-generation college attendance, learning challenges, or emotional problems—are more vulnerable to suffering in silence, not seeking help, and dropping out.[19] These students are more vulnerable to interpreting a bad grade or the bottom-half setback both seriously and personally, with a demoralizing freak-out: "I won't make it . . . I'm not smart enough to be in college." And their parents, who may have limited educations, may be ill-equipped to convince them otherwise. Only about a quarter of college freshmen born into the bottom half of the income distribution will manage to collect a bachelor's degree by age twenty-four.[20] In the divide between those who graduate from college and those who don't, the supposedly native ability of being smart enough or industrious enough to "make it" turns out to be a minor factor.

All college students are on an upwardly mobile trajectory, but only the minority students are subject to John Henryism—the kind of high-effort coping that can trigger exhaustion and defeat.[21] Overcoming the odds is often seen as evidence of the culturally much-vaunted "grit," But for students who have worked hard within a system that has denied them equal opportunity, succeeding against the odds comes at a high price.[22] Their specific risks include acculturation difficulties, academic gaps, lack of family awareness about college visits or financial aid applications, and lack of financial resources.[23] The fear of not making it/ failure mindset affects low-income and minority students differently. Their experience is not, "I got a B, my future is at risk," but a harsh reality: "I *literally* can't afford to fail, because if I lose my scholarship, or have to take a remedial course, my family can't afford the extra cost, and my dreams are lost."

The overtaxed neuroimmune systems of strivers from disadvantaged backgrounds make them disproportionately subject to everything from increased levels of the stress hormone cortisol to juvenile diabetes.[24] To keep this cadre of undergrads from dropping out, the typical intervention focuses on changing an overanxious mindset—fueled by unjustified shame at "not belonging" or "not making it"[25]—to a more confident one.

So What Can Be Done to Help?

Colleges have recently stepped in to stem the FONMI dropout tide. As colleges better identify the particular risk factors of traditionally underrepresented students, they are beginning to offer a variety of supports designed to increase academic success and graduation rates. At UT, professor Yeager, for one, has become a leading voice in the movement to help minority college students stay in school. He devised a failure-mindset "inoculation" that helps students defeat their doubts about belonging or about their ability to succeed.[26] Yeager recruited minority or first-generation upperclassmen to persuade by personal example. These upperclassmen fostered an empowering belief set change—"I can improve, I belong here, I can make it"—through disclosing their own earlier and similar struggles to the younger students. The result? The younger students felt an empowering change in their beliefs, which boosted their self-confidence. This inside-out approach—change your mindset, change yourself—happens to be a bedrock of cognitive behavioral therapy (CBT). Yeager also developed a computer-based peer group format using individual writing assignments to challenge self-defeating thoughts. The upshot: a steep downturn in UT's freshman attrition rate.

Colleges are increasingly implementing brief but effective student-to-student diversity education in freshman orientation. Counselors and staff are being trained to understand and provide support for the unique stressors of this population, including the "imposter" syndrome of "I don't belong here," feelings of cultural isolation or the disloyalty of leaving family and traditions behind, and the ongoing pressure of financial worries that many meet by working full- or part-time during the school year.[27]

Financial Stressor$

The pressure on a student to succeed is only amplified by financial burdens and looming student-loan debt.[28] First-generation students and students from lower-income families are particularly subject to worry about whether the sacrifices their parents are making are "worth it." A poor grade can lead to questioning the very value of a college education, and an increased risk of dropout. The student most adversely affected by this dynamic, of course, is the one who leaves college with no degree but plenty of debt.

No matter what rung of the SES ladder they occupy, both parent and child are affected by the awareness of financial sacrifice. At the affluent end of the spectrum, a sophomore attending an expensive K–12 private school told a group of parents, "We feel all this pressure to get into an Ivy League college." "Oh, no," the parents countered, "don't stress out over that." Unmollified, the student persisted: "Why else would you be spending all this money to send us to these private schools?" The parents fell silent.

In the middle of the economic range, middle-class parents who make up Gen X (ages 36 to 51) are being squeezed financially. Caught unprepared by the 2007–2008 housing bubble and credit crash, many will likely have to pay for college out of income, not savings. As a result, they will have to delay their retirements by 5 to 7 years.[29] Their children feel both grateful for their sacrifice and pressured by it.

Most burdened are students whose family incomes fall in the lowest economic quintile. Twenty to thirty percent of low-income high school graduates of urban school districts who had been accepted by— and planned to attend—four-year colleges didn't end up enrolling anywhere.[30] Colleges call this "summer melt." For those who do attend their first year of college, more than a quarter of college freshmen from low-income families do not return for a second year.[31] These students often face a morass of financial worries, with limited information about financial aid and heightened anxiety about asking so much of their parents.

Chris Lehmann, founding principal of the Science Leadership Academy (SLA), a Philadelphia magnet high school, notes the link between financial pressures and mental health stressors and college dropout:[32]

> *There's a financial pressure on students not to fail, which creates more stress. Because colleges are much more a mercenary experience than they were previously, students feel the pressure of how much money their parents are spending . . . or how much debt they may incur. If you're a kid who feels like you're faking it, and your family is spending thirty thousand dollars a year, and you're taking out twenty thousand dollars in loans, you may feel like a failure—and the pressure you're feeling not to fail is massive.*

Principal Lehmann describes an advisement system to assist each senior with an acceptance to debt equation to determine the viability of particular college and family finances:

> *At SLA, 46 percent are in a high economic-need category; 98 percent go on to college, with a 70 percent completion rate within six years. (That's much higher than the national average, especially considering our high degree of economic need.)*
>
> *We now tell kids that they need an academic safety school and a financial safety school. The hard part is that you don't want to limit yourself to your financial safety school; some of these big colleges have a high price tag but offer the most money.*

"We had a situation a few years ago," Lehmann recalls, "where a college was a top choice for one of our students. Though her single mother was well under the poverty line, the college said the family should contribute more than the mother made."

"This kid had set her sights on this school, so she was heartbroken. But she was an amazing student, and she had also gotten a wonderful offer with a lot of financial assistance from another school. Eventually we persuaded her to attend her second choice, but not before sitting her down with a loan calculator and saying, 'If you go to your first choice without financial aid, you're going to graduate with so much debt you're

looking at living in a cheap room somewhere eating ramen noodles.'"
This caring reality check anticipated and averted the risk of decreased
persistence and potential dropout for a student burdened by accumu-
lated student loan debt.

Counterintuitively, perhaps, enrolling in a rigorous program ups
your odds of graduating. Many low-income students "undermatch,"
meaning they neglect to apply to the most selective college that would
accept them—or, if admitted, they opt not to attend.[33] They may rule
out these colleges on the basis of their higher costs, unaware that substantial financial aid is available. Or they may believe, naïvely but
wrongly, that they won't fit in at a more competitive school, or be able to
thrive there. Before college, students and parents may be helped by
K–12 staff and by partnering national organizations such as College
Advising Corps (advisingcorps.org) and College for Every Student
(CFES; collegefes.org).

Whatever the source of a student's FONMI mindset barrier,
colleges are stepping in with successful interventions (failure inoculation, THRIVE, persuasion by tutoring, and personal example) designed to help students vanquish their doubts about not making it.
When combined with coursework assistance and/or counseling, these
lifelines promise to give students the resilience to persist despite setbacks.[34]

THE INOCULATION MINDSET

✖ Looking for a shot in the arm for an insecure student?
Try supplying him with these confidence boosters:

- An academic setback doesn't mean you don't belong or
  can't make it.
- Don't take a reversal personally—the majority of students
  have them.
- Older peers can teach younger students.
- You won't always feel this way.
- You can get help and improve.

Barrier 3: Emotional Problems

Asked whether they had experienced a "critical event," such as poor grades, money problems, or a job offer just before prematurely leaving a college, students most often cited depression as their reason for withdrawing.[35] What a shame, since depression responds to treatment. And other mental disorders that create barriers to belonging—among them social anxiety, autism spectrum, and social or communication disorders—can be mitigated by a regimen of counseling and/or medication.

As a hopeful sign, college students—never known for their quiet acceptance of a change for the worse—organized protests across the country in 2015 to demand additional mental health counselors and minority staffing on campuses. The latter stipulation arose from an especially troubling statistic: although minority students now constitute 40 percent of the total college populace, they report higher rates of depression than do white students but are less likely to seek help.[36] These figures underscore the challenge of caring for a population that is both underserved and at higher risk.[37]

I'm Okay and I Don't Need Help

Making campus mental health services widely available has become a national priority. Yet the vast majority of distraught college students still hesitate to seek help. One recent survey found that less than one-fourth of students with any mental disorder—and less than one-half of students screening positive for depression or anxiety disorders—had received mental health services in the prior twelve months. Of even graver concern, less than half of students who seriously considered attempting suicide in the previous twelve months had received any treatment during that period. According to reports from counseling center directors, 81 percent of students known to have died from suicide were never seen by campus mental health professionals.[38]

Similar findings emerged from an Internet treatment intervention program for seriously depressed college students.[39] Of the 165 participants, the one or more reasons given for not seeking help included:

"My problems are not serious enough to warrant assistance."
(66 percent)
"I don't have enough time." (27 percent)
"I prefer to manage my problems on my own." (18 percent)
"I'd rather seek help from my family or friends." (16 percent)
"There are pragmatic barriers to getting treatment." (16 percent)

In many cases, students simply lack the information or insight to recognize the need for help. Fortunately, the university of today is teaching students to recognize the signs of mental illness in themselves and their peers—especially mood, anxiety, and substance-use disorders. It is publicizing the availability of mental health services both on campus and in the community, and it is urging students in distress to take advantage of these resources.

One promising line of intervention aims to reduce the stigma of mental illness. Bred by societal stereotypes and biases, mental health–related stigma can be a two-pronged threat: it may take the form of an unspoken social stigma, or it may show up as a more insidious and internalized self-stigma—that is, a personal negative self-appraisal.[40]

Both social stigma and self-stigma can discourage a college student from seeking treatment, as demonstrated by a comprehensive longitudinal Healthy Minds Study,[41,42] of over 5,500 college students. Personal stigma also reduces the use of psychotropic medication, therapy, and nonclinical sources of support. Personal stigma makes a few groups even more vulnerable to help-rejection, particularly younger college students (freshmen and sophomores) with any of the following characteristics: male, Asian, international, very religious, or from a poor family. Parents and teens can benefit from a heightened awareness of their more reflexive resistance to help-seeking. The good news is that personal stigma decreases with age. It also improves with awareness and self-acceptance, and an open mindset to seek help when its needed.

The confusion between normal and troublesome (but treatable) moods can combine with the effects of personal stigma to keep an individual in need from seeking help. Parents may also have a positive bias about their student's moods and minimize an ongoing problem. That happened to Taylor, a socially reserved freshman girl we counseled who was well-liked in high school and always hung out with a few good friends.

Taylor and her mother thought she had conquered what they termed her "shyness." After all, Taylor was excited to leave home for college, a five-hour drive away. But when college backfired for Taylor, her mother confronted her own positive mental health bias—that is, her tendency to downplay or outright dismiss the very clear symptoms of Taylor's mental health issues:[43]

> *I thought I'd done a good job with Taylor's first college search, matching many metrics to her academic interests, social clubs, and activities. By "college" I imagined handsome, ivy-covered buildings surrounding a central quad, dorms filled with the smell of popcorn. I didn't consider community college or even a nearby commuter school.*
>
> *Taylor's first choice was a really big university. Knowing she was shy, I felt nervous about it, but the campus tour guide reassured us on that score: "You can't make a small college bigger, but you can make a big college smaller."*
>
> *It was a good line, but it proved not to be true. Taylor had a hard time making friends. She felt like she didn't fit in. She went to the counseling office a few times, but what she really needed were friends to hang out with.*
>
> *In hindsight—this was after Taylor had dropped out her freshman year—I had missed the obvious: If you question whether your child is resilient enough to weather the many challenges of independence, don't send her far away!*
>
> *Through my daughter's lonely experience, I've learned that what I'd been calling "shyness" was actually social anxiety, a treatable mental disorder. Back home, Taylor joined a therapy group that focused on overcoming the condition. After a second college search, she became a commuter student, then transitioned to dorm living a year later. This time, she was ready.*

As Taylor's mother discovered, "shyness" rings of normalcy, whereas "social anxiety" sounds scary, clinical, and stigmatizing. Yet her daughter's experience of feeling overwhelmed to the point of giving up is instructive, for it constitutes yet another tile in the larger mosaic of Emotional Problems Can Be Treated to Prevent Dropout. As Taylor and her mother learned, the decision to stay local and attend a community college—or to enroll as a commuting student in a four-year college—can build upon a student's earlier successes.

Those may strike some as "baby steps," but they are critical stepping-stones on the way to developing the self-confidence necessary to manage a later transfer to traditional campus life. Additionally, more students now attend a community college than any other form of higher education, as the more affordable price tag appeals to many families. More importantly, alternative pathways to success enable young people and parents to break out of a linear mindset.

Not All Those Who Wander Are Lost

J. R. R. Tolkien's quote from *The Fellowship of the Ring* reassures us that a detour from a linear college track does not mean a child has abandoned the path to success or to independence. The hushed reality is that parents from all walks of life have children who may require a more flexible route from cradle to mortarboard, including community or commuter college or college deferral. In fact, these alternate paths through higher education are more common than most parents realize.

A deferral, whether work or gap year, can be daunting for families that have never considered anything but a direct academic trajectory, writes Jeffrey Selingo, author of *There Is Life After College*: "Getting a bachelor's degree is so ingrained in our culture that students who do not march along are often admonished, questioned, and considered—or consider themselves—failures."[44] But the only reason more parents and students don't pursue temporary alternatives to higher education, we believe, is that they lack the support to resist the pressure to move in lockstep and the information they need to see how and why alternatives might be a better fit.

Mindset Review

This chapter has focused on the top three reasons students cite for dropping out of college: not belonging socially, fear of not "making it," and a negative mindset that may incubate and exacerbate mental health challenges. Next, we immerse ourselves in the riptide that students, parents, and families struggle against when problems first arise. A student who sailed through high school may surprise herself and her parents when anxiety strikes in college. Other teens may send distress signals prior to enrollment. We advise families to reach safety by exploring their positive and negative biases about their student and the related issue of the stigma of mental illness. We offer options they might never have otherwise considered, which can turn a mental health crisis or even a scrubbed liftoff into a maturation booster.

4

What to Expect When Johnny's Got Issues

Not everything that is faced can be changed, but nothing can be changed until it is faced.

—JAMES BALDWIN

In the spring semester of her freshman year, Adrienne Malloy sought counseling at her college mental health center. Her familiar anxiety had taken a nasty turn into feelings of failure and hopelessness: she felt she didn't really fit in with the friends she had made during freshman week; she was having trouble keeping up with the requirements of her major; her concentration was poor; and she wasn't sleeping well.

Following several appointments with no obvious signs of improved mood, her counselor referred her to the center's psychiatrist, who prescribed the antidepressant escitalopram. Adrienne then made the difficult phone call to her parents back home, two thousand miles away.

In response to their daughter's call, the Malloys contacted the center's psychiatrist, who could tell from their flood of questions that they were stunned and distraught:

"We sent a happy kid to college—what happened?"

"Her Facebook posts always look so upbeat—what are we supposed to believe?"

"How could my daughter be so depressed that she needs medication?"

"What is this medicine? Is it dangerous?"

The doctor listened to their concerns politely, then told them that the HIPAA campus privacy laws limited him from responding until their daughter gave her signed consent.

"HIPAA, what's that?" the Malloys wanted to know.

Following the call, the couple argued about the wisdom of psychoactive medication. Whereas Adrienne's father was a "better living through chemistry" guy, her mother saw the prescription as a mere quick fix. Mrs. Malloy, whose mother had been depressed for much of her childhood, strongly believed everyone was responsible for their own happiness. But she was also scared, relaying the story of a friend of a friend whose son had attempted suicide after starting a similar medication.

And both parents were full of self-reproach: "What earlier signs did we miss? Was this downturn preventable? What would Adrienne's recovery entail? How can we agree on the best plan?" And, unproductively: "Whose side of the family did this come from?"

Though her loving and supportive parents had done many things right, their initial responses—feelings of guilt, a tendency to blame, parenting differences—signaled trouble ahead. Unfamiliar with HIPAA, the medical records privacy law, they initially concluded her treatment would exclude them. And the family history of depression only complicated matters, by creating some distorted beliefs about mental illness: the Malloys were unaware that untreated mood disorders can sweep away the ability to work, to organize one's time, and even to manage such basic functions as sleeping and eating.

Another curveball: Mom and Dad never anticipated how Adrienne's depression would expose their parenting differences and strain their marriage. We'll return to the Malloys to explore the lessons they learned in order to participate in Adrienne's treatment and recovery.

Whether you're early or late to the game—alerted by a red flag that appeared in late adolescence, or surprised (as Adrienne's parents were) by a call from your college student hundreds of miles from home—this chapter can help prepare you for what may lie ahead. We'll review college mental health privacy laws and discuss the biases and stigma that thwart seeking help. And we'll invite you to assess the common mental health problems that may run in the family, while sharing some tips on how to avoid self-blame.

Parental Readiness

Despite the recent surge in mental health problems reported for this age group, parents like the Malloys often—and understandably—think, "Not *my* child. He's prepared; she's happy; he's got a good head on his shoulders. Mental problems don't run in our family." Yet positive biases, as well as their counterpart in negative biases, can delay treatment and worsen a college student's struggle. Many parents are unfamiliar with the advance planning needed to prepare for a possible college mental health problem. Parental readiness requires both practical steps—learning about college mental health services and privacy documentation—and introducing certain emotional practices that support a youth's resilience under the increased demands of independence.

So take heart. Experts have identified specific parenting styles and emotional prep that foster self-reliance, create safe spaces within the family, and strengthen the parent–child relationship. This chapter is designed to make you aware of them, with an emphasis on offering your adolescent or young adult the most effective help regardless of the type or severity of his problem.

Advance Treatment Planning

One of the most important—but most often overlooked—implications of an eighteenth birthday is that parents no longer have legal authority over the student as a patient. Many parents, among them Adrienne's, are initially confused by the privacy laws governing a college student's medical or mental health treatment. There are two main laws you should know about:

- HIPAA, the Health Insurance Portability and Accountability Act of 1996, protects the privacy of a medical patient's health records, whether hard copy or electronic. It generally prohibits medical providers, including college counselors, from sharing information with anyone—including parents—without the patient's (in this case the student's) permission. Although health care professionals have discretion to share information without the patient's permission, those who are "risk averse" will not. These safeguards mean that simply identifying yourself as the parent during a medical emergency will not necessarily empower you to make medical decisions for your child.

- FERPA, the Family Educational Rights and Privacy Act, protects students' *educational* records. This law explains why you won't receive a copy of your student's grades unless they specifically authorize it. But FERPA also governs confidentiality policies for college employees and guarantees that each college is free to make its own policy about when and how to notify parents of a student's trouble at school. For example, at some institutions, if a student is taken to a university-affiliated emergency room for alcohol poisoning, the parents may not become aware of the fact until they receive the hospital bill. FERPA also applies when a student studies abroad. Simply being his parent won't allow you to sign tax returns or leases for the coming year on his behalf.

The interaction of the two laws can be complex, so it pays to familiarize yourself with the basics (which are further detailed in the Appendix, including crisis planning). A little advance planning can help you take these privacy issues in stride. Before your college hopeful turns eighteen, have him fill out the crucial document known as an *advance directive*. It allows the student to stipulate who should be allowed to participate in his medical treatment and, should it come to that, who should be allowed to make decisions on his behalf.

You can obtain authorization forms from your student's physician or download the HIPAA Release Form online (http://www.nami.org/collegeguide.download). Remember to give your student the originals and keep two copies for yourself. Having your rising college freshman sign these documents should be a top priority, for it will give you both peace of mind.

Prepare to answer questions from your child about the future release of potentially confidential information. He may not be thrilled at the prospect you'll discover that too much partying sent him to the ER. You can counter this objection by reminding him you'd find out anyway when the hospital sends you the bill. Or she may not want you to know her poor grades are jeopardizing her scholarship. Again, point out you'll learn the bad news when the tuition bill arrives minus the scholarship.

It's natural that any young adult who prizes his autonomy will balk at sharing information. That's your cue to broach the notion of mutual trust: while he must respect your desire to lend support, you have to be counted on not to be judgmental or intrusive. College students need all sorts of reassurance, so let him know he'll be able to discuss any concerns before authorizing a medical or mental health provider to share treatment details.

In the case of Adrienne's mental health crisis, the Malloys found they were not totally shut out. Even in the absence of a signed authorization form, they were able to call Adrienne's psychiatrist and express their concerns. (His responses, by contrast, were limited until she had signed a release of confidentiality.) At her parents' request, Adrienne visited student health the next day and filled out the forms permitting more open communication.

Doctor Shopping

As if the family didn't have enough on its mind, Mr. and Mrs. Malloy also worried about Adrienne's prescribing psychiatrist; was he the best doctor for their daughter? They'd never met him, after all, and Mrs. Malloy remained unconvinced that antidepressants were the answer. Could Adrienne seek a second opinion, they wondered, without alienating the first psychiatrist?

Most college students have the benefit of an on-site treatment team through campus counseling services. Typically, a student may call in, or walk in and complete the paperwork necessary for problem screening on the spot. Next comes an appointment with a staff counselor, typically one trained as a social worker or psychologist. If the case is urgent, the student may then be referred to the counseling center's psychiatrist.

Campus counseling services often limit the length and frequency of treatment, though they often supplement in-person counseling with app-based mood lists, online meditations, and group therapy support. If more intense or specialized treatment is needed, the counseling center can refer the student to a vetted local provider. Whether the parent or the student conducts this "treatment shopping," it's important to feel free to ask the provider whatever questions may occur to you. The National Alliance on Mental Illness (NAMI) provides a very helpful list of questions to consider when seeking a mental health professional.[1]

At your first visit with a doctor or therapist, you're primarily seeking advice. But you're also interviewing providers, so it's reasonable to ask questions (see the list below for some samples).

Approaching mental health problems in a calm, value-neutral way will encourage help-seeking on a student's part. And that's a huge step forward, because the early detection of cognitive problems, poor coping reactions, and mood disorders is crucial to a student's recovery and long-term well-being.

QUESTIONS TO ASK A THERAPIST

Even when a therapist has a good reputation or a high level of education, the most important thing is whether you can work well together. The personal questions a therapist asks may sometimes make you uncomfortable, but the individual himself should not. You can use the following questions to establish that this person is a good fit for your concerns:

- How much education and professional experience do you have?
- Have you worked with people like me? For how long?
- How do you typically collaborate with a patient to establish goals and evaluate progress?
- How often will you meet with me, and how hard is it to get an appointment? May I phone, text, or email between appointments? What kind of improvements should I expect to see?
- Will the therapy be short-term or longer? Are you a staff therapist or an intern who may leave while I'm in treatment?
- May I pay on a sliding scale or at a discount? (Doctors and therapists would like to know ahead of time if you're concerned about your ability to meet insurance co-pays or deductibles; it's important to continue treatment without interruption.)

What Did We Miss?

When a young adult's mood, behavior, eating habits, or physical appearance change or take a downturn, parents often wonder, "What did we miss?" Yet it's usually very difficult for parents to distinguish between a benign transitional mood phase and a true disorder. Launching an adolescent is stressful.

The rapid changes in development give parents a raft of new behavioral puzzles to solve:

Is my teen's recent moodiness just a phase?
Is her new grunge look merely a fad?
Do declining grades signal boredom, undetected depression, or drug use?
Does noticeable weight loss mean a new diet or an eating disorder?

Clouding the picture, adolescents and young adults often don't know how to interpret their own mood or behavioral symptoms. They may assume—with consequences that can range from the regrettable to the tragic—that they are simply stressed out and will improve without treatment. In addition to minimizing their difficulties ("everyone is stressed out—it's not that bad"), they may believe they can work things out on their own without professional help.

While late adolescent moodiness is indeed often temporary and situational, it's also true that many mental health problems first crop up during the transition years from mid-adolescence through the mid-twenties.[2] Early intervention can reduce symptoms, avert crises, and prevent recurrences of mental health problems. So if you spot a red flag take action! (See early warning signs on the following page.)

Because we parents often feel helpless in the face of a young person's emotional distress, it's tempting to deny or minimize what we're seeing. We may try to reassure ourselves that an obvious problem is mere adolescent angst. Or we may tag a new personality variation with an old familiar label: "He's always been moody." "She got that temper from her mother." We may breezily borrow popular terms but incorrectly apply them clinically: "She's hyper." "He's manicky." So perhaps now is a good time to remind ourselves that parental assumptions about mental illness grow out of prevailing stigmas. Let's not fall into that trap!

EARLY WARNING SIGNS OF MENTAL HEALTH PROBLEMS

1. Increase in severity of symptoms of anxiety or depression
2. Major changes in eating, sleeping, or general energy levels
3. Mood swings that persist or worsen
4. Decreased concentration
5. Confused or bizarre thinking; paranoia
6. Withdrawal from friends and family
7. Significant weight gain or loss
8. Alcohol or drug abuse
9. Excessive anger
10. Suicidal thoughts or signs of self-harm
11. Unexplained physical problems, such as stomach pain, back pain, headaches, or fatigue

Mental Health Stigma

Mental health–related stigma can take the form of public biases and misinformation. This is readily apparent in the controversial link between violence and mental illness. The facts betray the bias, as researchers confirm that the association is vastly exaggerated in the public's mind. The reality is that the mentally ill are much more likely to be victims of violence than perpetrators of it.[3] At least the social stigma of "otherness" biases can be debated. More insidious is the unspoken, internalized bias of self-stigma that we hold about ourselves or our children with a mental illness. Both types of bias can exact a heavy toll on a student and his parents, delaying the search for help and impeding treatment.

Parents frequently hold both positive and negative stereotypes of mental illness. For example, when the Malloys learned of Adrienne's depression, their initial responses reflected positive biases: "I sent a happy kid to college—how can she be so depressed that she needs medication?" A positive bias may strike the layman as something desirable, but it actually echoes with denial: "My son is smart." "My daughter is happy-go-lucky." It may even betray a parent's instinct to disown mental health problems: "My daughter is successful." "My son is popular." And that's no help, because it sends an underlying message to the affected individual: "This isn't who you are. You're supposed to be happy—and not have these problems."

Negative biases can be equally unsupportive: "Nothing's wrong with him that a little hard work won't cure. . . . So dramatic! . . . Super sensitive . . . Just a phase." Whether positive or negative, these biases often arise from the societal and familial stigma surrounding mental illness.

Parents are often unprepared for the shame of social stigma and others' judgments of their child—and of themselves—when a mental health issue arises. To cope with their discomfort, embarrassment, and self-doubts, and to protect their child's privacy, they will often spin a positive public narrative: "Oh, yes, Kelly's been enjoying college, but she's decided to take a gap year." The real story, meanwhile, is that Kelly took a leave of absence to get treatment for an eating disorder.

It's therefore absolutely vital for parents to recognize and buffer themselves against stigma's invisible toll on all family members. No one blames the patient or his parents for purely physical illnesses such as diabetes, sickle-cell anemia, or celiac disease. Seeing these as beyond one's control, society tenders sympathy, not judgment. But the negative prejudices about emotional problems that we have allowed to infect our society often become internalized, attacking our sense of a "strong" self.

In the last fifty years, scientists have made great strides in understanding the relationship between neurobiology and mental disorders. They have mapped brain activities with real-time neuroimaging, identified specific genetic locations associated with cognitive problems, and identified more than one hundred medical conditions that may mimic the symptoms of mental illness.[4]

For all we've learned, however, popular culture still opts for blame over understanding the biology of behavioral symptoms. When a child, adolescent, or young adult experiences a mental illness, people often blame parents, parents may blame each other, and sadly sometimes blame the child. Blaming is a hot potato, "it's your fault," bias. Many support groups have coalesced to combat mental health stigma, educate the public, and provide emotional support for all family members. NAMI, for one, suggests adopting the following stigma-free pledge:[5]

1. Learn about mental health—by educating yourself and others.
2. See the person not the illness—striving to listen, understand, and tell your own story.
3. Take action—spread the word, raise awareness, and make a difference.

We strongly encourage every parent reading this book to seek out a support group, locally or online, that can help guide you through the process of diagnosing and treating your young adult's mental health problems. For starters, think how much better prepared you'll be to support your affected student. Online, grassroots, national, campus, and in-person resources are listed in the Appendix.

And the Malloys? This one has a happy ending: Adrienne received treatment and improved. When Mr. and Mrs. Malloy gained HIPAA access, they became better informed by Adrienne's treating psychiatrist and therapist. They learned what they'd missed: the earlier signs of her anxiety morphed in its chronicity and severity into depression. The Malloys faced their positive biases and got on the same page with each other as parents. In the process, they discovered ways to prepare Adrienne's younger brother for the challenges ahead. But how do parents change their attitudes and even harmonize conflicting parenting styles? We next meet the families of Mikki and Johnny to reveal the work involved in these happy endings.

"Managing" Mikki

High school administrators are familiar with the steep increase in severe anxiety in their students. Surveys across time tell this story. Beginning in 1985, only 18 percent of incoming college freshmen agreed that in the previous year, they "felt overwhelmed by all I had to do." By 2010 the number increased to 29 percent. By 2017, that number swelled to 41 percent.[6] Some students keep up the 95-mile-an-hour pace. Others, like Mikki, crash. It was fall midterms, senior year of high school—that high-pressure culmination of twelve years of testing, GPAs, SATs, and honors classes, all leading to college admissions.

That's when the frantic call came in from Mrs. Cuthbert.

"Dr. Hibbs, it's my daughter," she began. "Mikki is so anxious that she's missing assignments and tests. I'm embarrassed to keep asking the school counselor to give her an extension, because she probably thinks I'm just making excuses for her. I've tried to be supportive, but I'm frustrated, and her dad—oh, we're divorced—he thinks the problem is just *weakness*. He's mad at her, I'm worn out, and now Mikki won't talk to us."

That five-minute phone call revealed much more than the judgment Mrs. Cuthbert feared the school counselor might make; it also betrayed the negative stereotypes both parents held about mental illness.

As our session began the next day, Mikki surprised her mother by listing her parents among her top stressors: "Mom, you and Dad have said some really mean things to me. Like, 'You're disappointing your teachers—why are you doing this?' Then you get mad at me for needing to take a day off. After Dad called and told me I was being weak, I went into a panic attack, and you looked fed up and left me alone. I'm so mad at you, but I need you too much to be mad. I don't know what to do. You guys just don't understand!"

Mrs. Cuthbert responded defensively: "Well, your father's not here today, but I've been there for you ninety-nine times out of a hundred." Now both daughter and mother were scowling at each other.

With feelings running high, Dr. Hibbs hoped to reassure Mrs. Cuthbert.

"You're obviously a very caring mom. That shows because you want to help your daughter. There are no training manuals to tell parents what to do in this circumstance. I'm sure you're worried about Mikki's senior-year grades, but anxiety and panic are the joker cards in our mental health decks—they can disrupt our best plans. Each of you is doing your best. This is no one's fault." Dr. Hibbs paused, then asked, "Can you see that your daughter is more hurt than mad at you?"

Mrs. Cuthbert's face softened. "I'm scared," she quietly admitted. "I don't know how to motivate Mikki to finish well."

Dr. Hibbs hoped to put their minds at ease: "Mikki, if you need to get extensions or incompletes, that's an option we'll consider."

Mikki nodded her agreement, saying, "Okay, that would help a lot."

"And Mrs. Cuthbert," Dr. Hibbs continued, "I'd be glad to reach out to the school counselor, but I'll need permission in writing from you, Mikki, and Mr. Cuthbert. Most counselors are quite willing to make temporary accommodations for documented problems. It won't show up on Mikki's school record—and her anxiety is no reflection on you."

Then Dr. Hibbs turned to the daughter. "Mikki, we'll need to help you build some better coping skills before you leave for college. Talk therapy can help with both anxiety and panicky worries, like 'My life will be ruined if I don't finish with flying colors.' When we're anxious, we often believe the worst. So we'll work together to help you, your parents, and your school get on the same page and develop a plan."

Finally, she addressed Mrs. Cuthbert again: "Let's plan a parents' session to address the concerns you and her father have, and go over the basics you need to know about mental health issues."

The session was useful in revealing that Mrs. Cuthbert felt ashamed she couldn't "manage" her daughter. It also exposed a collision of parenting styles: whereas Mr. Cuthbert blamed his former wife for coddling Mikki, he also felt undermined because she resisted his rip-the-Band-Aid-off approach. If these parental attitudes went unchecked, Dr. Hibbs could see that Mikki risked internalizing a negative view of her struggles with anxiety. Her growing self-stigma could result in hopelessness and lowered self-esteem; it might even disrupt her willingness to continue treatment.

In these sessions, Dr. Hibbs emphasized that Mikki's recovery would hinge on her parents' willingness to educate themselves and reduce their own mental health biases. The Cuthberts listened uncomfortably at first, but soon took the first steps toward stigma reduction: they signed onto NAMI's StigmaFree Me campaign, and compiled histories of their own (and their extended families') mental health problems. To the extent that parents are able to quell their own fears, take stock of their biases about mental health problems, and normalize the importance of asking for support when it's needed, they can boost a student's resilience—and with it her willingness to seek help.

By demonstrating their support in attending sessions together and taking the StigmaFree pledge, the Cuthberts took the first steps in helping Mikki. Ahead of them lay a problem that is common to all parents, whether married, divorced, or stepparents: ending the shame-blame game. The cross-blaming "It's your fault, not mine" can emerge with history-taking. Next we ask you to reflect on your own family history of mental health problems, as you check your responses to "shaking the family tree."

Shaking the Family Tree

Reducing stigma starts at home. Parents can help dismantle such biases by exploring and openly accepting the history of psychiatric problems within the family. To transform parental worry into treatment support, let's turn to the seemingly innocent act of history-taking.

Understanding your family's mental health history is crucial to helping your child. When you first learn that your child has social, emotional, or behavioral problems, it's not long before you ask yourself, "Who does he take after? Which side, close or distant branch, of the family does this come from?" With these questions, you're "shaking the family tree"—that is, searching for clues. And when you first seek a professional opinion, a physician or mental health professional will likewise shake that tree by probing the medical histories of the individual and his family.

This line of questioning is routine and necessary to insure a prompt diagnosis and proper treatment for your child. Yet the history-taking—and its prospect of a psychiatric diagnosis—often feels threatening to parents. They commonly experience a mixture of fearfulness ("Will my kid be okay?") and helplessness ("What can I do?").

As the family tree fills out, it's essential for parents to avoid the temptation to blame themselves or other family members. Worries about a child's state of mind can all too readily slip into self-defeating questions: "Did I cause this? What did I do wrong? What did I miss? Wasn't I a good parent?" Stepparents may add an additional twist to the situation: "*My* kids are fine—it's *yours* who have the problems." To avoid the "shame and blame game," resist both of these urges: don't judge yourself, and don't judge the other parent or partner. Assigning blame or looking for scapegoats is never healthy. In fact, it only makes difficult matters worse.

Parents should also be aware that while many mental health problems have a genetic component, biology is not destiny. Genetic expression in the brain's structure and neurochemistry is subject to a dizzying array of influences that science is still exploring. These encompass a wide variety of biological factors interacting with environmental influences. The environment is both "around us" (in school settings, peer relationships, and social media) and "between us" (in the culture of family life).

Make a List—and Check It Twice

Below is an informal and preliminary screen for your family's mental health history. Use it to note any condition that "runs in the family," paying close attention to your feelings as you go. Exploring the mental health history of one's family is enough to make anyone feel defensive, but we think you'll find that this review greatly accelerates the process of getting the most appropriate help for your student.

MENTAL HEALTH CHECKLIST:
SHAKING YOUR FAMILY TREE

	Self	Parent	Grandparent	Other Relative
ADHD				
Alcohol/substance abuse				
Anxiety				
Autism				
Bipolar disorder				
Depression				
Eating disorder				
Panic attack				
Personality disorder				
Phobia				
Schizophrenia/ psychosis				
Smoking				
Suicide attempt				
Suicide				

Shaking the family tree compels us to examine our family mental health history in order to understand it more objectively. Because biological psychiatry and diagnostic criteria were rudimentary until the last few decades of the twentieth century, mental disorders often went undiagnosed—or, worse, they were mischaracterized as "weakness of character." Keep that context in mind as you consider which relative just "didn't seem right," was a "very difficult personality," or was deemed "a little bit off." This exercise may surface all sorts of interesting things:

assumptions and judgments, explanations of behavior and character, even stigmas about mental illness. It's important to explore all these issues in a calm, thoughtful, and nonjudgmental fashion—otherwise you'll miss important information that could be helpful in addressing the current concerns you and your child are facing.

Many parents and students who've come to us over the years have described the loneliness and pain of being subjected to social bias. As if coping with a learning difference, a behavioral problem, or an emotional disorder had not handed them enough to deal with, youth often face the additional burden of "being different," which typically imposes social rejection and isolation. Feeling totally alone is arguably the worst part of a mental health crisis.

Fortunately, college counseling services are often excellent sources of social support: there, a student can find groups targeting stress, anxiety, depression, and substance use. Other campus support groups may be available to help students who feel marginalized by their ethnicity, gender, or sexual orientation. The powerful crucible of shared experience encourages learning from—and leaning on—one another. The message is clear: the raft that no one wants to float away on can become a lifeboat of belonging and mutual support.

Parenting Challenges: Safe Spaces in the Family

Each developmental stage of childhood, adolescence, and emerging adulthood presents new demands on parents. Perhaps none of them is greater than learning how to relate to—and help—your child weather a mental health crisis. As we noted in the last chapter, a student's best buffer against the many challenges they'll face is knowing that the parent–child or the family's relationships hold safe spaces: a space for feeling understood and supported, not isolated or alone. For the sake of your child's recovery and your own resilience, be prepared to adjust your expectations, your parenting habits, and your basic interactions with this young person whose behavior has suddenly become confusing, worrying, or exasperating. The discussion that follows can help you fine-tune your parenting style to guarantee the healthiest outcome for your student—and the strongest possible bond between parent and child.

Parenting Styles

Mothers and fathers have strong—and often conflicting—views about the best way to guide a teen into adulthood: Should we take an understanding approach or a disciplined one? How important are traditions? What's the right balance between self-sufficiency and support? What parents most want to know, however, often turns out to be the very thing that's most difficult to discern: What works best in relating to *their* child?

The good news is that most parents don't need to sweat the small stuff as much as they do. After all, the point of keeping our children safe and secure early on is to enable them to take reasonable risks as they mature, thriving in and adapting to the new world they will inherit.[7] And today's parents can benefit from decades of research on the best parenting styles.[8] Groundbreaking research by psychologist Diana Baumrind in the 1960s and 1970s, for example,[9,10,11] showed that the most competent teens and young adults had been raised by what she characterized as "authoritative" parents. These parents are firm but warm. They set high expectations for maturity and good behavior, but they are also emotionally responsive. According to Baumrind's findings, responsiveness is the opposite of knee-jerk reactivity; it emphasizes warmth, flexible and reasoned communication,[12] and the ability to recognize and regulate your emotions. You might think of this parenting style as "attuned relating."[13]

Authoritative parents are engaged in the lives of their children. They offer guidance on values, family traditions, and education. But the authoritative parent does *not* use perfection as the minimum performance standard: authoritative parents who show love and warmth—and who set reasonable expectations—make "good enough" parents. And that's good enough to produce safe relationship spaces to foster the development of adolescents and young adults who are emotionally stable and possess good coping skills.

A few parenting styles, by contrast, can result in poor self-control, low self-esteem, and overt aggression.[14] "Permissive" parenting—a laissez-faire style that is highly responsive but sets a low bar for expectations—has a negative effect on child development (because children benefit from firm and reasonably high expectations). Another problematic approach is the "authoritarian" style of parenting, generally associated with a student's poor academic achievement and depressive symptoms. Authoritarian parents are low on warm responsiveness and high on harsh demandingness.

Finally, kids raised under the "disengaged" parenting style seem to fare the worst. Bound up in their own problems, disengaged parents are both unresponsive and undemanding, and are largely uninvolved in the daily care and lives of their children. Adolescents and young adults raised by disengaged parents often struggle with poor academics, substance use, and legal run-ins. Moral of the story: when parents don't care, neither do their kids. Curious to assess your own parenting style? The website of the Gottman Institute, among others, offers a free self-test online.[15]

Ready for a Makeover?

Most parents employ a mix of parenting styles, improvising as the child and situation seem to require. It's normal to occasionally feel insecure about your parenting decisions, but what happens when you realize that your entire approach is too permissive, authoritarian, or disengaged? Every parent–child relationship benefits when a parent sets out to improve it, but perhaps none gains more than when a student has substantial emotional or behavioral issues.

So what's the biggest takeaway from the last half-century of research into parenting styles? Simply this: neither "tiger moms" nor "drill sergeants" pose the largest threats to adolescent autonomy and parent–child trust. No, the most problematic parenting behaviors are those characterized by parental intrusiveness, manipulation through guilt, withdrawal of love, unrealistic expectations, coercion, highly negative emotionality, and personal attacks. Think of the movie *Fences*. The flawed and obstinate father deeply hurts and alienates his son and his wife through his competitive undermining and personal attacks on the son. Or the film *Black Swan* in which the overbearing mother's perfectionistic standards and relentless demands take center stage over the emotional health of her ballerina daughter. These parents inflict tremendous pain on their loved ones by their rigid interactional styles and uncompromising attitudes.

What if you decide you want to change your own parenting style? It can be done—but it will take practice. By evaluating your current style and making specific and conscious adjustments, you can move toward a more desired approach. Start here:

- Evaluate your expectations: Are they realistic?
- Explore your parenting beliefs: What's the right balance between love and demands? What's the best way to motivate my young adult?
- Modify your behaviors: Do I tend to lead with praise or with criticism?

Most parental mistakes, whether those of permissiveness or rigid control, are driven by our emotions. When we feel tired, anxious, or overwhelmed, we may react by minimizing or dismissing what our kids tell us. It can be exhausting to deal with a healthy adolescent who both needs us and defies us. So when a college student alerts us to a deepening emotional downturn—be it a balky roommate, romantic troubles, or the shock of poor grades or a disciplinary action—it takes a very special effort to hear and acknowledge the underlying painful emotional reality.

Doesn't every parent strive to make his child feel less troubled by life's demands? With our protection and guidance, we hope they'll turn out wiser and more capable than we were at their age. We hope to be better parents than our own were, sidestepping the mistakes they made and communicating better with our kids. We'll "be there" for our children.

Yet anxiety, depression, an eating disorder, or substance abuse are great equalizers—forceful reminders of our illusion of protective control. Under such stressful circumstances, we often react less than nobly. Our first response when a child experiences emotional trauma may be one of defending ourselves from the explosions of tiny death stars blowing up *our* hopes and dreams for our child. Other knee-jerk reactions may range from "OMG!" to the deterioration into dismissiveness, shaming, and blaming to what we call "rescue mode"—that is, leaping into problem-solving before simply offering our calm support.

Psychologist John Gottman is known for his research on emotionally focused parenting. His view is that a parent should be emotionally aware enough to allow a young person to express negative emotions, whether anger, deep sadness, self-doubt, anxiety, or fear. By learning a specific set of listening and problem-solving behaviors, Gottman writes, any parent can become "an emotion coach"—one who relates in positive ways while reducing critical or blaming habits. Keep the following traits in mind as you consider how you are most likely to respond in specific situations—and how you might try a new approach.[16, 17]

THE EMOTIONAL COACH

- Is aware of and values a young adult's emotions
- Does not poke fun at or make light of the young adult's negative feelings
- Does not say how the young adult *should* feel
- Uses emotional moments as a time to listen to the young adult, empathize with support, and offer guidance and perspective that leads to a constructive response

---

Nixing the Negatives

Looking for a quick and simple way to evaluate how *you* relate to your college student? Ask her to answer this question: "How critical of you do you consider your mother/father/relative to be?"[18]

Not at All Critical   **Very Critical Indeed**

0   1   2   3   4   5   6   7   8   9   10

One proven way to improve your parenting and family life is to reduce the negatives that may have crept into them. This lesson is particularly crucial when a college student struggles with an emotional problem. Encourage him to share disappointments and failures. Be a responsive, warm listener; this builds trust and resilience. Even if your son or daughter is away at college when a problem occurs, how positively you respond—nixing the critiques or second-guessing—can dictate how proactively they will seek help and how willing they will be to share experiences with you in the future. This is true regardless of the specific events or circumstances that precipitated the current crisis—nonjudgmental, active listening generally works best. Instead of trying to solve their problems for them, it's best to form an alliance and establish open and honest communication—not an easy task for sure, but one that's vital before effective crisis management can occur.

Next we meet Johnny Hopkins and his parents. The time had come to decide on his readiness to head for college straight out of high school. Granted, he was making good progress in his treatment for anxiety, ADHD, and substance abuse, yet we urged the family to weigh the pros and cons of either enrolling or deferring college in the fall.

When Johnny's Got Issues, His Parents Need Help

"We've had to accept many things from childhood to young adulthood. Our first shock was that our child could have a learning disability. That was my introduction to the limitations and obstacles for him. Then I began to grasp that his path would be different from what we imagined."

—JOHNNY'S MOTHER[19]

Johnny's parents, Cindy and John, thought his troubles were behind him. As a mixed-race couple, the Hopkinses had fretted early on that Johnny might encounter the same racism his father had. By settling in an urban neighborhood with a good school district, however, they hoped to shield him from racial prejudices. Like many in his generation, Johnny made friends across racial and economic lines, and his largely white classmates seemed to accept him.

Tutoring helped Johnny overcome an early reading delay, later diagnosed as dyslexia. In middle school, his impulsivity and difficulty in concentrating met the criteria for attention deficit hyperactivity disorder (ADHD). Yet by senior year of high school, he had a high GPA and competitive SAT scores, putting him on track for a good college. His relieved parents even allowed themselves to hope he might land a scholarship; if not, they knew, his college expenses could easily eat half their income.[20]

But then, trouble: Over winter break of his senior year, Cindy and John learned their son had turned in so few assignments that he had received poor grades for the fall semester. Though Johnny denied it, his parents suspected he was smoking pot several times a week. Cindy and John grew frantic. "He couldn't have picked a worse time than the very last semester that counts," they silently lamented. "What can we do?"

Johnny's problems had created a long history of friction for the couple. Before his ADHD diagnosis in middle school, Johnny had developed a bad habit of procrastinating, abetted by the occasional lie about completing his assignments. For two years, Cindy pulled "second shift" after dinner, sitting with Johnny and helping him complete his homework. John, for his part, was fed up. Within the boy's earshot he exclaimed, "Just let him flunk!"

But Cindy couldn't. She saw her son's distress and intuited that something was wrong. Where was his passion? What did his sulky, irritable moods and easy default to video gaming portend for his future? Without her active support, Cindy worried, would their son falter?

During those years, a parenting chasm opened up. John faulted Cindy for being too lenient, while Cindy retorted that his "tiger dad" style was harsh enough for two parents. Cindy favored understanding and flexible consequences, but John peppered their son with barbs: "You're a quitter. You're lazy, always playing those games." And Mr. Hopkins frequently invoked the nuclear option: "You lost your privileges. You can't play your games, and you're grounded for a month."

After Johnny's ADHD was treated and he caught up on his coursework, however, the couple's differences went underground. At last, John felt proud of his son. Finally, he was a *striver*, just like his dad.

And now, this: Johnny's problems were back, but magnified by the looming college-admissions season. "Have we done enough to prepare our son for the increased demands of college?" Cindy wondered.

Her protective stance was at dramatic odds with John's blame-casting: their son had screwed up, making college out of the question next fall. His solution? Johnny should get a "Joe job" after graduation. Maybe working at minimum wage would knock some sense into him.

Unable to resolve their different approaches, the Hopkinses agreed to seek counseling.

The first sessions with Dr. Hibbs were diagnostic: What's the core problem here? Are the family backgrounds relevant? And what is the recommended treatment? Sure enough, in compiling mood, attention, and anxiety inventories on Johnny and his parents, some essential clues emerged.

Cindy's Family Tree

Cindy's mood checklists may have been "boringly normal," as she remarked, but her family's psychiatric history was anything but. Her carefree adolescence had come to an abrupt end when her mother admitted herself to a psychiatric hospital for severe depression. Her mother had tried various medications—even shock treatments—before doctors hit on the right mix of medicine and therapy. A month later her reenergized mother had returned home. Cindy felt grateful she had dodged this mood bullet—and she'd presumed that Johnny had too.

John's Family Tree

While Cindy seemed open to the interview, John was considerably frustrated and openly challenging: "Look, we're here to help Johnny, so I don't know why you're asking about me and my family. If you're digging for some problem, forget it."

The history-taking had hit a nerve. John's resistance, like that of many parents, was part protectiveness of his own parents and part mental health stigma. Aware that mental health literacy can remove the shame of such a stigma, Dr. Hibbs responded: "I don't want to do an archaeological dig into the past to throw your parents under the bus. But family mental health histories can provide important clues for understanding your son." She paused, waiting to see if John was persuaded.

"Okay," John allowed reluctantly, "but I still don't know all that much." He then recalled that his father had been a heavy smoker, while his paternal uncle was known as a drinker. Beyond that, he said, he was unaware of any overt emotional problems. John's paper-and-pencil questionnaires, however, uncovered a central clue. "Doc," he observed, sounding both surprised and concerned, "looks like I was an anxious kid. More labels. This is bad. I'm not crazy, you know."

Dr. Hibbs moved to clarify matters: "These labels don't mean 'crazy.' The public sometimes assumes anyone with a mental health diagnosis is either crazy or dangerous, but neither is true. Psychological labeling is just a shorthand way to describe what symptoms a person experiences—and which treatment would be most effective."

As John reflected on the findings, he began to recognize features of his childhood anxiety. He recalled hating fireworks (too overwhelming) and being scolded by his parents for crying too easily.

"I guess I had reason to be nervous as a kid," John added, almost as an afterthought. "I was light skinned, and the darker kids made fun of me even through high school, calling me 'Albino' or 'Oreo.' I hated it. I was never good at getting teased. I'd get really mad, but I wasn't good at fighting either. I'd get teary, and then I'd get harassed for *that* in turn.

"The white kids at high school were friendly in class, but I was never invited to any of their parties. I didn't want Johnny to endure what I had. I thought things would be easier for him, because times have changed some."

John's parents, who were proud of their hardworking son, hadn't thought of him as anxious.[21] In his mid-twentieth-century upbringing, psychology had not yet evolved to explain the mental hiccups that can result from chronic stressors in adolescence and young adulthood. Nor were parents inclined to dig deeply for psychological roots in an era when mothers were held largely responsible for childhood emotional problems.

Interpersonal reality—how we understand one another, quirks and all—seems automatic. Yet we puzzle its many pieces into a unique storyline about relationships, values, and beliefs. As parents we transmit this familial narrative to our children, who tend to incorporate it in their own lives as objective truth. John's storyline—and, crucially, the one he constructed for Johnny—excluded the "indulgence" of emotional disturbances. John's parents had been *strivers* (the same word he used to describe himself), comfortable in their belief that anyone could overcome difficult circumstances with hard work and sheer gumption. In their narrative, anxiety played no part. Their son was normal, just as they were.

All this explains why John had never considered himself an anxious child until the hour, decades later, when he sat in Dr. Hibbs's office and shook his family tree. Like many people with moderate anxiety, John had learned over time to manage it through exercise and relentless striving. His achievements guaranteed that he would be admired and accepted. As the Hopkinses came to see their histories more clearly, they grew more receptive to a new explanation for their son's problems.

Johnny's Issues

"So, Doc," John asked, "which side of the tree did Johnny fall out of—the anxious branch or the depressed one?"

In addition to his ADHD diagnosis, Dr. Hibbs explained, Johnny had an anxiety disorder.[22] And ADHD typically worsens anxiety, Dr. Hibbs pointed out; instructions "drop out of orbit" and are difficult to retrieve, complicating learning and task completion.[23] The anxiety fueled Johnny's procrastination, his irritability, and his tendency to expect catastrophe at every turn: "I'll flunk out. . . . You'll never believe me since I lied. . . . I'm a loser." It also very likely contributed to his marijuana use. Dr. Hibbs had another key puzzle piece to add, but she paused to let the Hopkinses respond.

Cindy had nodded throughout this description; Johnny's behavior was beginning to make more sense. But John shook his head, saying, "So, it's my fault that this is who he is." Dr. Hibbs was accustomed to instances of self-reproach from parents whose adolescent has just been diagnosed, so she reassured John: "Anxiety and attention deficit problems are what Johnny *has,* not who he *is.* You've experienced anxiety yourself, yet you've done very well in life. Give yourself credit that you've sought treatment early for your son."

"But it came from *me,*" John fired back. "Don't tell me to feel good about *that.*"

"Whether it's genetics or overprotective parenting," Dr. Hibbs replied, "we know that children whose parents struggle with anxiety are at higher risk for the same condition.[24] For all you know, one of your parents may have been coping with ADHD or anxiety. Your dad was a heavy smoker, right? Did you know that just under half of all smokers have a mood disorder? Just think about what a powerful mood agent nicotine is. And it helps ADHD symptoms too. But better treatments are available for anxiety and ADHD. I'll introduce you to some parenting and problem-solving strategies that can reduce and even prevent anxiety in kids."

"There's one more thing," Dr. Hibbs continued. "On his questionnaire, Johnny scored very high on the John Henryism scale.[25] He strongly believes statements like, 'When things don't go the way I want them to, that just makes me work harder.' Or, 'I've always felt that I could make of my life pretty much what I wanted to make of it.' Minority or mixed-race students like Johnny are more vulnerable to the risks of anxiety and depression that the continuous striving to prove themselves can create.

"Until this crisis, Johnny was a goal setter. Until recently, he was persistent in managing his anxiety and his ADHD. He navigated setbacks, made the honor roll, and resisted temptations like smoking weed. I think Johnny may be sending us a message: he desperately doesn't want to disappoint you, but he's plain worn out. With his permission, let me quote you something from my interview with him:

"'High school sucks. Why can't I just mess around with my friends, and figure out what I'm interested in, instead of all this constant pressure? I'm so sick of it I don't even know if I want to go to college. At least right now. If this is what it's like to be an adult, then I'll be Peter Pan.'"

John looked sad, but some of the tension had gone out of his posture. "I never even considered he might be so stressed," he reflected. "I guess I thought he was just like me—head down, always going for the next goal. My son believes those 'work harder' mantras because *I* taught them to him."

John paused, then asked, "So what's the best treatment for Johnny?"

Dr. Hibbs replied, "Well, Johnny's already taking medication for his ADHD. When anxiety enters the mix, you begin by teaching coping strategies. Those might include mindfulness, insight, and perspective-taking. If the anxiety remains too severe, we might add other medications as well.[26] But good family relationships are equally important; they can provide a buffer from the pressures he feels.

"I'd like to refer Johnny to Dr. Rostain for a further diagnostic and medication consultation," Dr. Hibbs concluded. "When an anxiety disorder like his is involved, the combination of therapy and meds is generally better than either treatment alone. And we still need to understand the role of anxiety in his marijuana use. Maybe he was trying to tell us something about his readiness for college—his therapy will need to explore that."

The Hopkinses followed up one afternoon with Dr. Rostain, who confirmed the diagnoses of a generalized anxiety disorder, ADHD, and now substance abuse disorder. As John sat quietly absorbing the news, Cindy wept for a few minutes. Finally, she asked Dr. Rostain, "Why am I so upset? You're telling me this is treatable, and that Johnny will learn how to cope better. You're telling us he'll be okay in his life, right?"

"Yes, Johnny will be okay," Dr. Rostain reassured her. "That's not why you're crying. You're crying for the loss of your wished-for 'perfect child.' Most parents hold cherished dreams for the future that their child will someday fulfill. It's painful for us to face a changed reality in which their journey toward that bright tomorrow is stalled or derailed."

Cindy's tears reflected the momentary loss of her long-held hopes for Johnny's college career. Understandably, she was scared; she wanted to shield her son from unnecessary struggles, yet she had no way of knowing what lay in store for him. Like many parents, the Hopkinses had assumed that Johnny would be as successful as they had been. Now they understood he was stressed to the point of sabotaging himself through substance use. As Dr. Rostain confirmed, Johnny felt calmer and less preoccupied when he smoked marijuana. He would need to clean up this habit and find other ways to manage his anxiety.

Larger tasks loomed too: How could Johnny free himself from the relentlessness of striving? Was there a different way to define his value to himself—and to his parents? To reinforce this idea, Dr. Rostain remarked, "It's February. Let's consider taking some of the pressure off Johnny by considering alternative colleges, or perhaps even alternatives *to* college."

The Hopkinses needed time to absorb their emotional reactions following these meetings. True to the pattern of many parents in their predicament, their thought process went something like this:

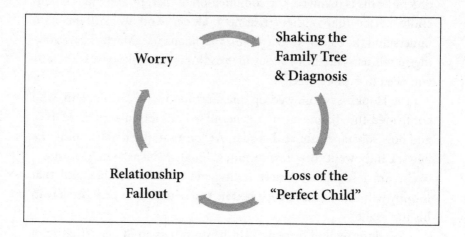

Parents' Emotional Reactions

It all made for a heady emotional brew: the Hopkinses' worry was mixed with regrets about what they had missed—and what they had misunderstood. They felt sad about their own bias, namely the belief that emotional disorders couldn't happen to *their* child. At the same time, they were heartened to learn they could play a crucial role in their son's good mental health.

Following Johnny's diagnosis, the family counseling focused on three priorities:

1. Helping Johnny curb his marijuana use, which was masking his anxiety, not treating it
2. Parenting style makeovers
3. Assessing readiness for college

Although his parents couldn't change Johnny's biology, they *could* improve their relationship problems. A more positive family environment would reduce Johnny's anxiety and stave off a relapse. Their first step was to modify their expectations for Johnny's academics, relieving the pressure of his John Henryism.

Ever the good students, Cindy and John realized they faced a steep learning curve. Cindy graded her parenting A- for being warm and loving, but gave herself a C for over-parenting. Even after Johnny's ADHD diagnosis, Cindy stood ready for second-shift help with his homework, as a human reminder prompt, and as an alarm clock. She now understood that her natural tendency to "help" wouldn't prepare him for college—or, indeed, for life. Her "help" offered a pseudo-protection for her son's struggles. Left unchecked, Cindy's personal-assistant role implied that Johnny wasn't capable, thus deepening his dependency. She now resolved to tolerate her own qualms in order to allow Johnny to make his own mistakes, and find his own solutions.

Cindy's compensatory strategy of over-parenting is very common in families where adolescents struggle with anxiety, ADHD, or executive functioning deficits. This accommodation style offers short-term solutions at the expense of an individual's long-term self-sufficiency. And when over-parenting jells into a way of life, it can be as tough for the young person to step up as it is for the parent to step down.

As Cindy worked to dial down her over-functioning, her husband undertook a separate effort. As he owned up to his anger and frustration with his son, John graded himself harshly, with Bs to Ds for parenting. His son had given him a score of 8 out of 10, or "very critical." It was no wonder, he now saw, that Johnny should seek out his mother, because his father led with negatives—hostile teasing and blame—whenever he was frustrated with him. Newly aware that Johnny's anxiety and procrastination were limitations to be treated rather than character flaws that warranted his disapproval, John set out to change his hurtful habits. He wanted to show more patience with Johnny, so "Keep calm and carry on" became his new motto.

And then there was the issue of their marriage. Both Cindy and John gave themselves Cs on the spousal scorecard. Their polarized parental roles undermined each other, taking a toll on their partnership. They set these goals to reverse course:

Tips to Reduce Negative Emotions
- Don't judge or be dismissive.
- Be tolerant and forgiving of others' shortcomings as well as your own.
- Recognize that the family member with a psychiatric diagnosis is not to blame.
- Resist the urge to overprotect.
- Remain engaged, but don't put your teen in the middle of an adult conflict.
- Get help for your biases about mental illness.

- Assess your caregiver burden and take care of yourself, too.
- Remain hopeful.

Cindy would rein in her over-parenting, she hastened to reassure her husband. Her "help" on Johnny's homework had actually been anything but, hindering his task of learning to address his academic weaknesses on his own.

John, for his part, felt relieved that his wife had finally acknowledged his concerns, and he agreed to reduce his reactivity and become more emotionally available and responsive. He read parenting literature, and the two of them plugged into parenting forums online. Their efforts to redefine their parenting and improve their relationship took a few months of active effort, but the strain between them eased as they learned to make these changes.

Hard Choices: What About College?

The importance and influence of the family environment is hard to overstate. In the journey from problem to treatment, the Hopkinses learned that they too had issues, just as all parents do. They confronted their biases and relinquished their narrow definition of success. They reassured Johnny of their renewed support, and encouraged him to reduce chronic striving and develop better coping skills to manage anxiety. Improving these emotional skills and increasing his resilience would be essential for a successful college launch.

Unanswered by late spring, however, was whether Johnny would be ready for the four-year academic marathon of college in the fall. In an individual session with Dr. Hibbs, Johnny confided that he didn't want to go. Sure, he'd been accepted by a good university, but he needed a break from academics. Understandably, he was reluctant to share this news with his parents; wouldn't they view it as just one more disappointment? Johnny especially dreaded the judgment of his father—the man who had branded him a "quitter" and a "pothead." "I want to prove my father wrong," Johnny said. "I want to make him proud."

"So avoiding your reality—that you're not ready, and that you feel pressure not to let your parents down—is another John Henryism to overcome," Dr. Hibbs replied. "Exploring your options is a good idea. But instead of 'powering through,' as you usually do, what if you make yourself and your parents proud by asserting yourself? Maybe your parents would be up for that. Standing up for yourself would certainly be a better coping strategy than relapsing into heavy marijuana use at college. Going to college before you're ready is often a recipe for dropping out."

Knowing his parents as he did, Johnny correctly anticipated they would resist the idea. Sure enough, Cindy tried to brush aside her son's worries—"Oh, you'll do fine at college"—while father John darkly hinted that waiting might mean never going at all.

To break the impasse, Drs. Hibbs and Rostain held a parents' session where they encouraged the Hopkinses to talk to other parents, including those who had disregarded their children's reservations and pressured them to enroll. One story in particular hit home: getting through college had been ugly for Levi. Early on, he told his high school counselor that he wasn't interested in going to college right away: he didn't feel ready, and though his parents were insisting on a premed major, he was uncertain what he truly wanted to study.

The counselor suggested to Levi's parents that he defer admission. They overrode his concerns, and off he went, three thousand miles away. The next four years were characterized by skipped classes, missed exams, smoked bowls, and bouts of depression. A month before graduation, Levi was hospitalized during a bad acid trip. He managed to graduate—but still felt aimless. Levi had been deprived of a fundamental developmental stage: he had needed to grow up before attending college.

To sidestep Levi's fate, the Hopkinses began to explore the burgeoning trend of a gap year. This detour from an educational straightaway may make parents anxious, but the fact is that young adults are more mature after a stretch of working, traveling, volunteering, or exploring other interests. Long before gap years were more formally organized, many students worked to save money for college. Colleges today are more receptive to this maturational interlude between high school and college. And a handful of colleges and organizations—among them the American Gap Association and USA Gap Fairs—promote this pause between academic hurdles. But because formal gap programs can be costly, you'll want to investigate work-travel programs as well, including AmeriCorps, City Year, and WWOOF-USA.

Ultimately, Johnny and his parents decided that he would defer college for a year, continuing his therapy and combining volunteer and part-time work while living at home. In the process, Johnny learned to reduce the anxiety-inducing pressure he put on himself; he drastically cut his marijuana use, and he developed better coping strategies. Twelve months later, he finally felt ready for college. And his parents? Johnny's struggles taught them to be better parents. They got on the same page as parents and learned to neither over-function nor give up. They developed a more complicated understanding of the contributors to Johnny's stress in his biological, familial, and societal contexts. Johnny and his parents emerged from the turbulent riptide that had threatened to pull them apart, now together and closer.

Like many talented students, Johnny simply lacked the social-emotional and executive functioning skills necessary for a successful launch. In our next chapter, we'll take a closer look at one of the key factors for "making it" in college: executive functioning.

5

How to Plan—
and How to Follow Through

*"I'm going to graduate from college on time no matter
how many years it takes me."*

—A STUDENT WITH ADHD

Arjun sat in Dr. Rostain's office on a day in early November with a troubled look on his face.

"Dr. Rostain," he began, "there's something I need to tell you. . . ."

A first-semester college freshman who had been coming in regularly for help in managing his attention deficit hyperactivity disorder (ADHD), Arjun was an affable young man with a winning smile and a laid-back style of interacting. With encouragement, he haltingly revealed that he had gotten into "some academic trouble."

Pressed to elaborate, Arjun replied, "I've been skipping English composition because I'm so far behind on my writing assignments. And I'm not doing so hot in calculus, either; I currently have a D in that one."

Arjun had been struggling to attend his morning English class, he confided, because he had been staying up until all hours playing a particularly engrossing online video game. And even though he was having trouble understanding the calculus professor's lectures, he had not yet made any move to talk things over with him.

Arjun was well aware he should be going to class, keeping up with assignments, and meeting with his professors whenever he had questions about the course material. He also thoroughly understood the perils of late-night game-playing. And despite the resources available to him—he was entitled to academic assistance from the student learning center, as well as extended time for schoolwork under a prearranged academic accommodation—Arjun had failed to follow through on his best intentions to make up lost ground. Compounding matters, he had also put off divulging the full extent of his difficulties with Dr. Rostain until this late stage in the semester. The situation had gone from requiring mere remediation to demanding full-blown crisis management.

So, how did this train jump the tracks?

Arjun exhibited all the classic symptoms of a college student with problems of executive functioning, or EF. In layman's terms, he had trouble putting his intentions into action—that is, doing what he knew he needed to do. EF problems are found in roughly half of those with ADHD, which itself is present in more than 5 percent of U.S. college students. EF problems, such as the double trouble of distraction and procrastination, also exist in individuals without ADHD, many of whom are not diagnosed either because they've found "workarounds" or because they select environments that are not too demanding. When such individuals move into settings that demand more EF, they become symptomatic. The condition represents a severe and persisting impairment because it often translates into a host of negative life outcomes: lower educational achievement and occupational attainment, chronic relationship problems, low self-esteem, and high rates of mental health disorders.

Among college students, disordered EF is one of the surest predictors of poor academic performance and dropout. This chapter presents some of the insights that specialists have recently uncovered about EF, explaining the role it plays in the lives of college students just learning to carve out their identity as independent adults far from home. Students with EF deficits *can* avoid the pitfalls that interfere with their academic and personal success; we'll tell you how that's done.

Understanding the Command Center of the Brain

Most clinicians view EF as the capacity to carry out independent actions in an effective manner. Neuropsychologist Muriel Lezak, for example, defines EF as "those capacities that enable a person to engage successfully in independent, purposive, self-serving behavior."[1] ADHD expert Russell Barkley, for his part, boils EF down to an individual's "self-directed actions that are used to self-regulate,"[2] which in turn means being able to "choose, enact, and sustain actions toward a goal."[3]

In other words, EF enables us to manage our pursuit of long-term goals in the absence of immediate rewards or consequences. Another way to consider EF is to ask: "How *efficiently* do I do what I set out to do?" The more efficiently one executes the multiple tasks involved in reaching a goal, the better one's EF in that domain.

But what gives rise to EF? And how can you tell whether these capacities are working properly?

The neuroscience of EF is fascinating in its own right, and knowing a bit about its basic operations can help one better understand the cognitive, behavioral, and emotional functioning of a college student in pursuit of his or her daily life activities.

The structures and interconnections that make up the "central executive network" of the brain develop slowly over time, not becoming wholly operational until early adulthood. Eighteen-year-olds are still maturing and their EFs are not completely formed, which is why it's important for young adults to have some supervision in their transition to independence. Normally, by age twenty-five or so, the process is complete. It is therefore crucial to enable this process to run its course, for the brain's executive network is the command center that allows individuals to exercise willful control over their thoughts, emotions, and behavior. Otherwise, any damage to this area—whether from injury or disease—can trigger forgetfulness, distractibility, poor concentration, impulsiveness, poor organization, timing deficits, or loss of working memory.

In neurodevelopmental conditions such as ADHD and autism spectrum disorder (ASD), among others, the maturation of this network is delayed or disturbed, and EF deficits are frequently the result. Indeed, recent studies have found that structures in the brain's prefrontal, cerebellar, and parietal networks are underperforming in individuals with ADHD. On a more positive note, however, there is growing evidence that stimulant medications like Ritalin (methylphenidate) can improve the performance of these circuits.[4]

Does all this mean we can blame our genes for the development of an EF disorder? No: the mechanisms that guide normal brain development are subject to three main forces—genes, environment, and experience—and their interaction over time. A person's susceptibility to disordered EF is therefore only partially determined by his or her genetics. The environment exerts a much greater influence.

Prenatal exposure to certain substances, for example—including nicotine, alcohol, recreational drugs, chemicals, and infectious agents—is known to foster wide-ranging EF deficits. Postnatally, trauma, neglect, poverty, social adversity, inadequate schools, health problems, and family stress have all been shown to have a negative impact on the brain's executive networks. The reverse side of that environmental coin, of course, is that many protective factors—among them physical health, economic security, high-quality schools, and positive family relationships—can spur the brain's precious executive network to flourish.

As youths mature, they are given more opportunities to exercise their executive functioning under progressively less supervision. They learn to organize their activities, plan their schedules, prioritize their efforts, and allot their attention and energy to a growing array of duties. By the time they get to college, ideally, young people will have demonstrated the capacity to self-regulate their behavior—that is, to act *reasonably* responsible and independent without constant supervision from others.

Regrettably, students whose entire lives have been micromanaged—by their well-meaning parents, teachers, or both—often arrive on campus with insufficient practice at making plans and following through. This can make for a sobering discovery when they awaken to the reality that they are unprepared for the sort of day-to-day EF skills that college life requires, notably using a daily planner and a to-do list, regulating one's sleep/wake cycle to meet the demands of the college setting, and preparing ahead for long-range assignments and examinations. Especially likely to experience EF difficulties in college are students with ADHD, ASD, learning disabilities, or other neurodevelopmental conditions. Many of these students are eligible for academic accommodations under the Americans with Disabilities Act (ADA) but these must be disclosed prior to arriving at college in order for them to receive instructional assistance and/or curricular modifications.

Before they disappear from your sight in the fall of freshman year, students who are eligible for ADA accommodations should make a clear commitment that they will meet regularly with the appropriate providers of student support services on campus. You always want to make sure you're receiving all the benefits to which you're entitled. As

Arjun's story makes clear, though, many special-needs students drag their feet when it comes to seeking assistance: either they have persuaded themselves they don't need the help, or they are too embarrassed or ashamed to ask for it.

So if a student's essential contribution to vanquishing an EF deficit is her willingness to seek help, where does that leave the educational institution itself? Institutions have become increasingly—and understandably—reluctant to double as mental health providers, but there are at least half a dozen arenas in which schools can bolster the learning efforts of a student with compromised EF:

1. **Instructional adjustments.** The student can request that his schedule be modified to provide sufficient study time between classes. He can also ask for certain in-class accommodations, such as preferential seating, extended time to take a test, or note-taking services.

2. **Optimized living arrangements.** Quiet dorms, single rooms, and optimal location on campus (i.e. near classrooms or the dining hall) can be very helpful.

3. **Academic scaffolding.** Designated study spaces, preferred access to tutors, and scheduled "study halls" can enhance a student's learning experience.

4. **Opportunities to learn and practice EF skills.** Most schools offer "College 101" courses that teach basic organizational and time-management skills. Students with EF challenges should get an "enriched" version of these classes.

5. **Coaching.** Individual or group coaching can enhance EF.

6. **EF-oriented cognitive behavioral therapy.** CBT to promote EF is a promising new clinical innovation that helps individuals overcome their negative thoughts and dysfunctional behavior patterns.

Several new approaches for addressing EF impairment seem to be catching on. In our own practices, for example, we have found it best to address EF deficits by giving an individual various prompts and cues that help him stay on track. For Arjun this involved first creating be-havioral scripts of brief instructions to help him face common situa-tions where he tended to get "off task."

When Arjun resolved to spend less time playing video games late into the night, for instance, he and Dr. Rostain devised a script in which he spelled out that he would not log on to his favorite game until after he had completed a certain assignment. This gave him an incentive to dive into his schoolwork promptly rather than putting it off. The script also stipulated a maximum time limit—ninety minutes, at first—for his game playing. By following the script, Arjun could get to bed at a reasonable hour and avoid sleeping through that problematic English comp class the following morning. This script is an example of an intervention called implementation intention strategies (IIS). This method empowers individuals to anticipate obstacles and come up with methods for overcoming the common barriers of distractions, interrup-tions, motivational deficits, or inefficiency in tackling problems.

Arjun also utilized environmental cues to remind him of key tasks he needed to accomplish. Environmental cues include visual prompts, such as whiteboard lists; auditory reminders, such as cell phone alarms; and internalized cues—catchphrases like, "Let me take just ten minutes to get started on this assignment." These cues can help individuals with EF disorders increase the likelihood that they will start promptly on a project. Cues also boost efficiency, by prompting a student to stay on task longer and return to work more quickly after getting interrupted. Finally, reminders can assist someone with disordered EF to maintain motivation in the face of adversity and identify alternative strategies when problems arise.

Clinicians incorporate IIS and cueing to enhance a student's execu-tive functioning, as well as ADHD coaching and cognitive behavioral therapy, the two most commonly used interventions for college students with EF disorders.

Is Coaching the Answer?

While many studies of EF focus on the subset of ADHD students, you may be surprised at their wide applicability to a broad array of stu-dents. A growing body of research has pinpointed coaching as a most important resource for college students with EF difficulties to improve their chances of success.[5] According to educational psychologist Frances Prevatt and her colleagues,[6] such coaching is designed to help these students stay on track in a dozen different target areas:

TARGET AREA COMPONENTS

Academics	Studying, note taking, memory skills, writing, paying attention and focusing in class, accessing accommodations
Time management	Setting and keeping goals, scheduling, overcoming procrastination, setting reminders, using calendars and planners, being on time
Organization	Organizing home and study areas, finding places for everything
Career planning	Evaluating and identifying a career; planning steps to reach a career goal
Healthy habits	Maintaining healthy eating, sleeping, and exercise routines
Life skills	Managing finances, managing a home or apartment, becoming independent from parents
Problem solving	Breaking down tasks, identifying barriers, making good decisions
Psychoeducation	Educating oneself about ADHD, engaging in self-advocacy
Social settings	Managing and establishing healthy relationships, communication, emotional control, and self-esteem
Medication	Managing medication
Motivation	Utilizing self-reinforcement to accomplish goals
Handling stress and anxiety	Managing life skills to lessen anxiety and depression associated with impairments

Source: Adapted with permission from *Coaching for College Students with ADHD* by Frances Prevatt

Studies of college students with ADHD (and EF difficulties) show that those who attended coaching sessions regularly—and, crucially, put into practice the coping strategies they learned there—were able to improve their academic performance and sharpen their executive functioning skills. Small wonder, then, that more and more campuses are offering ADHD coaching classes at their student learning and mental health centers. Likewise riding to the rescue are nonprofit organizations such as the Edge Foundation, which provides online tips and resources about ADHD coaching for students of *all* ages.

Although specialists may throw around technical terms such as "behavioral interventions," ADHD coaching often boils down to a return to good old-fashioned basics: how to break a complex task into its constituent—and therefore accomplishable—component steps:

1. How to pick a starting point in such a way as to guarantee you get traction on a project
2. How to move from an off-task activity to one that is very much on task

Consistent with the sports metaphor implicit in the term, ADHD coaching also puts students through drills customized to hone their skills: "coachees" get a chance to practice setting aside time to plan, making a to-do list, using a daily planner, and identifying common obstacles to getting started. ADHD coaching may even get as granular as helping a student arrange the most productive physical work space possible.

"I'll Take Care of It Tomorrow"

Individuals with EF difficulties have a troubling tendency to take procrastination to extremes. Motivational expert Piers Steel, author of *The Procrastination Equation,* defines the behavior this way: "to voluntarily delay an intended course of action *despite expecting to be worse off for the delay.*"[7] (Emphasis added.) What, you might reasonably ask, would make someone repeatedly postpone important tasks despite knowing that doing so will almost certainly cause them harm?

Part of the answer lies in the lopsided reward system of those with disordered EF. Confronting a priority task that they find challenging or anxiety-provoking, they tell themselves, "Not now"—and feel an immediate surge of relief at this decision to postpone. That simple act of deferral is highly reinforcing: it instantly removes the negative stimulus—that is, the unpleasant thought of tackling a daunting task—

and this in turn opens the floodgates of relief. In the digital age, this often means web surfing, online TV watching, checking social media, or playing a favorite video game. These are surefire ways to get away from an unpleasant task and find instant gratification. The obvious problem here is that precious time gets wasted without even realizing it because of the high degree of engagement and stimulation that digital media provide.

Other forms of procrastination may include losing track of a high-priority task because of poor time management, forgetfulness, or disorganization; hyper-focusing on (also known as perseverating over) a less important task; and failing to recognize the importance of a task until the last minute (a scenario that patients often describe as feeling "underwhelmed" and which we've termed "brinksmanship"). Finally, procrastination may take the form of having to be in just the right mood, with everything in just the right place, before getting started—a syndrome some therapists dub "front-end perfectionism." Admittedly everyone procrastinates from time to time—it's what leads us to put off the diet or the exercise program we know we need to get moving on. But people with EF difficulties exhibit "pathologic procrastination"—that is, they do it repeatedly even when they're on the brink of disaster.

No one can overcome procrastination until they have identified the "escape behaviors" being used to sidestep the task at hand. In Arjun's case, he and Dr. Rostain quickly agreed that his wee-hour RPGs (role-playing games, usually online) were paradoxically keeping him from playing a more active role in his academic life. While he was clearly getting lots of reward from the game playing (enjoyment, sense of mastery, social interaction), he was also losing sleep, skipping out on meals and exercise, and doing very little of what he came to college to do: study. They therefore zeroed in on revising the behavioral script that had brought Arjun to near-ruination halfway through his first college semester.

The options were clear: Arjun could limit how long he played the game at night; he could go "cold turkey"; or he could permit himself to play the game for shorter periods of time—and these would be allowed only *after* he had completed certain key tasks, such as meeting with his professors or going to the study-skills center. Concluding that he was not yet ready to stop playing the game altogether, Arjun chose option three.

He also engaged in a highly effective behavior-modeling exercise that students in crisis should be encouraged to try on their own: he wrote out the email he would send to his English and calculus professors, and he rehearsed the conversations he would have with them about his plans to complete missing assignments. By witnessing the concrete steps involved in breaking a seemingly impossible task into its component steps, Arjun succeeded in moving from crisis-avoidance mode to crisis management.

If you've ever gotten ready for a dreaded job by straightening the room, doing a load of laundry, or meticulously aligning every last object on your desk, you are familiar with "procrastivity"[8]—Dr. Russ Ramsay's term for avoiding a high-priority task by engaging in one of far lower importance, simultaneously justifying the dodge by reassuring yourself that the avoidant behavior is, after all, productive. Procrastivity tasks tend to be manual or physical undertakings. They can be achieved in a brief span of time, giving the person performing them a clear—and rewarding—sense of accomplishment.

Now, what if you could trick your mind into attacking a high-priority task by persuading it the job was actually mechanical, not mental, in nature? Rather than trying to write an overdue term paper in a single sitting—an impossible task, most of us would agree—why not work out a bargain with yourself that you will complete the *physical* actions of going to your study space, sitting down, and merely reading the assignment for a few minutes? And what if you further agreed to spend the next ten minutes on the *physical* action of writing the first few lines of the paper? After ten minutes of concentrated effort, if things are going well, the writing session can be extended for another ten minutes. If not, a separate ten-minute writing session is simply planned for later in the day.

This entire stratagem may strike you as elaborate, yet it has a very straightforward point: you are creating a realistic time frame, with clearly defined start and stop times and rudimentary short-term goals. When blended together, these elements make the high-priority task appear to be the manageable undertaking it truly is.

Mindset Melding

Another proven way to address executive function problems is to very deliberately change your frame of mind about whatever challenge you happen to be facing in the current moment. All of us—parents and students, specialists and laymen—alter reality to some degree to suit our own purposes—a dynamic that psychologists call *cognitive distortion*. In addition to engaging in excessive procrastination, individuals with EF deficits are prone to several types of cognitive distortions:

1. **Magical thinking**: "I'll get it done somehow."

2. **Magnification/minimization**: "Working on this term paper is going to be a nightmare—especially since I can't write."

3. **Invidious comparisons**: "My friends seem to have this class nailed, but I can't figure out what's going on—I must be an idiot."

4. **Emotional reasoning**: "I have to be in the right mood to get going on this project, but I'm just not there yet."

5. **Perfectionism**: "I can't really get started until I know exactly how this whole thing is going to play out."

Most of the college students who come to us for assistance report having engaged in one or more of these warped thought patterns. As a first step in helping them break free of such fatalistic thinking, we peel apart the cognitive distortions that are creating avoidant behaviors.

Next, we work together to poke holes in these negative thoughts, inviting the student to serve as a "defense attorney," promoting an efficient mindset. In a fair trial, we point out, both sides of an argument get to be heard, yet procrastination rationales tend to present a lopsided view of the evidence.

Listening to the procrastinator mindset alone almost invariably ushers in a decision to put off working on a priority task. So, what reasoning might the defense attorney bring forward on behalf of getting started? How would an efficient mindset counter the claims that the task is too difficult, that the outcome is unlikely to be successful, or that "working best under deadline pressure" makes a lick of sense? By encouraging individuals to contrast the reality of a troublesome behavior against its cognitive distortions, alternative and more efficient ways of task management emerge.

"Slow Down, You're Too Fast"

Finally facing up to a difficult task—especially one that your mind has been taking active countermeasures to avoid—can be an understandably stressful experience. We have therefore devised an array of clinical methods to "embrace the suck," if you'll pardon the Millennialism. The first step is to acknowledge, and *accept,* the sense of unease that billows up like a dark miasma as soon as one contemplates tackling a challenging project. Rather than waiting to get going until the procrastinator is in the mood, we urge individuals to "own" their feelings of dread and dive into the deep end despite them.

"Mindfulness," rather than a voguey trend, is an ancient practice, and precisely what's required here: a calm moment in which to draw a deep breath and simply catalog all the feelings being currently experienced about a stressful situation. This recognition of the fact that a pressing task is feeding distraction or inattention frees the person to tolerate and reduce the stress without resorting to escape behaviors. In a sense, the procrastinator is learning to resist the urge to self-distract by noticing their feelings rather than acting on them.

Another advantage of analyzing a stressful situation in this fashion is that you *decelerate* the brain's response. Slowing things down enough to recognize that your feelings are merely one aspect of the scenario—not the scenario in its entirety—usually provides a sense of relief from the discomfort, or at least a reduction in its intensity. And this in turn carves out some breathing room—a space in which a struggling student can identify the next small step that will be just enough to get moving in the right direction.

Planning to Act

Earlier in the chapter, we learned how Arjun used an implementation intention strategy (IIS) to achieve a goal. This is a decision, in advance, about which precise steps a person will take to accomplish a task—and *when* to take them.[9] IIS shifts the student's focus from the *goal* of a task to the *mechanics* of completing it.

Imagine that the goal in question is to read a certain number of pages for a class in, say, twentieth-century U.S. history. Rather than becoming overwhelmed by the sheer magnitude of the undertaking—"They expect me to absorb every detail of Watergate in a single night?!"—the student consults his IIS and sees that its first stage calls for him to sit down at his desk and read for an uninterrupted block of ten minutes. By the same token, if the larger goal is to complete a substantive writing project, the reassuringly incremental IIS directs the student to repair to her study space and spend a concerted ten-minute stretch brainstorming ideas for the paper.

The secret to a successful IIS is that it empowers the student to write himself a behavioral prescription. By consciously identifying in advance the tipping points most likely to facilitate getting started on a task or keeping at it, the IIS empowers a person to plan exactly how they will handle distractions or interruptions. Again, granularity is the name of this game: the IIS is composed *by the student* in such a way that it forces him to answer questions like these up front:

1. Knowing yourself as you do, what will help you get started?
2. What disruptions might derail this plan once you start down the track?
3. What is your plan for returning to work if you get interrupted?

Ideally, IIS puts tools in the hands of an EF-challenged student that enable him to build his own framework for problem solving: "If X happens, I will do Y." In Arjun's case, crafting an IIS helped him to spot and quarantine certain external temptations, namely those represented by the dorm mates with whom he enjoyed playing video games. Here's the script he devised to inoculate himself: "If my friends come over and ask me to join them in a session, I'll tell them I'm tied up for the time being but will hit them up as soon as I finish the day's assignment." Recognizing that Arjun needed to stay focused on his academics, his friends supported his IIS by dialing back their invitations to play; they even moved their game play to another location.

Arjun was a capable student who had fallen behind in his academic commitments because of numerous EF problems commonly seen in young adults with ADHD. Yet concerted efforts to address the most detrimental of his EF effects—notably procrastination and poor planning—allowed Arjun to begin practicing more effective methods of accomplishing what he knew he had to do. With the additional help of an ADHD medication that targeted his distractibility, Arjun was soon back on the road to meeting the academic challenges of college life. Arjun continued to use the skills he had learned, and three and a half years later, he graduated on time, with a very decent GPA and a wonderful career-building job in the tech industry.

PART TWO

OF CRISIS

and RECOVERY

6

Risky Business: The Adolescent Brain

*"I discovered that hospitalizations for alcohol detox
had become routine on the campuses of even the most
academically renowned schools."*
—BARRETT SEAMAN, FROM *BINGE: WHAT YOUR
COLLEGE STUDENT WON'T TELL YOU*[1]

If a college student seems enticed by risky behavior, blame it on her brain. Thanks to a quirk in the way the human nervous system matures, the brain's reward mechanisms come online much earlier in the decade of emerging adulthood than do those responsible for inhibition and control. The result is the well-known array of adolescent and young adult risk-taking and thrill-seeking that parents bemoan but frequently misunderstand.

At Joey's first appointment, he was slouched in his chair, openly sobbing. "How could this have happened to me? What am I supposed to do now?" Haltingly and painfully, Joey told Dr. Rostain about some recent events. The local police precinct arrested him after he'd crashed his parents' car and failed the alcohol breath test. He was on his way back home from a friend's house and took a curve too fast. Very fortunately, there were no oncoming cars; he was driving alone and avoided injury because the front and side air safety bags inflated. But the car was totaled and he was facing DUI charges. Finally, he'd hit bottom, and was starting to come to terms with the serious consequences of his behavior.

Joey's parents and his attorney had contacted Dr. Rostain and requested a psychiatric evaluation. A review of his history and academic record revealed that Joey was a very intelligent, socially popular, and talented student-athlete on involuntary leave from college. After "one too many" violations of the school's drug and alcohol policy in the fall of his sophomore year, Joey had moved from probation to suspension.

Joey started drinking and smoking pot in his freshman year of high school. Initially, he limited his substance use to weekend indulgence with friends at parties and get-togethers. By senior year, Joey's alcohol consumption increased in frequency and included drinking alone in his room at home. At one point, his mother found an empty vodka bottle in his bedroom and questioned him about it, but he convinced her he was holding on to it because he liked the bottle's design. He admitted that he and his friends drank occasionally but he insisted that he had it under control and that there was nothing to worry about. After all, he reminded her, he'd been accepted into his first-choice college and awarded a soccer scholarship.

Like other incoming freshmen at most U.S. colleges, Joey completed his school's mandatory Alcohol 101 course online and arrived on campus ready to enjoy his newfound freedom. At his second party, held off-campus by a popular "jock fraternity," he ended up in the local emergency room with minor injuries sustained from trying to climb a tree (while drunk). Later that fall, his friends from the soccer team carried him to the ER after he passed out at another frat party. Joey was diagnosed with alcohol poisoning and kept for observation overnight. Following discharge, he appeared before the school's disciplinary officer who issued a warning citation and mandated an advanced course on alcohol and substance use. Joey rationalized these incidents, convinced he didn't really have a drinking problem. He told himself that he was just keeping up with his peers and, unluckily, he got caught.

In his freshman spring, Joey was accepted into the school's most storied fraternity (think *Animal House*). As a newly inducted member, he pledged his allegiance by spending over twenty hours per week completing chores, doing "favors" for upperclassmen, and engaging in hazing activities that included very heavy drinking followed by "pranks and partying." Though his grades dropped significantly that semester (from 3.8 to 2.9), Joey described it as "the best time of his life." After all, this was what college was supposed to be.

In the fall of his sophomore year, Joey's drinking and pot smoking increased dramatically. He began to skip classes regularly in favor of sticking around the fraternity house. He frequently skipped soccer practices and found ways to get around the random drug screenings. One of his coaches shared a concern that Joey seemed "down" and recommended he go to see a counselor, but Joey disregarded the advice. During his fraternity's Halloween party, Joey blacked out and fell down a half-flight of stairs. He was taken to the same ER he'd visited the previous year. His blood alcohol content was 0.4 percent. He was admitted to the hospital with alcohol poisoning. Following discharge, the school disciplinary committee met with him to inform him that he had forty-eight hours to leave campus and could not petition for readmission without clearance by a substance abuse treatment program of his choice.

When Joey's parents questioned him about the circumstances of his hospitalization and his subsequent suspension from school, he acknowledged that he'd had "a little too much to drink" at the party. He protested that the school was making a big deal out of a stupid mistake, and that he really wasn't a problem drinker. His parents helped him locate an outpatient drug and alcohol program near their home.

Joey's participation in treatment was half-hearted at best. He knew what to say to convince his counselors that he was taking the program seriously, but in his own mind, he was convinced he wasn't a substance abuser. He assured his parents that he was making progress and they believed him—that is, until he crashed their car, was arrested for drunk driving, and needed an evaluation and treatment to hopefully avoid jail time.

Following a thorough psychiatric evaluation, Dr. Rostain recommended admission to an inpatient drug and alcohol treatment facility for treatment of substance use disorder (SUD). It was clear to him that Joey's longstanding use of alcohol and marijuana was chronic and severe enough to warrant intensive treatment, especially in view of the life-threatening behaviors that he was engaging in regularly and repeatedly under the influence of substances.

This chapter examines the hazards, as well as the contexts, fueling the risk-taking behavior of college students. It answers Joey's questions—"Why and how had things gotten to this point? What might have been done sooner to avoid the crisis? And now what?" We take a quick look at how key changes in brain biology and anatomy dictate the development of thoughts, emotions, and behavior in youth. And how these changes translate into a young adult's natural susceptibility to rash actions commonly displayed in alcohol or substance use in high school or college. We'll give you a sense—prepare to have your eyes opened—of the social contexts in which this risky business gets transacted, spelling out the consequences of misuse and abuse. We'll help you to understand how a seemingly typical behavior, like college drinking, can morph into a serious illness (SUD). We'll enable you to take stock of your student's ability to manage the risks of alcohol and substance use (ASU), and provide important conversational tips for the discussion of safety issues. We'll also explain what parents and peers can do to prevent harmful use, and how anyone can intervene when they witness it happening. At each step along the way, we'll furnish valuable resources designed to help you and your student survive this often harrowing but ultimately hopeful journey.

Wired for Thrills

Magnetic resonance imaging (MRI) studies over the past two decades have revealed that the brain undergoes a dramatic rewiring from ages 12 to 25. These changes occur in a wave from the back of the brain to the front, transforming the neural networks that govern reward, behavioral self-regulation, and social relationships. Yet as any parent who's ever had a what-were-you-thinking "discussion" with their teen knows all too well, this cortical remodeling project betrays one glaring design flaw: the brain regions associated with arousal coalesce more rapidly than the prefrontal-cortex areas that regulate impulsivity and encourage advance planning.

The upshot? Goaded by its accelerators—that is, its increased drives for pleasure, social interaction, and sexuality—the adolescent and young adult brain lacks the braking capacity it needs to curb its urges to take risks, especially in social contexts.

The relative immaturity of adolescent frontal lobes means that behavioral restraint—thinking through the consequences of an action before taking it—gets "outvoted" by the mechanisms that facilitate reward-driven behavior. Planning ahead and using good judgment—the twin pillars of mature executive functioning (EF; see Chapter 5)—are simply not yet developed enough to rein in the brain's reward circuits. This explains why risk-taking emerges as such a prominent feature of this stage of development—and why problems such as addiction, anxiety, and depression show a rise in prevalence and severity during this period. These emerge when negative experiences accumulate, eventu-

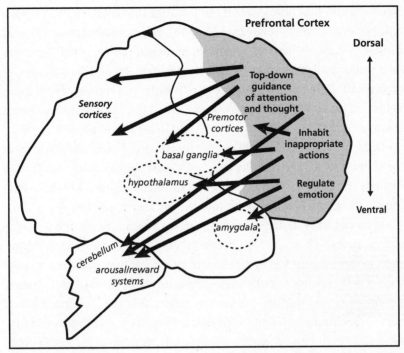

Source: A. Arnsten and K. Rubia, *Journal of the American Academy of Child and Adolescent Psychiatry* 2012[2]

ally overwhelming the young person's coping abilities and leading to excessive stress, then to distress and, eventually, to mental disorder.

As adolescence performs its makeover of brain anatomy, the functioning of that organ changes in three vital ways:

1. Information processing becomes faster, more efficient, and more precise.
2. Reasoning capacity expands to include deductive logic, abstract thought, and a keener sense of time.
3. Real expertise is attained in acquiring skills and solving problems.

From an evolutionary standpoint, these changes equip teens to grow into the mature adult roles required for individual and group survival.

Laurence Steinberg of Temple University has probed why risk-taking increases from childhood and adolescence, only to decline from later adolescence into adulthood.[3] Asking study participants in three age groups to drive as quickly as they could through twenty intersections over six minutes—don't worry, a video driving simulator was used—

Steinberg and his colleagues set out to gauge the balance of risk versus task performance in teens (ages 14 to 18), young adults (19 to 22), and adults (24 to 29). Whenever a traffic light turned yellow, as it did at every intersection, subjects had a choice: they could stop and wait three seconds for the light to turn green, or they could try to run the yellow light. When they beat the yellow, they incurred no time penalty; whenever a crash occurred, by contrast, a six-second delay would ensue.

But more than traffic-light colors were involved here. The study measured the percentage of risky decisions each subject made under two distinct conditions: when driving the simulator alone and when driving it with an audience of peers looking on. (See figure below.)

Who did the worst? Fourteen- to eighteen-year-olds in the presence of their peers. When an fMRI machine was added to the driving experience, marked changes lit up the reward circuits of the adolescent brain—but not in those same circuits among the young adult or adult participants.

The practical implication of this research is that it is normal—if nerve-wracking for parents—for risk-taking to override rational judgment in mid to late adolescence, especially in the presence of friends. This may affect how tightly parents decide to set limits for their 14- to 18-year-olds, particularly in arenas known to be highly vulnerable to impulsive or peer-influenced behavior. (Driving and parties come to mind.) At the very least, it gives us a clearer picture of just how compromised a young person's brain truly is when confronting a social situation that encourages risk-taking. This is even more the case when the individual is "young for their age" as is seen in ADHD, ASD, depression, and anxiety disorders.

Stoplight Task Performance

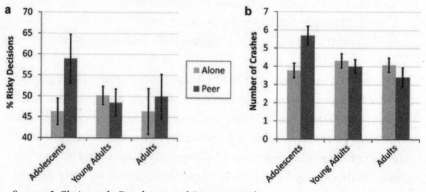

Source: J. Chein et al., *Developmental Science*, 2010[4]

Substance Use and Abuse

Substance abuse takes a heavy toll on both grades and graduation rates. National surveys conducted over the last decade (see appended web references) confirm that ASU is widespread among U.S. adolescents and young adults. Underage drinking is the rule rather than the exception, while *binge drinking*—defined as having five or more drinks on any one occasion in the past month for males and four or more for females— occurs in roughly 1 out of 5 high school seniors and nearly 1 out of 3 college students.

Make no mistake; problem drinking in college is more than just easily lampoonable hangovers or walks of shame. As many as one-fourth of all college students report having suffered academic consequences from drinking: missed classes, blown assignments, substandard performance on papers or exams. Some 40 percent of binge drinkers reported performing poorly on a project or test, compared with just 7 percent of students who never binged. Equally disturbing is the National Institute on Alcohol Abuse and Alcoholism (NIAAA) estimate that a flabbergasting 1 in 5 college students meet the criteria of alcohol use disorder (AUD) (see College Fact Sheet in Appendix web links).

Some kids reassure their parents: "Don't worry, I don't like to drink. I just smoke weed." Regular marijuana use (defined as daily or near-daily consumption) was reported by 1 out of 5 high school seniors and college students; other forms of illicit substance use, including the unauthorized use of prescription drugs, emerged as a persistent behavior for more than 1 out of every 10 people in this age group.

Of perhaps even greater concern, young adults do not perceive the potential harm in these indulgences. For pot consumption in particular, the transition from high school to college often involves a decrease in risk perception and a simultaneous increase in availability.

Pot use can also exact a heavy levy long-term. Recent research has turned up evidence that chronic marijuana use may have negative effects on intelligence, cognition (including EF), and motivation. There is also the risk that usage may devolve into a use disorder—known better by its less clinical name, "addiction." And especially in genetically vulnerable youth (25 percent of the population), habitual marijuana use is associated with higher rates of other substance-use disorders, as well as with an eleven-fold increase in the onset of psychosis and schizophrenia.

"Work Hard, Play Hard"

Young people live in a society that sends out mixed messages about ASU. On one hand, they encounter dire warnings about the dangers of excessive consumption, while on the other they're invited to buy fine wines, craft beers, name-brand vodkas, and even artisanal varieties of cannabis. Tragically, the social pressures of college life may be getting the upper hand in this battle—with risky business the victor.

To gain a thoroughgoing view of just how perniciously campus ASU breeds overconsumption, one need only visit a popular website like collegepartynation.com. Claiming to offer "Everything You Need to Get Your Party On," its fifteen clickable tabs dish the 411 on drinking games, drinking shots, party drink recipes, drinking toasts, party themes, bartending terms, and bar tricks. Here you'll learn the eight variations of beer pong, as well as how to mix seventy-nine different shots classified under seven headings, among them Birthday Shots, Dessert Shots, Random Shots, and Very Easy/Girl Shots. At the bottom of each web page, of course, lurks a cynical disclaimer: "**Please Drink Responsibly.**"

In a similar vein, dozens of websites host videos of college weed parties replete with graphic demonstrations of smoking bongs and blunts in dorm rooms, frat houses, hotel suites, parks, and the like. It's easy for students to find instructions online of how to grow, buy, smoke, eat, or cook with weed, as well as how to handcraft a panoply of pipes, bongs, and other devices to consume weed. In short, welcome to college, where there's always a party going on!

What's most striking about these descriptions of college ASU is how closely they mirror the reality of campus social life, especially on weekends. Sociologists Daniel Chambliss and Christopher Takacs spent eight years shadowing a cluster of nearly one hundred undergraduates as they made their way through Hamilton College, a small liberal arts school in upstate New York, then recounted what they had learned in *How College Works*.[5] The excerpt below characterizes the sort of American academic environments that normalize, wittingly or not, social drinking:

> *Early on a weekend evening, a group of friends will gather in someone's dorm room to "pregame," in the metaphor taken from sporting events: dress up, drink a while, and talk themselves into going out on one of the odysseys that characterize the party*

scene. They psych up, they talk about what they plan to do; they try on this dress, or that shirt and pants, testing them out on friends before later trying them out on strangers. And odysseys they are— the group moves from place to place, one party to the next, to a game, then to a party or two, then to the late-night diner, then back to a dorm room, in search of the adventures that lend the weekend its special appeal. . . . The weekend odyssey is a journey filled with the excitement of new rewards, and some risk (although one can always leave), but it's an amazingly immediate (if not always accurate) way to check one's status and competence: Am I cool? Attractive? Do I have friends? A few or a lot?

Walk across any college campus in America on a weekend evening and you'll hear the clink of glasses and bottles or smell the pungent waft of weed floating from the windows of fraternity and sorority events or spontaneous get-togethers in dorm rooms and off-campus apartments. As the night wears on, the laughter gets louder, the conversations more disjointed, the body movements of partygoers less coordinated. People start leaning heavily on one another, toppling over in fits of giggles. Falling-down drunks are helped to their feet and steered to the nearest couch or armchair, or perhaps dropped insensate onto someone's unoccupied bed. And as the bars close and the sponsored parties end, the streets fill with revelers staggering toward the inevitable "after-party," the ultimate goal being to keep the bacchanal going until early morning.

In an essay for *The Chronicle of Higher Education* titled "A River of Booze: Inside one college town's uneasy embrace of drinking,"[6] Karin Fischer and Eric Hoover detail a very liquid weekend at the University of Georgia. Through interviews with the campus police chief, a student manufacturer of fake IDs, a bar owner, a veteran tailgater, and a campus health educator, they paint a multilayered portrait of a social scene awash in alcohol. Despite the best efforts of law enforcement, health promoters, and college administrators, the piece ruefully concludes, the prevailing campus culture encourages college students to drink to excess.

Fake-ID mills . . . happy hours that seem to last days . . . lax enforcement of noise ordinances . . . Greek-letter systems fed by a constant freshet of alcohol:[7] these are the forces conspiring to create a hidebound campus culture that rebuffs change. Whether your student is headed for her freshman year or Ph.D. orals, therefore, it's obviously never too late to engage in a dialogue about what underlies this culture—and whether it is truly impervious to change. The most crucial question to pose is what relationship your student has to this culture, and whether or not he or she perceives the true hazards it poses to their health and well-being.

It's All a Blur

One particularly troubling trend is the current vogue—we're really not sure what else to call it—for drinking until blackout. In an opinion piece written for her campus newspaper and published in *The New York Times*, Ashton Carrick, a senior at the University of North Carolina, stated her belief that students who drink until they pass out do so in response to the inordinate pressures of college life. She also painted a chilling picture of how normalized the practice has become:

> *So the mentality behind the decision to black out boils down to the simple question of why not? No one will stop you. You're in a familiar environment. You assume that if you black out, someone will make sure you get back home. And most of the time you do get home, which makes it seem a lot lower-risk than it really is—and allows it to be repeated every weekend. . . . The way we as students treat the blacking out of our peers is also partly responsible for its ubiquity. We actually think it's funny. We joke the next day about how ridiculous our friends looked passed out on the bathroom floor or Snapchatting while dancing and making out with some random guy, thus validating their actions and encouraging them to do it again. Blacking out has become so normal that even if you don't personally do it, you understand why others do. It's a mutually recognized method of stress relief. To treat it as anything else would be judgmental.*[8]

And if the individual enablers of excessive ASU don't get to you, the institutional enablers just might. Fraternities, sororities, drinking clubs, and sports teams have historically been accused of promoting hazardous consumption. As Carrick notes, the game favored at the frat parties was cuff and chug, "where you are handcuffed to a partner until the two of you finish a fifth of alcohol. For the super competitive, Sharpie pens were used to tally the number of drinks on your arm, establishing a ratio of drinks to the time it takes to black out. A high ratio was a source of pride among the guys."[9]

Little has changed from 1993 when a national survey of over 17,500 students revealed that more than 90 percent of fraternity houses engaged in binge drinking. Then, as today, researchers concluded that "efforts to reduce hazardous use of alcohol on college campuses (e.g. campus regulations and educational programs, legislation) seem to have had little effect on members of social fraternities and sororities . . . and scant evidence that campus officials hold fraternity members accountable for their irresponsible, and often illegal, behavior."[10]

Michele Goldfarb, the University of Pennsylvania's former director of student conduct, acknowledges that Greek-letter institutions "take on service projects and improve campus culture." Yet by "distancing and separating students so they socialize less with the rest of the student body," she continues, "they can have a very negative impact. Plus, their drinking culture creates expectations of heavy drinking. Frat parties are characterized by excessive drinking games—chugging beer out of funnels and hoses, drinking spirits poured from ice towers—that prevent individuals from controlling their consumption. It's crazy and dangerous, but accepted—even expected—that you will drink to excess."

In fairness, say officials of national fraternal organizations, not every fraternity or sorority in the land is out of control, and the balance of their contributions to college life is positive. Most local chapters claim to have strict rules governing alcohol consumption and substance use, as well as policies for handling infractions. To remain in good standing, they must demonstrate adherence to safety guidelines and codes of good conduct—and violations may trigger a permanent loss of charter. Yet as current studies show, Greek-letter institutions continue to pose thorny challenges to college administrators—and a real question mark to parents trying to keep impressionable or impulsive kids out of harm's way. Numerous unintended deaths from hazing incidents and over-drinking at fraternity parties have appeared in the news, shedding new light on the inner workings of these age-old rituals. Yet it remains to be seen if these highly publicized cases will slow the rivers of alcohol that flow through most of America's colleges.

The Law of Unintended Consequences

The price students pay for ASU is steep. More than 1,800 college students die each year from alcohol-related unintentional injuries. Some 700,000 are assaulted by another student who has been drinking, 110,000 report having been too drunk to know if they consented to sex, and 97,000 report having experienced an alcohol-related sexual assault or date rape.

Being aware that drinking invites sexual misconduct can help college students avoid or address a crisis of this kind. A 2006 study identified the factors that contribute to "party rape": off-campus parties (especially frat houses); alcohol; and sexually predatory males interested in controlling the availability and flow of that alcohol. Stir in such volatile ingredients as peer pressure, status-seeking, and the absence of any stigma about losing control in public and you have a sure-fire recipe for sexual assault. One of the undergraduate men interviewed for the study confirmed:

> Girls are continually fed drinks of alcohol. It's mainly to party but my roomies are also aware of the inhibition-lowering effects. I've seen an old roomie block the door when girls want to leave his room; other times I've driven women home who can't remember much of an evening, yet sex did occur. Rarely if ever has a night of drinking for my roommate ended without sex. I know it isn't necessarily and assuredly sexual assault, but with the amount of liquor in the house I question the amount of consent a lot.[11]

The bottom line, parents and students alike should know, is that consensual sex becomes a dubious notion when one or both partners are under the influence of alcohol or any other substance. Indeed, it was the prevalence of date rape and party rape that mandated passage of the Campus Sexual Violence Elimination Act in 2013. This law requires every institution of higher learning to educate students, faculty, and staff about rape prevention, acquaintance rape, domestic violence, dating violence, sexual assault, and stalking. It also places a larger share of the responsibility for response, disciplinary actions, and prevention education squarely on the shoulders of colleges themselves. There are major changes being proposed to make this law more equitable for those students accused of inappropriate sexual behavior, but despite this, campus culture and national opinion are moving in the direction of greater protection for victims of sexual assault.

To educate yourself more about the scope and degree of this problem, visit the website of the National Sexual Violence Resource Center (www.nsvrc.org). This site informs the public about issues such as campus sexual assault, with sobering statistics meant to preempt future sexual assaults. For example, did you know that 9 of every 10 campus victims knew their attacker? Or that 3 in 4 self-reported perpetrators had been drinking just before their most recent incident?

Excessive drinking harbors yet another routine peril of alcohol: poisoning (if near-death can be called that). At high levels, alcohol can have toxic effects that range from vomiting, slow or irregular breathing, hypothermia, and mental confusion to stupor, coma, and death. Recall that Joey was taken to the hospital in a stupor after attending a frat Halloween party. Had his frat brothers not been so quick to respond to him, he very easily could have died that night.

On campuses across the country, it has become commonplace for officials returning to work on Monday morning to update themselves on the weekend's tally of emergency transports for alcohol-related and other drug overdoses. Fortunately, most of these interventions save lives. Goldfarb recalls the case of a drunken freshman basketball player being escorted back to his dorm room from a party by a teammate. The athlete's roommate and the hall RA instructed the teammate to drop him on the bed so he could sleep it off as usual. The teammate refused to comply. Hoisting the near-comatose player onto his shoulders, he carried him to a hospital ER several blocks away, where doctors intubated him—and informed his rescuer that the player almost certainly would have died had he been left unattended.

The close call became a wake-up call: upon recovering, the player became active on the university's alcohol task force, speaking out about the dangers of excessive alcohol consumption and urging fellow students to face up to their own risky drinking habits. New medical amnesty rules have saved countless lives by shielding students who seek emergency medical help for fellow students from being prosecuted or disciplined for underage drinking.

Faced with the terrifying enormity of a campus problem that looms out of their control, parents may lecture, scold, threaten, or simply worry themselves sick. We'll address more effective ways for parents to talk with their young adult about substance abuse issues at the end of this chapter.

"Not the 'Study Aid' We Had in Mind"

America's Adderall epidemic has gotten all the press, but college students have in fact been repurposing prescription medications as study aids for over eighty years, when scientists introduced Benzedrine sulfate (racemic amphetamine) as a treatment for depression. Within months, undergrads were using it to cram for finals, prompting an alarmist tocsin in the May 10, 1937, issue of *Time* magazine; "pep-pill poisoning" was now the newest source of worry for college directors of health: "Students who collapse, faint, or develop insomnia are under suspicion of using the substance."

During World War II, Nicolas Rasmussen recounts in *On Speed: The Many Lives of Amphetamine,*[12] both Allied and Axis troops used the drug to stay alert during prolonged battles. And for the next thirty years—until it was declared a narcotic in 1971, with the Drug Enforcement Agency classifying it as a "controlled substance"—amphetamine was widely used by students, soldiers, and dieters.

Because stimulants improve concentration, reduce sleepiness, and increase physical stamina, they are often put to use as cognitive enhancers by students and truck drivers, nurses and doctors, athletes and soldiers. You may have heard this nonmedical stimulant medication usage referred to as "off-label use." To keep things simple, however—and to conform with the recently released Surgeon General's report *Facing Addiction in America*[13]—we use the term *stimulant misuse.*

College students who misuse stimulants take them to improve attention, perform better on tests, improve study habits, and stay awake. A recent meta-analysis of twenty surveys of ASU in college students found a strong bond between stimulant misuse and cigarette smoking, problematic alcohol use, and cannabis dependence.[14] Of even greater concern were reports that some students snorted the stimulants in a bid to accelerate their effects. That way madness—or at least misery—lies: snorting can "pump up" intracranial pressure enough to bring on strokes or other malfunctions in blood-brain circulation.

Stimulant misuse is particularly virulent in Greek-letter institutions. One study[15] revealed that 8 percent of fraternity members at a large state university had legal prescriptions for ADHD medication—double the national incidence of ADHD in college students. And a staggering 55 percent—roughly three times the national average—reported stimulant misuse. Not surprisingly, 9 in 10 of the respondents indicated that stimulants were easy to obtain, while an equal proportion believed they were at most only slightly dangerous.

In one fraternity house, a patient of Dr. Rostain's recounted, the brothers kept a glass bowl in their designated study room containing a cornucopia of prescription drugs, most of them stimulant medications. An illustrated menu beside the bowl identified specific tablets and capsules.

Sharing prescription drugs, or "diversion," is a seemingly commonplace campus practice. In two-thirds of reported cases of illicit use, peers with ADHD medication prescriptions were the source of the stimulant supply. In another investigation, only one-third of undergraduates with a script for ADHD meds had *not* diverted them.[16]

How do these trends affect students on a personal level? With collegiate academic pressures rising every day, stimulants offer an easy path to scholastic achievement but a dysfunctional response to psychological stress. Indeed, investigative reporters for both *The New York Times*[17] and *The New Yorker*[18] have faked the symptoms of ADHD in order to obtain a stimulant medication under false pretenses—and prove just how prone to abuse the entire system is.

"This Is Your Brain on Drugs"

Remember those scary public service announcements from the 1980s in which a man cracked a fresh egg onto a hot griddle and somberly intoned, "This is your brain on drugs"? The message, deliberately simplistic, was that substance use fries the user's brain. Not only were the ads ineffective, they may have been counterproductive: most young people—the target audience—simply laughed at the hyperbole.

Yet the acute and chronic changes that take place in brain structure and function after exposure to psychoactive substances retains its urgency for the parents of college students today. This is especially so when you stop to consider how "normal" (technically speaking) ASU is for young adults. It's therefore worth taking a moment to look at precisely what happens when the brain encounters pleasure-inducing substances, for it helps to explain why certain personality types ("novelty seekers") tend to engage in problematic use—and why a subset of these go on to develop abuse, dependence, or addiction, which are collectively referred to as SUDs.

Facing Addiction in America[19] offers a highly readable chapter on the neurobiology of substance use, misuse, and addiction. The Surgeon General's report explains how three key regions of the brain interact in various ways to guide human adaptation and promote survival. Whenever an individual encounters a pleasure-inducing substance—whether chocolate, ice cream, or alcohol—these three processing centers are specially but differentially activated.

Non-problematic substance use allows people to experience the rewards of consuming a favorite food or beverage without suffering longstanding negative consequences. Addiction, by contrast, is a repeated pattern in which bingeing and intoxication lead to negative results and withdrawal, which sets up the brain to crave its next high.

Initial experiences with an addictive substance are highly reinforcing. Repeated use dulls these effects, however, requiring larger or more frequent amounts of the substance to achieve the same sensation. After a time, withdrawal from the substance sparks negative emotions, prompting the individual to use again to reduce his distress. Eventually the person becomes preoccupied with obtaining the substance, negative consequences be damned, and the habit becomes entrenched. The loss of ability to stop using is a hallmark of SUDs.

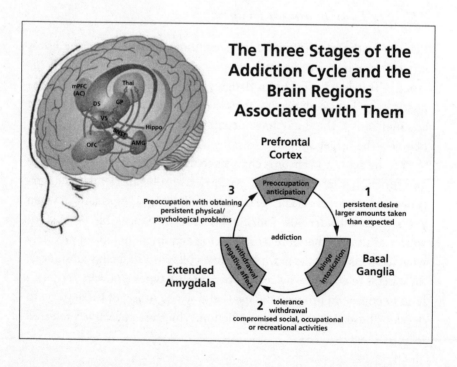

DSM-5 CRITERIA FOR SUD

1. Taking the substance in larger amounts and for longer than intended
2. Wanting to cut down or quit, but being unable to do so
3. Spending a lot of time obtaining the substance
4. Craving the substance
5. Repeated inability to carry out major obligations at work, school, or home because of substance use
6. Continued use despite persistent or recurring social or interpersonal problems caused or made worse by the very substance
7. Stopping or reducing important social, occupational, or recreational activities because of substance use
8. Recurrent use of the substance in physically hazardous situations
9. Consistent use of the substance despite acknowledgment of its persistent or recurrent physical or psychological difficulties
10. Tolerance (defined as a need for markedly increased amounts to achieve intoxication or markedly diminished effect from continued use of the same amount)
11. Withdrawal in one of two forms: the characteristic withdrawal syndrome or in instances when the substance is used so as to avoid withdrawal

Source: *Diagnostic and Statistical Manual of Mental Disorders* (Fifth Edition)[20]

When only two or three of these symptoms are present, clinicians categorize the disorder as mild. If four or five symptoms occur, it is moderate. And if six or more are present, the condition is severe. The *DSM-5* stipulates eight different types of SUD: alcohol, cannabis, hallucinogens, inhalants, opioids, sedatives/hypnotics/anxiolytics, stimulants, and tobacco. Genetic factors are thought to account for 40 to 70 percent of individual differences in risk, and early life stressors such as exposure to trauma or loss of an important relationship are highly correlated with addiction.

Of critical interest to parents, early exposure to a substance boosts the odds of becoming addicted to it later on. But *Facing Addiction* qualifies that risk tendency: "Although young people are particularly vulnerable to the adverse effects of substance use, not all adolescents who experiment with alcohol or drugs go on to develop a substance use disorder." This is one of the most central concerns of parents, educators, and clinicians: how to reduce the risk of young adults becoming addicted, and how to recognize when someone is crossing the boundary between acceptable and dangerous ASU.

The Surgeon General's report also notes that many well-supported, cost-effective prevention programs reduce the rates and severity of SUDs, and are especially effective at staving off alcohol misuse and abuse.

Why Prevention Is Measured in Ounces

Given the prevalence of ASU among college students, how can parents prepare their young people to face the risks? It's abundantly clear that abstinence approaches such as "Just say no" just don't work. The so-

WARNING SIGNS OF EMERGING SUD

1. Skipping classes (especially from oversleeping)
2. Decline in academic performance
3. Excessive fatigue; sleeping all the time
4. Reduced memory and/or concentration ability
5. Vague or evasive replies to direct questions about ASU
6. Unusual neglect with respect to physical appearance
7. Unusual and drastic weight loss/gain
8. Slurred or incoherent speech
9. Bloodshot eyes; frequent nosebleeds
10. Unusual smells on the body or clothing
11. Suspicious injuries (especially head trauma)
12. New onset of tremors or seizures

cial experiment known as Prohibition was largely unsuccessful in preventing alcohol consumption by the American public, just as the
War on Drugs has failed to curtail the use of marijuana and other substances. And let's face it: simplistic slogans or threats of sanctions from
an authority figure do nothing to help your college student make good
decisions in the heat of the social moment. Instead, parents need to
be pragmatic: adopt an authentic, down-to-earth framework for holding
truthful conversations with your young adult about alcohol consumption, binge drinking, and illicit substance use.

An excellent resource for accomplishing this task is *A Parent
Handbook for Talking with College Students About Alcohol* by Robert
Turrisi, a counselor at Penn State's Prevention Research Center. After
developing the manual, Turrisi and his colleagues tested it in several
clinical trials. To their relief, it proved effective in reducing problem
drinking *if utilized prior to arriving at college.* (The handbook's impact
was lower with students who had already experienced college life.) Although the bulk of the discussion that follows is drawn directly from the
Parent Handbook, parents should note that its contents can also easily
be accessed online at www.bucknell.edu/Documents/Communication
/WHPS/BU_ParentAlcoholHandbook.pdf. (Our thanks to Dr. Turrisi
for making this valuable resource so freely available.)

The handbook lays out communication tools and strategies to
empower parents and teens to talk about alcohol use in a constructive, open-ended fashion. The bedrock of this approach is that communication between parent and student can have an immediate and lasting
impact. Despite the common misperception that teens will tune out the
older group's views, parents *can* make a difference in preventing alcohol
abuse—binge drinking in particular. A recent national college health
survey revealed that parents were the number-one source that students
turned to for important information.

But what's the most effective way of getting your message across?
For an in-depth review, the handbook presents the most relevant statistics and communication strategies, and links readers to websites such
as the one maintained by the National Institute on Alcohol Abuse and
Alcoholism (www.niaaa.nih.gov). Below we'll offer the most crucial
takeaways for effective conversations between parent and youth.

What Parents Can Do

Inform yourself about the facts, and be ready to discuss them in a non-judgmental, non-confrontational manner. It's imperative to convey open-mindedness during the initial conversation. To effectively communicate, express your wish to hear and understand your student's experience. Reassure the young person throughout that you respect their views and trust them. Ask the young person to relate their experiences, then prompt them to say what they think about them in retrospect. Don't expect your child to agree with you.

You may not be prepared for—or approve of—what you're about to hear, so discipline yourself to suspend critical judgment and listen without defensiveness. Above all, parents should resist responding with anger. Research shows that more drinking goes on among teens who come from homes where parents tend to lecture too much, or where the teens fear punishment or harsh disapproval. Conversely, when young people feel they can trust their parents and are trusted by them, they tend to drink less.

Parents can use the conversation tips to lay the groundwork for a positive outcome to any uncomfortable conversation.

Parents should also be prepared to field questions about their own past behavior and drinking as a student. There's no hard data on how best to handle this issue, so trust your gut. Given the high sensitivity of the young adult's "bullshit detector," honesty and authenticity is likely the best strategy.

Does this mean any disclosures on your part must be forensically graphic? Not at all: you simply want to convey the certainty that you have firsthand knowledge of what they're going to face, and that you've got their back should they run into any difficulty. If you're not yet prepared to discuss what happened when you were a student, say so. And of course, you owe your child a realistic history of any family addictions, so have this talk as soon as you humanly can.

Parents can assist teens to create a ready response that will enable them to *automatically* resist social pressure to drink. Ask your student to imagine himself in a campus setting where everyone present is drinking or getting high; what will he do? You can armor him with some simple or tension-defusing one-liners that serve as handy "outs" to the pressure situation in question, such as "I'm not a drinker" or "Sorry, man—alcohol is my kryptonite." No doubt your child will coin better

CONVERSATION TIPS FOR TALKING ABOUT ASU WITH YOUNG PEOPLE

1. **Choose a good time.** Wait until both parties can have a reasonably relaxed and calm discussion. Perhaps parents could take their child to lunch: a neutral terrain where they can sit down and hear each other out.

2. **Phones down—both of you!** Listen intently, without multitasking. Permit the person to speak without interruption, and focus exclusively on what they are saying in the present moment.

3. **Verbalize respect.** Whenever appropriate, tell your son or daughter that you are proud of them for being able to handle tough situations.

4. **Appeal to common goals.** Remind your child that you are on their side. Emphasize shared objectives—for example, you both want the student to stay healthy and safe—and use these as the basis for guidance and recommendations.

5. **Avoid conversation killers.** "No one in this family would ever do that" is out of bounds, so it should be off the table.

6. **Acknowledge that conflict is natural.** Realize that disagreements are opportunities to learn the other person's stance, not threats that should put you in a defensive crouch.

7. **Agree to disengage,** temporarily, if things don't go well.

8. **Use body language** mindfully and appropriately. How you position yourself as you talk can send an unmistakable message about your attitude.

9. **Shun debate mode.** Here's a little dialogue trick: try not to start any sentence with the word "you" (it can make the other person feel attacked). If talk evokes a mini-debate, try suggesting that both sides are clearly approaching the same topic from different angles.

ones of his own. This sort of "instant-response shield" is especially vital for young women, who want to avoid drinking scenarios where sexual assault may result.

Parents should disabuse teens of common misapprehensions: no, exercise can't sober you up faster, and neither can coffee (the latter merely yields a wide-awake drunk). Nothing can speed up the rate at which the liver metabolizes alcohol, and during that period the alcohol continues to distort brain function, judgment, vision, and motor skills. This is crucial knowledge to have, given how notoriously bad people of all ages are at assessing their own level of impairment. It likewise wouldn't hurt to review the possible dangerous side effects of combining alcohol with even run-of-the-mill medications such as aspirin and sedatives.

Finally, don't hesitate to make your own values clear. Explain exactly what you believe is okay—and what is not. If you decide to allow a teen to drink at home in controlled amounts, be aware of studies showing that teens permitted this leeway tend to drink more often (and more heavily) outside the home. And—flying in the face of your strongest parental instincts—be prepared to talk candidly about the so-called positive reasons (at least from the student's perspective) for why they might choose to drink: celebrations, feeling less inhibited, and fitting in. The reasoning: parents lose credibility when they opt to focus exclusively on the negative aspects of drinking. This devil's-advocate approach can also help young adults frame these "positive" motivations in a more realistic perspective.

The main takeaway? Talking to your kids about alcohol comprises much more than a single conversation, but an open dialogue will most likely yield a trusting and respectful exchange of experiences and perspectives.

Leaf Me Alone!

Regrettably, few evidence-based guides exist for the parent who wants to constructively talk about pot with their young person. Coming closest is the Marijuana Talk Kit, a free tool you can download from the Partnership for a Drug Free America (www.drugfree.org/MJTalkKit). The kit offers a number of conversation starters designed to answer teens' questions about marijuana. It also advises parents how to respond to arguments or rebuttals teens may have, what to avoid saying, and how to use empathy and positive framing.

CAN WE TALK?

✻ If you're not a fan of scare tactics but want to lay bare the negative consequences of drinking in a matter-of-fact way, try one of these entry points to a talk with your teen. All are adapted from *A Parent Handbook for Talking with College Students About Alcohol* by Robert Turrisi.

1. **Legal hassles.** At a loud party with drinking and other drugs present, neighbors' complaints to the police can result in the arrest of everyone present who is intoxicated. Public reports of an arrest are not just embarrassing, but in the Internet age they can be vexatiously enduring. An arrest can also dump a heavy financial burden on parents, who must pay legal fees and take time off work to attend a court appearance. Rare is the student who thinks about this aftermath beforehand, so walking through the consequences in advance can be a powerful deterrent.
2. **Loss of control.** Drinking to excess makes you vomit and pass out. No one at a party wants to be responsible for you in that condition.
3. **Rape.** Drinking can lead to sexual assault—either to you or by you.
4. **Alcoholism.** Drinking may lead to becoming an alcoholic—a development that's possible, astonishingly, after only a few drinks. Because most teens cannot tell a social drinker from an alcoholic, parents should explain the signs of problem drinking. (Teens whose genetic makeup predisposes them toward alcoholism may develop into problem drinkers relatively easily. If that describes your own family background, you owe it to your child to alert them to the danger today.)
5. **Death.** Speed kills, but so does the sauce: even a single night of heavy drinking can lead to unsafe sex, a fatal car crash, or choking to death—a routine outcome when an individual vomits while lying prone after heavy drinking.

According to the "talk kit," weed is still risky for teens, and there are both effective and fruitless ways to explain why that's so. The kit also directs parents to additional resources, such as the educational materials available from the website of the National Institute on Drug Abuse (www.nih.gov/news-events/news-releases/nida-offers-tools-talking-teens-about-marijuana). For video clips illustrating communication skills parents can use to broach the topic, visit www.drugabuse.gov/family-checkup.

A knotty issue when it comes to addressing marijuana use is the drug's recent head-spinning cultural makeover. Decriminalization, medical marijuana, and the explosion of commercial dispensaries have spawned an entirely new industry seemingly overnight, with a welter of cannabis products on offer, from plants and oils to baked products and candies. And don't even get us started on "glassware."

While social media may extol the virtues of easy access to cannabis, new medical research is uncovering hidden threats to mental health in high-potency, THC-rich products, along with the expected smorgasbord of respiratory and other physical-health problems that derive from smoking or vaping weed. Eventually this information will make its way into new prevention modules that parents can use with their young adults. And as legal sanctions against marijuana use fall away, schools and communities can be expected to ratchet up their prevention efforts to levels rivaling those of alcohol-awareness programs.

And if all the talk has been to no avail? If, say, your son or daughter is starting to show signs of problematic drug or alcohol use, what then? Where do you turn for help?

Facing the Music

The following case illustrates the mental health complications of poorly regulated ASU for a college sophomore who also had difficulties with anxiety and self-injurious behavior. For many young women, the too-common scourges of eating disorders and self-harm often overlap with substance abuse. It's important to understand how to interrupt these mutually reinforcing cycles. Jasmine first met Dr. Rostain just after spring midterms. Despite a heat wave, she wore a long-sleeved blouse over her jeans—perfect camouflage for the fresh cuts covering her arms and legs.

During that first session, Jasmine spoke openly about how scratching herself had quickly led to cutting behavior. Whenever she felt overly stressed, she admitted, she got a tiny rush from cutting before the pain set in. The ritual had started during winter finals, when it was a simple matter to hide the marks beneath layers of winter clothing. But at home during spring break, both her mother and a girlfriend had spotted light cuts on Jasmine's forearms and voiced their suspicions.

At first she dismissed their questions: "Oh, the cat must have scratched me." But when her mother confronted her with the discovery of a razor blade in a bathroom trashcan, Jasmine confessed the truth. Relieved that her secret was out, she agreed to seek help.

As part of their treatment contract, Dr. Rostain and Jasmine developed the following plan of action:

1. Identify the triggers of her self-injury.
2. Ascertain the emotional function of the harmful behavior.
3. Develop better coping strategies.

Step 1 was easy: Jasmine quickly identified the triggering circumstances as exam preparation and alcohol. She would study until exhausted, then have a few beers to unwind. Disinhibited by the alcohol, she would then cut herself. Jasmine knew what was needed to change this pattern—better distress tolerance and better impulse control—but she was not confident that she could develop them.

Dr. Rostain suggested that Jasmine capture her thinking and feelings from the last cutting episode in a journal. The exercise exposed Jasmine to her surprisingly critical inner voice, which berated her as a "stupid idiot" whenever she got frustrated with class material or homework assignments. In such moments of distress, however, her journal now became a substitute for the bottle. Writing gave her a mechanism to calm her mental state, challenge her critical voice, distance herself from her anguish, and resist impulsive actions.

Jasmine also wrote down reasons to avoid cutting herself, then consulted this list each day. She practiced mindfulness meditation, with a focus on the simple action of drawing and releasing each breath. To augment her coping skills and minimize her opportunities to cut, Jasmine intentionally studied with fellow students or on her own in the library. In neither setting would she have access to alcohol.

But recovery, like life's forward path, often zigzags. Two weeks before the end of her second semester, with finals approaching, Jasmine got extremely drunk at an off-campus party with friends. Spying a knife there, she cut new lines on her arm.

"I blew it," Jasmine lamented in her next therapy session.

To help her regroup, Dr. Rostain and Jasmine discussed the conditions that jeopardized her commitment to herself. She had downplayed alcohol's role in her cutting behavior, Jasmine acknowledged, so Dr. Rostain asked her to troubleshoot some possible solutions: "What can you do the next time you're drunk—not have a knife around? Not drink eight shots of tequila?"

Jasmine began to envision what the next risky situation might be, and questioned whether getting so drunk was a good idea. Already, she confided, she had awoken in a young man's bed with no memory of how she got there—a liaison that filled her with recriminations.

Dr. Rostain pursued the point: "We've looked at how you can study and not hurt yourself; now let's think about how you can *have fun* and not hurt yourself. You've got some decisions to make about that. Remembering how bad you feel will be another basis for you to be mindful. You might want to make a deal with a friend, telling her, 'You have my permission to take that fourth shot out of my hand.' That will help you set limits when you're not as capable as you might be without any alcohol in you."

Rather than insisting on total abstinence—which he knew wouldn't work for Jasmine, because she wasn't yet ready to walk the sobriety path—Dr. Rostain was suggesting a strategy that has proven effective for individuals who have embraced a plan to limit their alcohol intake but need the support of a trusted other to help them put it into action.

Intrigued, Jasmine agreed to this plan to support her goal and avoid self-injury. To begin closing the alcohol gateway, she resolved to match her intake to that of a best friend who routinely switched to soda after a single beer. If that friend wasn't around, Jasmine planned to enlist the aid of other close friends. She informed them of her vow not to cut herself and asked for their help. Her friends agreed to take that "one drink too many" away from her, should the occasion arise in their presence.

Not every therapy story ends in success, but this one did—or has so far. Jasmine's strategy worked. It also drove home her need to continue cultivating new coping skills—ones that could help her handle future situations in which her better judgment might not be all she needed to manage risk.

Ch-ch-ch-changes

Jasmine's story illustrates how essential it is for young people who get into trouble with ASU to acknowledge they need help—and *act* to change their risky behavior. By the time she showed up for her first appointment, Jasmine had reached the "ready for action" stage. This priming of the pump enabled her to develop a treatment contract and start modifying her behavior.

The Stages of Change Model[21] provides a handy gauge for appraising an individual's readiness to change some aspect of their behavior.

1. In the **Precontemplation stage,** the person is blind to his own behavior and resentful or dismissive of any hint that they might need to change. This phase often goes by the label of "being in denial." Individuals at this stage commonly blame others for their difficulties or feel powerless to improve their situation.

2. In the **Contemplation stage,** the person acknowledges he has a problem and begins thinking about solving it. Because Contemplators still have trouble identifying the source of their problems, they cannot clearly see a solution at hand. They also tend to sound vague about any plans to get moving on a change agenda. Even as they express a desire to get unstuck, Contemplators aren't yet ready to do anything about it other than thinking.

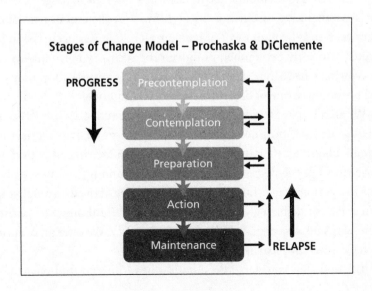

3. The **Preparation stage** signals a shift from considering making a change to planning a course of action that will usher in that change. People at this stage are open to discussing various ways to change their behavior, and they are willing to weigh the pros and cons of each action plan. As they become energized by the prospect of change, their anticipation begins to shine forth as excitement, anxiety, or increased motivation.

4. During the **Action stage,** a person begins to take responsibility for modifying his behavior. Because assessing the effectiveness of their course of action consumes a great deal of time and energy, individuals at this stage typically need a lot of support from a significant other to persevere in the face of obstacles or setbacks.

5. The ultimate phase in anyone's journey of personal transformation is the **Maintenance stage,** requiring the individual to remain vigilant for signs of a relapse. Indeed, unless someone is committed to maintaining their new pattern of behavior, they run the risk of regressing to a Precontemplation or Contemplation stage; this happens! As a matter of fact, most successful treatment for SUD sees the patient cycle through the Stages of Change more than once.

Fully aware of this pattern, clinicians involved in treating patients with SUD are trained to spot the early harbingers of a relapse and point them out to their patients. In Jasmine's case, she managed to avoid excessive drinking or cutting through finals at the end of her sophomore year and through most of the summer. Relapses occurred in late August and early September, but given the recovery mechanisms and processes she had already put in place, Jasmine's outlook for junior year and beyond was one of determined resolve and hope.

What can parents do if they suspect their student is in a crisis involving alcohol, pot, or some other substance? In Joey's crisis, his parents played a crucial role in helping him to face his addiction and move through the decisive stages of inaction and refusal to seek help into the action stage. Like many parents, they moved through their own stages of disbelief, distress, and fear of the unknown to take the many steps necessary on behalf of Joey's recovery. We offer an overview of the lessons they learned here.

The first step is to face the situation head-on and find out what is really going on. Expressing love and concern and sharing candid observations about how the young person appears to be having a hard time are important in establishing rapport and opening the lines of communication. Before jumping to conclusions or demanding explanations, it's crucial to talk calmly and directly about your genuine desire to help in whatever way makes most sense.

The second step is to invite the young person to share whatever he feels comfortable disclosing about how he is feeling and what is going on with him. Even if his initial response is to minimize his distress or deny there's anything wrong, it's important to gently confront him with whatever evidence you have that things don't seem right and that you're worried for his health and safety. It may take several invitations before your young person discloses he is having issues that are interfering with his ability to cope with school or with life.

The next step would be to offer to arrange for a visit to a mental health provider who is able to evaluate the situation more fully. In most cases, parental input will be solicited during the assessment process, and you will be able to share your observations and concerns with the provider. If either inpatient or outpatient mental health treatment is recommended, it's important to be available at every step to support your young person's journey to recovery. This will likely include attending family meetings and participating in recovery-oriented parent support groups. While this will inevitably involve a great deal of time, energy, fortitude, persistence, and financial commitment, it is vital for your young person to see that you are fully in his camp and are dedicated to helping him achieve full recovery from addiction.

If a more difficult scenario emerges in which your young person remains in the "precontemplation" stage and refuses to acknowledge the need for help, it would be helpful for you to consult directly with a mental health provider specializing in difficult-to-treat SUD in young adults. The provider should be able to offer guidance and support in your efforts to engage your child in treatment, especially by helping you to mobilize the energy and emotional resources you'll need to effectively mount a challenge to the status quo. They should also be able to offer a game plan for confronting your young person's resistance to or outright denial of the need for care.

In the upcoming chapters, we'll meet other students whose harbingers of mental illness begin or are accompanied by the sidekick of substance abuse. Sometimes it's alcohol or drugs, for others it's a life lived online. We'll reveal the underlying mood disorders and the helping hand parents can lend, and prepare you for the bumps ahead that line the road to recovery.

For More Information
- http://www.collegepartynation.com/
- http://pubs.niaaa.nih.gov/publications/UnderageDrinking/UnderageFact.htm
- https://www.niaaa.nih.gov/alcohol-health/special-populations-co-occurring-disorders/college-drinking
- http://pubs.niaaa.nih.gov/publications/CollegeFactSheet/CollegeFactSheet.pdf
- https://www.collegedrinkingprevention.gov/
- https://www.drugabuse.gov/related-topics/college-age-young-adults
- http://www.aep.umn.edu/index.php/aep-tools/college/
- http://www.drugfree.org/wp-content/uploads/2015/03/Marijuana_Talk_Kit.pdf
- http://www.samhsa.gov/data/sites/default/files/NSDUH-PreventionandInit-2015/NSDUH-PreventionandInit-2015.htm
- https://www.drugabuse.gov/publications/marijuana-facts-parents-need-to-know/letter-to-parents
- http://www.cdc.gov/vitalsigns/heroin/

7

Anxiety and Depression

"Anxiety is the Wheel of Misfortune."
—STUDENT WITH AN ANXIETY DISORDER

Anxiety tops the list of mental health disorders among college students.[1] Over half of all students who show up at college counseling offices cite anxiety as a reason they're seeking help. In close second place is depression, often accompanied by problems concentrating and sleeping.[2] In a nationwide survey of college students at two- and four-year institutions, an alarming 30 percent reported being "so depressed it was difficult to function in the past year."[3] These rates reflect an upward trend over the past four years.

Compared with their parents, the college students of today are 50 percent more likely to say they feel overwhelmed.[4] What's behind the rising tide of anxiety disorders and depression for this generation of college students? They report multiple stressors, including academics, social media, romantic relationships, "debt serfdom," and increased competition in the looming specter of adulthood. Yet these students—many of them experiencing their first bout of a mood disorder—often don't understand the nature of their illness.

Like most of us, these students are merely "visitors to" anxiety or depression, acquainted with only the mildest symptoms of these mood disorders. They are very likely unaware that anxiety disorders come in eleven varieties identified by the *Diagnostic and Statistical Manual of*

Mental Disorders (*DSM-5*), the American Psychiatric Association's diagnostic reference. Depressive disorders, for their part, merit eight specific classifications in the *DSM-5*.

Many parents are likewise caught off guard, normalizing a student's anxiety disorder as high-strung, run-of-the-mill stress, or being fooled by a depressive episode that first masquerades as freshman angst, irritability, rebelliousness, or risk-taking with drugs or alcohol. Parents often bond and commiserate about expressions of adolescent moodiness, but they may be out of their depth in trying to decide how to handle shape-shifting moods that are often difficult to diagnose and stubbornly persistent.

Having gained a great deal of experience on the front lines of college mental health, we'll share some of the lessons and strategies we've picked up along the way in this chapter. You'll meet Karin and Harry, whom we treated for anxiety, self-injury, and depression. Through the worrisome struggles of these young people and their parents, you'll learn a number of strategies to deal with anxiety and depression when they occur.

Worry or Disorder?

According to the National Institute of Mental Health, nearly one-third of both adolescents and adults have been affected by an anxiety disorder.[5] Anxiety has been called the common cold of psychological problems: almost everyone catches it at some time or another. And similar to a cold, anxiety's impact can range from mild to moderate to severe, and from transient to chronic. Anxiety is so common, in part, because it has an evolutionary function—to detect and avoid danger. For some youth, anxiety can be a realistic response to abusive family members, or an unsafe contemporary political climate, or exposure to violence in a dangerous neighborhood. For other students, the rising incidence of anxiety signals an overestimation of the perceived danger in failing to meet unrealistic goals in a culture of hyperachievement.

Yet, a certain amount of anxiety is good for us and motivates us to study for tests, to begin and complete long-range assignments, and to take the risks necessary to become an adult.

So what's the difference between a productive amount of anxiety and a debilitating dose?

Everyone worries—the average is fifty-five minutes per day—but those with generalized anxiety disorder (GAD) worry in a way that consumes up to five hours of their day.[6] Part of the challenge of diagnosing and treating anxiety is therefore discerning the difference between normal anxiety and the more pernicious clinical variety.

Whereas momentary anxiety is a normal reaction to a real or perceived danger, an anxiety disorder creates a chronic experience of perceived threat. "Anxiety disorder" is an umbrella term covering several different manifestations: panic attacks, obsessive thoughts, social anxiety, specific phobias such as agoraphobia and claustrophobia, and then the broadest category, GAD. The latter of these is one of the most commonly diagnosed psychiatric conditions in childhood and adolescence. Scientists have determined that many childhood experiences—from the trauma of a one-time violent event, to the onset of a serious or chronic illness, to overprotective parenting—can foster the development of anxiety disorders.

So can genetics: if you have a parent or a sibling with an anxiety disorder, your chances of having one are five times higher than the general population.

Left untreated, the milder form of anxiety—irksomely familiar to the worrywart or poor sleeper—can worsen as responsibilities pile up, and autonomy opens up, in the college years. GAD, for example, is that wheel of misfortune that seems to land on "Disaster Ahead!" with every spin. In its early form, an anxiety disorder may show up as torturous decision-making: "Should I wear the green shirt to class or the blue one?" Later on, it may devolve into catastrophic thinking: "OMG, I got a C on that midterm! I've blown my med-school chances—I'm such a failure!"

The American Academy of Child and Adolescent Psychiatry provides a checklist of emotions and behaviors that may signal the presence of various types of anxiety disorders.[7]

Signs of generalized anxiety disorder (GAD)
- Excessive worry that interferes with your work or social life
- Worries that pop up and spread contagiously, not limited to a specific concern

- Worries that bombard you and you can't be reassured
- Three or more psychological or physiological symptoms: irritability, tension, problems with sleep, or trouble concentrating

Signs of phobia

- Extreme fear about a specific thing or situation (for example: dogs, needles, germs, bridges)
- Fears that cause significant distress and interfere with usual activities (for example: walking up several flights of stairs due to a fear of elevators)

Signs of social anxiety

- Fears of meeting or talking to people
- Avoidance of social situations
- Restricted number of friends outside the family

Other signs of anxiety

- Many worries about things before they happen
- Constant worries or concerns about family, school, friends, or activities
- Repetitive, unwanted thoughts (obsessions) or actions (compulsions)
- Fear of embarrassment or making mistakes
- Low self-esteem; lack of self-confidence

How Should (and Shouldn't) a Parent Respond?

Because anxiety is such a common, even universally felt experience, we can too easily normalize it. Instead, these warning signs signal a need for professional assessment and treatment. When reacting to an adolescent or college student who shows signs of anxiety, parents often make one or more of three common mistakes:

1. *Modeling anxiety of their own.* This occurs when a parent over-reacts to a possible threat: "What do you mean you're going to *Miami* for spring break? Haven't you ever heard of the Zika virus?!"

2. *Minimizing or dismissing the reason for the student's anxiety.* This response challenges the very root of the student's concern: "What

do you have to be so worried about? You're blowing things way out of proportion. Nothing really bad has ever happened to you." Not only does a negative reaction deny the validity of the individual's experience, but it also ignores the parent's possible genetic contribution to their offspring's predisposition to anxiety.

3. *Over-accommodating the child's distress.* The opposite of downplaying imposes an equivalent burden on a young person. Parental over-accommodation unintentionally adds kindling to the flames by helping an anxious youth avoid a worry rather than master it on his own. Let's say a student has stomachaches on test days. An over-accommodating parent might allow the child to stay home. In an extreme case, the parent might transfer their child to a progressive school without grades or start homeschooling them. Over-accommodation promotes avoidance of whatever is seen as stressful, and can lead to greater vulnerability to anxiety, since many challenges are unavoidable.

If you find yourself modeling anxiety, or minimizing or over-accommodating your child's distress, it's best to seek a professional consultation. If a child's symptoms are nothing more than passing worry, the visit will provide reassurance. And if there are legitimate grounds for concern, early treatment can begin before the condition progressively worsens. Next we meet Karin, whose mild anxiety took a turn for the worse in college.

Freshman Year—When Perfect Wasn't Good Enough

Karin Sutton was the commencement speaker at her high school graduation. She had breezed through high school, avoiding the party scene and never letting "senioritis" affect her studies. Her parents were fiercely proud of her, and Karin, an only child, expected nothing less of herself than a stellar college career. But the powerful link between her achievements and her self-esteem, compounded by her worsening anxiety, inexperience with risky behaviors, and her intolerance for unavoidable disappointments, nearly proved to be her undoing in college. Karin's experience is an almost textbook case in what therapists term *destructive perfectionism.* It illustrates how situational anxiety can dovetail with increased demands and rigidly unforgiving expectations. Warning signs of anxiety emerged before college.

Early in Karin's senior year of high school, her parents were disturbed to see that their daughter had pulled out many of her eyelashes and was now working her way through her eyebrows. It wasn't a deliberate disfigurement, Karin reassured her parents; she simply had a nervous tic of pulling at them whenever she felt stressed by an upcoming test. With their encouragement, Karin consulted Dr. Hibbs for several sessions to better manage her test anxiety.

In the first informational session, Dr. Hibbs invited Mr. and Mrs. Sutton to join Karin, in order to provide family history as well as to understand the parent–child dynamics. Mrs. Sutton confirmed that these symptoms were relatively new, adding that Karin had a tendency to be too hard on herself. Beyond the pressure of college acceptance, neither Karin nor her parents reported any additional stressors, nor any family history of mental health problems. Mr. Sutton, mimicking his more disengaged parenting, deferred to his wife for much of the session and joked, "At least I'm off the hook, 'cause the mom's the boss."

In a follow-up individual session, however, Karin revealed hidden family conflicts. She was upset by her mother's fussing over her, by her father's high expectations and critical attitude, and by her parents' chronic bickering. Asked how she managed, Karin replied she simply shut herself in her bedroom and played her music louder to drown them out. There were two possible goals of therapy: symptom relief and the larger goal of improving parent–child relationships. Karin opted for the former, and rejected the family focus—at least for now. After all, she stated, "I'll be leaving home soon and I don't want to stir things up with them before I go. I have enough on my plate." Dr. Hibbs, like many therapists, was familiar with beginning where the client is most comfortable, and then as trust is built, expanding the treatment goals as needed for a long-term best outcome.

Symptom relief began with brief behavioral skills. Dr. Hibbs suggested that Karin use a stress ball to give her hands something to do when she was studying—a substitute activity to avoid pulling her eyelashes and brows. She liked Dr. Hibbs's reminder: "Your hands and your face aren't friends; keep them away from each other." Dr. Hibbs also taught Karin a short mindfulness exercise she could use in the run-up to a test, with the goal of self-soothing through a focus on the breath.

The most dramatic reduction in Karin's transient anxiety came with her early acceptance to her first choice, a nearby Ivy League university. Now that she'd run the gauntlet of college admissions, she felt she could ease up.

Karin appeared to be in the high percentage of mildly anxious teens who benefit from brief, symptom-focused therapy. With a reprieve from her symptoms, Karin felt she no longer needed a venue to discuss her stress. In their final session that February, Dr. Hibbs credited Karin with what she'd learned and the progress she'd made, reminding her she could always return if the need arose.

The next fall, Karin's freshman year got off to a promising start. She made friends with a few girls on her hall and settled into a daily routine of early-morning exercise, a careful diet, and a rigorous class and study load. "I can set my watch by your schedule," her friends teased her. Karin took it as a compliment. As her academic demands increased, she wore "Type A" as a badge of honor. She regarded her ability to keep "rising to the occasion" as a strength.

Then four weeks into the semester, her downward spiral was precipitated by a dinner on parents' weekend. Karin's mother and father broke the news that they were separating. They had tried couple's therapy, they told her, and suggested she might want to see Dr. Hibbs again to sort out her feelings.

"Why should *I* go back to therapy?" Karin blurted out. "It didn't help *you guys* any! It won't change a thing—you're still going to split up."

As Karin's mother began softly crying, her father protested, "Look, we waited to tell you because we didn't want to ruin your senior year."

"Yeah, well, thanks for ruining my first semester of *college*!" Karin fired back. The Suttons left the restaurant in a tense and gloomy silence.

By the next day, however, Karin seemed to have brushed off her parents' looming separation as no big deal. She told them that for all their customary squabbling, their announcement had taken her by surprise. But she knew they loved her, she comforted them—and the fact that she loved them hadn't changed. They parted with hugs.

A Narrow Escape

A few weeks and a bad cold later, Karin became convinced that her persistent cough portended cancer. *Didn't my uncle and maternal grandfather, both heavy smokers, die of lung cancer?* she fretted. She visited student health, where a nurse pronounced her lungs clear of fluid; the cough was just the lingering effect of her cold. Only temporarily reassured, she soon sought a second opinion from an off-campus physician, who again found nothing. Karin's newfound preoccupation with cancer seemed beyond her control. She didn't tell either parent about her daily ruminations; instead, she reasoned, *Why bother them? I'm just stressed out.*

Her intrusive thoughts made it hard to concentrate. To cope, she exercised even harder, studied even more. One evening, in a funk after "bombing" a chemistry exam (on which she actually got a B-), Karin decided a party might shake off her down mood. That's when she broke all her rules:

- Never pregame with vodka shots.
- Always go to and leave a party with a friend.
- Don't drink or do drugs at a party.
- Don't go to a guy's room when you're high.

Karin narrowly escaped being raped that night. Feeling drunk but enjoying the flirtation, she left the party with an upperclassman. When making out led to his roughly undressing her, she repeatedly protested, "No, no, no," but the alcohol had left her woozy and powerless to fight him off. Very fortunately, the assault ended abruptly when his roommate walked in on the scene: "Hey, man, leave her alone! Can't you see she's out of it?!" Dazed, Karin pulled on her underwear, lowered the dress now wrapped around her armpits, and stumbled barefoot across campus to her dorm room. Still inebriated, she found a razor and slashed across her left wrist.

Freaked out by the blood, she ran down the hall to the resident advisor's room. The RA accompanied Karin to the emergency room of the university-affiliated hospital, where she received fifteen stitches.

The ER doctor was all too familiar with the high rate of college students who harm themselves.[8] Karin's compulsive perfectionism, combined with her worsening anxiety, had become destructive. She'd cut herself in a moment of panic and self-loathing.

Deeply ashamed, Karin hid the attack and its aftermath from her friends and parents. Yet her trip to the ER had scared her into acknowledging the need for professional help. The morning after, she called Dr. Hibbs and requested an appointment.

The Road to Recovery

A few days later, in her session with Dr. Hibbs, Karin tearfully berated herself for her behavior that fateful night. She confided the ongoing ruminations about her health, and despaired that her image of having it all together was a farce. Karin further revealed that she could no longer suppress her sadness about her parents' breakup. Thanksgiving was approaching, but it felt like just one more pressure point: "Which parent will I have dinner with? What will that be like? How can I be there for both my mom and dad and have time to see my high school friends too?"

"Have you told your parents about your trip to the ER?" asked Dr. Hibbs. "Or about your feelings of sadness?"

"They have no clue," Karin replied morosely. "They're separated now, and I don't want to bother them with my bullshit."

Karin's psychotherapy would address her shame, self-blame, and obsessive thoughts. It would also grapple with her recent acknowledgment of her tendencies toward destructive perfectionism. Later, when Karin's mood improved, she would involve her parents in the search for a more open and honest relationship. The use of psychoactive medication might be needed to best support her talk therapy focused on insights and behavioral changes.

As part of her assessment, Dr. Hibbs recommended that Karin consult with Dr. Rostain. A week later, Dr. Rostain evaluated Karin and recommended that she begin a trial of sertraline—a proven SSRI (selective serotonin reuptake inhibitor) used to treat GAD and moderate depression.

Combined with Karin's individual therapy, Dr. Hibbs recommended an on-campus dialectical behavior therapy (DBT) group. This treatment approach incorporates the practices of mindfulness, emotion regulation, and interpersonal effectiveness. DBT's goal is to cultivate a sense of inner fortitude in the face of setbacks.[9] DBT has proven to be especially effective in helping adolescents and young adults improve distress tolerance and social problem-solving skills.[10]

By challenging negative thoughts that are clearly distortions of objective truth, DBT can also be effective in moving an individual toward accepting disappointments, either with themselves or with others. Knowing that other students in her group therapy were also struggling, Karin gained solidarity and perspective. And she strengthened her coping skills in her individual psychotherapy through a number of take-home assignments.

One ongoing assignment included an approach called "mentation," or consciously observing one's state of mind. Karin began to recognize the mental agitation she felt when her inner critic took over. She learned that whenever she got frustrated with herself, her mind started spinning like a hamster wheel in a negative feedback loop of self-accusations. She practiced mindfulness techniques to return to a calm mind, where she was able to distinguish "dirty pain" from "clean pain."

"Dirty pain" is a shaming inner critic. It packs the double whammy of unexpressed and painful emotional experiences that shame prevents one from sharing. Karin's negative self-talk was full of self-judgment: "I shouldn't feel so sad if my parents divorce, because I'm white and privileged; my parents were together throughout my childhood; they're still going to pay for my college. I shouldn't feel so broken up about that night: I wasn't raped; I was stupid and drunk."

Just as Karin did, many students from more affluent backgrounds experience feelings of guilt and self-contempt when they are anxious or depressed. Well aware of their privilege, they reproach themselves: "How can I complain? I have it all." This form of comparative suffering, or dirty pain, dampens the willingness to seek help.

"Clean pain," describes the healthy ability to recognize that disappointments are not only inevitable but necessary for growth. Clean pain entails the willingness to share and accept a difficult reality. To the extent that Karin's mental suffering had resulted from her attempts to deny painful realities, self-acceptance would equip her with a new form of resilience that would require self-acceptance. Her path forward would embrace the energizing objective of setting goals with a new sense of meaning and purpose, in lieu of an oppressive daily "to do" list.

Identifying and tolerating her disappointments and limitations topped the list. To recover from her assault, Karin found that speaking with Morgan, a member of her DBT group, was tremendously helpful. Karin identified with Morgan, who had been raped and subsequently dropped out of college for a semester. Morgan helped Karin see that despite her regrets, she wasn't to blame, and she deserved the sympathy of others, whether friends or parents. For Karin, clean pain would allow her to seek the compassion of others.

For Karin, dirty pain had meant receiving a grade that was merely good, which her perfectionist makeup defined as "not good enough." Dirty pain also limited feeling good about earning an excellent score—it fell into the category of "meets expectations." Clean pain would mean accepting her worth, independent of stellar academic performance. She was, after all, a human being—not just a human "doing." Dirty pain likewise emerged in her habit of compulsive exercise and dieting, to manage both her weight and her body image. Clean pain would mean accepting the reality that she did not have a model's thin body type.

Karin's gradual acceptance of these realities lessened her suffering. Next, she faced the dirty pain that arose from denying her sad and angry feelings about her parents' separation. Karin had suppressed these feelings by convincing herself that being sad was a waste of time. In an attempt to protect herself and her parents, she had pushed these painful feelings deep inside. Clean pain allowed her to feel, to grieve, and then to share her sadness.

Now that Karin was recovering from disappointing herself, perhaps she could risk disappointing her parents. Throughout her life, she had displayed her loyalty to her mother and father by trying to meet their expectations—how else to explain all the ceaseless striving for academic laurels? Karin had equated not disappointing them with being valued and worthy of their love. Challenging that belief would make her parents partners in her recovery. Developing the skills to face rather than avoid difficult realties was a basic component of Karin's treatment. Now was the time to put this new learning to the test.

Turning Family Binds into Loving Bonds

Dr. Hibbs offered to hold a family session to support Karin in an important dialogue with her parents, and through the process release her from the binds of perfectionism. The goal of a family session, she reassured Karin, would be to help each family member establish closer relationships: rather than avoiding conflict, they could trust one another to disclose their true feelings in a constructive way.

Karin declined the offer, explaining she wanted to talk with her parents by herself. She worried that a group session would make her parents feel implicit blame: "Did our separation create our daughter's problems?"

So Dr. Hibbs changed gears, running through some role-playing dialogues to prepare Karin for her conversation with her mom and dad. Even if Karin didn't get the support and reassurance she longed for, she had to dismantle this unspoken but powerfully guiding expectation that she could never let them down. Her success in telling her parents about this impossible bind would help her disable the perceived threat of an imperfect—and therefore unlovable—self.

Dr. Hibbs encouraged Karin to let her parents know that their separation had been painful for her; and, if it seemed safe enough, to divulge her recent ordeal. After all, Dr. Hibbs prompted, why not give her parents a chance to care about her? Hopefully, their responses would help deflate her self-judgment and shame along with the destructive value she placed on herself to be perfect. Karin nodded her understanding.

At their get-together, Karin opened the talk by disclosing the double bind she felt from that fall "separation" dinner—"We have bad news for you, but don't upset your mother, and Dad is mad that you're hurt." Bracing herself for more tears from her mother and defensiveness from her father, she was relieved to encounter understanding instead—and their willingness to hear out her feelings. The Suttons told her that they regretted not imagining the impact of their announcement—and how upsetting it had clearly been for Karin. Their new openness to her feelings reflected the post-separation parenting guidance from their counselor: *Don't judge; validate your daughter's sad or angry feelings; don't get on the defensive.* Sensing their shift, Karin felt free for the first time to share what she had been working on in therapy: her struggles with anxiety and perfectionism, and the assault and self-injury that occasioned her ER visit. Her parents' sympathy and support were a true comfort.

Over the course of two hours, Karin and her parents had their first heart-to-heart talk in years. Rather than automatically orienting herself to her parents' needs, as she'd done in the past, Karin broached what she thought she might need over the rapidly approaching Thanksgiving break. That would be the family's first holiday together in the wake of her parents' breakup. She made a few key requests:

- "I'd like to stay in my childhood home rather than moving between homes."

- "I'd prefer not to travel to the two extended families for two holiday dinners."
- "I need to spend more time with my high school friends."

By stating her needs, Karin broke the symbolic link between being loved and being "perfect." Indeed, her parents had anticipated one of her requests, and planned to host Thanksgiving dinner for both sides of the family.

The process of building up her resilience—to accept disappointments, to face possible parental disapproval—brought palpable relief. Redefining what made her a good daughter, a good student, and a worthwhile person laid the groundwork for increased security and self-acceptance. At last, Karin could relax the rigid academic and personal regimens that had contained her anxiety.

In time, Karin would come to regard her breakdown as a breakthrough. By confronting her anxiety, she managed to relinquish her perfectionism. She became more compassionate and empathic, both to herself and to those around her—a young woman vulnerable enough to share her feelings and ask others for help. And perhaps most important of all, together, she and her parents had built trust and deepened their relationships at a pivotal time in all of their lives.

Is It Sadness or Depression?

For some students, chronic or severe anxiety can tip into depression. The two conditions often coexist, sharing such features as negative mindset, catastrophic thinking, worst-case assumptions, irritability, fight-or-flight reactivity, and self-defeating behaviors. Whereas mild anxiety can focus the mind and activate and mobilize task completion, severe anxiety paralyzes people with indecision. When it persists, depression sets in and triggers an even more intense reaction: a system shutdown that induces an individual to crawl into bed and hibernate. Worry gives way to despair.

As we tend to do with anxiety, most of us normalize depression, viewing it as that run-of-the-mill blue mood that leaves us sluggish and momentarily down in the dumps. For most people most of the time, the storm blows through and the sun returns. This passing familiarity with a low point leads us to think, almost moralistically, that anyone can snap out of it with enough effort.

So what's the difference between normal, garden-variety lows and the diagnosable mood disorder of depression?

Depression is not momentary sadness; it is not grief. Neither is it the opposite of happiness. Depression is the loss of meaning, vitality, and hope. Clinical depression comes in degrees from mild to moderate to major, with or without suicidal thoughts, as a one-time event or in recurrent episodes. Severe depression remains invisible, stigmatized, and almost unimaginable to most people. Mercifully, relatively few of us know the debilitating effects of despair and with it the loss of friends and interests; the problems concentrating, studying, or working; the sleep and appetite disturbances; the physical and psychic pain.

If you've never seen major depression firsthand, you may initially feel like a helpless witness to your depressed child's pain. But you must be more than a silent sentinel—you must act, advocate, and maintain hope.

So first off, be alert to changes in behavior and social interactions that could signal depression. In the best-case scenario, a young adult will have the insight to recognize what he's going through—and clue you in.

That was the case, eventually, with Clark, a science major at a large private university, who vividly recalls the onset of his depression—and the very dark corridors down which it would lead him:[11]

You might ask yourself, "What is depression?" After all, the word is used for everything from passing sadness to an existential crisis that has long ceased being a state of mind but has become your very state of being.

The trouble with this state is that it changes not only your mood but also your thinking and the meaning of most things around you. Many of the things that might cheer you up or have substance no longer mean anything—and that's part of why suicide feels like a viable option.

It didn't occur to me that I was suffering from depression until speaking with my parents over the course of several very difficult weeks. I began counseling and started medication very soon.

From then on my parents offered to help me in whatever way they could, but I didn't really want to see them much at that time. It was easier to ignore the pain than to acknowledge it and try to work through it, even with the added assistance.

Every time they came to campus and tried to help, it was just a reminder that there were people who cared about me more than I did. And for some reason I didn't find that very comforting. It just made the sting of depression even worse.

The onset of depression is not unlike the end of a film, where you sit in the empty theater alone, in the dark, and the lights don't come on after the credits have rolled. And it seems like there's nothing left to do in the world. So you guess you'll go home and sleep. The next day, you wake up to again face the reality that you are not the marvelously fortunate protagonist of the film you watched. Instead, you are the protagonist of your own sad little movie. You lie in bed, wondering why to ever get out of it in the first place—after all, it's so warm and soft. Somehow you get up and go to the kitchen and look for something to eat, but eating seems like a chore and nothing appeals to you so you decide you'd rather not eat at all.

And that's depression.

When you realize you have nothing else to do and can think of nothing you'd enjoy, you decide you'd rather go to bed so you can dream about being the protagonist in that film rather than in your own life story. And that's depression too—when you'd rather be anyone else, or simply not be, than be yourself.

Depression clouds your mind and tricks you into believing your own life is outside your control. It fools you into thinking even your most valiant efforts will have no substantial improvement on your day-to-day. I believe that what makes depression so debilitating is its capacity to sap your ability to persevere.

After several months of weekly psychotherapy and group therapy, as well as a regimen of antidepressant medication, Clark completed his college year and gradually recovered from depression. As his wise and insightful words make clear, capable students often mistake depression for typical college stress. Or they may not recognize the deeper significance of its symptoms, which can include loneliness, loss of focus, or substance abuse. Parents or students should seek help if several of the following depressive signs persist:[12]

- Frequent tearful or sad mood, sometimes accompanied by suicidal thoughts or expressions
- Loss of meaning or hope
- Mental confusion and reality distortions with catastrophic beliefs
- All-or-nothing negative thinking
- Lethargy; persistent boredom
- Loss of concentration and motivation
- Inability to enjoy previously favorite activities
- Social isolation; poor communication
- Low self-esteem
- Feelings of guilt
- Extreme sensitivity to rejection or failure
- Increased irritability, anger, or hostility
- Difficulty with relationships
- Frequent complaints of physical illnesses such as headaches and stomachaches
- Frequent absences from school; poor performance in school
- A major change in eating or sleeping patterns

Depression's Storyline

Depression is as ancient as humankind, and has centuries of storylines—theories of mind that explain its causes and the best ways to treat it. Our understanding of depression has changed dramatically in just our lifetimes due to decades of medical research. It turns out there's more to depression than a simple cause-and-effect explanation. The development of new tools to study brain chemistry and the interconnected brain circuits that regulate our emotions has led to the current prevailing view: depression results from an interplay of situational stress, loss, and family and interpersonal environments that interact with inherited tendencies toward melancholy, anxiety, panic, and obsessive rumination. An individual's coping skills and available supports can buffer these variables, but only to a certain degree.

In the early twentieth century, doctors hadn't yet uncovered the biological changes we now associate with depression. Some early mod-

els of depression emphasized childhood experiences and inner conflicts; others pointed to behavioral learning theory such as the trapped
feeling of "learned helplessness"; or social-cultural causes, for example
being in a disadvantaged or stigmatized class. To parents of affected
youths, it's helpful to know these earlier theorists were at least partially
correct: parenting *does* matter, as do behavioral patterns and the social
context of daily life. However, medical research was needed to fill in the
missing pieces of the puzzle.

Major breakthroughs in biological theories of mood disorders such
as depression occurred in the years after World War II, when lithium
was found to be effective in treating manic states. In the 1950s, doctors
discovered that iproniazid—a medication formerly used to treat
tuberculosis—could alleviate depression. And by the 1960s, medical researchers developed medications that acted on neurotransmitters, the
chemicals that carry information between brain cells. These new medicines included drugs such as monoamine oxidase inhibitors (MAOs)
and, later, selective serotonin reuptake inhibitors (SSRIs).

With the 1990s came an even clearer picture of the biological ori-
gins of depression: neural circuits, a group of closely interacting neurons, normally function to buffer stress and stabilize mood. Depression
can result when they are impaired. Gene expression plays a role too,
making some individuals more susceptible to stressors than others.
There are also various types of depression that result from different
disease mechanisms. Functional neuroimaging technology reveals
differences between the mood-regulating circuits in depressed subjects and those in unaffected individuals. And when you use the
same technology to scan the brains of patients who have been successfully treated for depression (either with medications or with talk
therapy), these neural pathways reflect a return to normal functioning.
The most effective treatments address more than just one of these elements in play.

Depression may also be rooted in a person's coping skills within a
particular social environment. We all acquire coping skills on the road
from infancy to adulthood. As babies, we cope by crying, alerting adults
to feed and care for us. Children add temper tantrums, followed by
counting to ten, then asking nicely. Later on, we cope by learning which
behaviors are expected and accepted in our families, in our friendships, and at school—and, later still, in our romantic relationships and at
work. We cope by first understanding our own thoughts and feelings,

then those of others. We develop the ability to talk about our mental states.

But no one copes well under all circumstances. Sometimes we cope impulsively, become our own worst critic, or blame others. We may escape into fantasy, online games, or social media. We may misuse or abuse substances. Because these poor coping strategies momentarily relieve stress, they can easily become a default behavioral mode. They're a feel-good habit that's not good for you.

The unfamiliar and relatively unstructured college environment presents an array of new social and academic challenges, and not every student packs a coping skill set equal to meet them. College coping often mirrors the Facebook-user experience of projecting a rosy image online while adopting risky, copycat behaviors in real life. First-year and transfer students, trying to make friends quickly and rig an instant social safety net, are especially vulnerable to this tendency. And many students lack the one crucial coping skill they will need: the self-awareness to seek help when stress morphs into distress, because the next stage can be clinical depression.

Lessons for Parents
- Pay attention to your young person's expressions of loss.
- Be aware of changes in mood and social withdrawal.
- Don't be afraid to ask about suicidal thoughts—asking does *not* increase the tendency to act.
- Encourage your student to seek help.
- Don't judge; *do* believe—and provide resources.

Treatment Options

As you'll gather from Harry's saga that follows, loss often precipitates depression. Long before college, parents help their children build a scaffolding for understanding and coping with loss. The first rung of loss is often the death of a pet. A child's need for sturdy support escalates with the death of an older family friend or beloved grandparent. The impact and duration of grief depend on the meaning of each loss, and how a family navigates the daily void a particular loss creates. In addition, losses that may seem manageable from an adult's perspective—a change in the family's location or circumstances, an illness in the family, parental divorce or remarriage—often take an outsized toll on a child, especially at times when one loss cascades upon another.

And finally, even a significant childhood loss can never cushion a young adult from the pain of his own making: an identity crisis; failure to meet the expectations of self, parents, or others; a sports injury that threatens an athlete's career dreams; the slow drift or sudden rejection by friends or romantic partners.

Though a momentous loss can often touch off a first depression, the illness doesn't require the kick-start of a bad event to recur. This is especially so in the absence of an adequate social safety net. It's as if an earlier episode "primes" the brain to slip back into depression. This is one reason why the most effective treatments for depression combine medication (when indicated) with talk therapy that challenges negative thought patterns. The resulting gains in distress tolerance and resilience couple with mindset awareness, and help an individual to be on the lookout for catastrophic thinking. And for its power to promote healthy primary relationships, family therapy is a key component of treatment, as Harry's parents learned.

Harry's Story

Aspiring track star Harry Ballard toured several colleges before accepting the admissions offer from a large, prestigious public university. The fit wasn't perfect—the place felt impersonal and overwhelming—but it boasted a Division I track team and offered him the best scholarship. Harry tried explaining his reservations to his parents, but they reminded him of the huge loans he would incur without such generous scholarship aid. Pushing his hesitations aside, he accepted.

Waterskiing on their family vacation early that summer, Harry partially ruptured his hamstring muscle. He had a 50–50 chance of healing without surgery, his sports-rehabilitation physician told him. So Harry redoubled his efforts in physical therapy; he was intent on making the track team's active roster for the fall semester.

Though his parents urged him not to rush things, by summer's end Harry felt stronger and eager to run again. He was counting on track to keep him in shape and introduce him to a new circle of friends.

On a training run two weeks into the fall semester, Harry suffered another hamstring pull. This recovery period would be twice as long as the first, and the second episode put him at even higher risk of reinjury. His new teammates were sympathetic, but as he watched them bond during training and meets, Harry felt left out.

And he found it hard to make friends outside the track team. His roommate and suitemates were okay, but they didn't have much in common. The fire code required closing all hallway doors, limiting random meetings with the other students on the floor. And though the community rooms were impressive—furnished with flat-screen TVs, a ping-pong table, and sofas—they were almost always empty. Everyone brought their own entertainment devices (TVs, laptops, Xboxes, and, of course, smartphones) from home. Indeed, the posh environment seemed custom-designed to promote isolation by stifling real-world socializing.

As disappointing as dorm life was, his classroom experience was worse. Harry's injury resulted in stabbing pain when he was seated, but he felt self-conscious about standing throughout each class period. Between classes he holed up in his room, often lying on his bed and fretting about his future: *What if I don't heal? What if I need surgery? What if I get reinjured? What if I can't run track? My parents can't afford the tuition here without my scholarship.* Before long, these ruminations about the future cycled into depressive thoughts about himself. His inner critic called him a poser, a phony athlete.

Harry had no friends on campus with whom he could share his problems. He didn't feel close to anyone and blamed himself for his loneliness, telling himself, *Who would want to hang out with a downer like me?*

Through it all, Harry's Facebook updates remained breezy. But he did confide his unhappiness to one person—his high school girlfriend, Julie—but that didn't help much: she was happily ensconced in her own college a few hours away, and every time Harry looked at her Facebook wall, he felt even worse. Julie was tagged in photos at one party after another, red Solo cup in hand, laughing with a bunch of guys. The couple had agreed to date around at college, but now that Julie had apparently moved on, Harry felt rejected. Even the posts from fellow high school friends made him feel worse; they were having the fun college experience Harry had always thought *he* would have.

Yes, his parents called frequently, but talking to them about his problems didn't help. Why couldn't they simply *listen*? Instead, his mother defaulted into "Cheer up!" mode—a warm and fuzzy form of "Get over it"—while his father delivered a sort of brusque, "Toughen up" retort to most complaints. Unknown to Harry or his parents, chronic medical conditions put young men at greater risk for depression and suicidal thoughts.

Despite a family history of depression, the Ballards had never discussed mental health concerns with their son. They so powerfully projected a good life for Harry that unhappiness was not an option. Whenever they called, he extemporized: "I'm busy," he would tell them, or "I'm studying." In truth, he was skipping classes and handing in assignments late. Harry had never experienced a down mood as debilitating as this one.

Lonely, worried, and in pain, Harry let a mountain of dirty clothes pile up by his bed. Empty hours spent online upended his typically organized routine. His occasional marijuana use in high school now became a daily habit, further dulling any motivation.

Likewise conspiring against him was the age-old cultural definition of "strong" masculinity. This ethos discourages the sharing of feelings within male peer groups at college, and predisposes young men from seeking mental health care. Indeed, conforming to the masculine norms in the chart below is significantly correlated with lower mental health (less self-esteem and social well-being, for example) or even negative mental health—including substance abuse and depression.[13] And wanting to "be one of the guys" and belong to a peer group reinforces these norms, making it harder for college students like Harry to seek help.

Masculine Norms	Negative Mental Health	Lower Mental Health	Less Inclined to Seek Help
Self-reliance	X	X	X
Power over women	X	X	X
Playboy	X	X	X
Emotional control	X	X	X
Winning	X	—	X
Risk-taking	X	—	—
Violence	X	—	X
Dominance	X	—	—
Pursuit of status	X	—	—

Lost in depression's fog, Harry didn't seek help. Instead, help found him: he failed a substance-use screening required for all track team members. His coach told Harry he'd be dropped from the team unless he agreed to counseling and random drug tests. Because track was Harry's last tie to his former sense of positive identity and self-esteem, he agreed.

Harry was fortunate that the university had a dedicated sports psychologist on staff who deemed his case severe enough to connect him with Dr. Rostain. Before each session, Harry filled out a Beck Depression Inventory (BDI)—a widely used paper-and-pencil self-assessment used to monitor a patient's degree of depression. Harry's initial BDI score was "moderately depressed"—sufficient, as Dr. Rostain pointed out, to rob him of many executive functioning skills. Harry had taken for granted that he would always manage the basics: bathing, washing his clothes, and organizing work and play. But these seemingly effortless activities of daily living now demanded an enormous expenditure of effort. His marijuana use—which Dr. Rostain ascribed to depression and social anxiety—wasn't helping, either.

Now it was Harry's turn to question Dr. Rostain: "I'm confused. Depression makes sense—but social anxiety? I always had lots of friends in high school. I wasn't nervous around them. What's this new problem?"

"When your injury took away your old way of coping and making friends—through sports—it became much harder for you to meet people," said Dr. Rostain. "Your social standing changed from active athlete to DL [disabled list], creating an 'ambiguous loss.' That's a loss you feel very keenly, but which others may not perceive. Loss of any kind creates anxiety—including social anxiety, which in turn creates a state of hypervigilance and social unease, especially when you feel like an outsider. The brain reads your physiological response to this anxiety—a faster pulse, stomach butterflies, tightness in your chest—and assumes you're in danger. It puts your body into fight-or-flight mode. And once that starts, it's hard to stop."

Beyond identifying the loss of running as a source of well-being and stress relief, Dr. Rostain helped Harry recognize that he had lost the track team as a sure path to social belonging. Harry's loneliness and anxiety-driven thoughts had led him to believe his situation would never change, and that somehow it was all his fault. In his darker moments, he had begun to feel he simply wasn't cut out for college. Overwhelmed, he had withdrawn academically and socially—and had turned to pot as a balm.

On that front, Dr. Rostain asked Harry to consider whether his heavy marijuana use was an effective coping mechanism.

"I know I have to quit to stay on the team," Harry protested, "but smoking helps me feel calmer."

"An antidepressant medication can do the same thing," said Dr. Rostain, "but without increasing your passivity like pot does. Apathy is the opposite of what you need right now to extend yourself socially and recover from your depression."

Dr. Rostain prescribed the antidepressant bupropion, known to improve mood, restore energy, and boost the ability to concentrate. Approximately one-third of all individuals diagnosed with depression take antidepressant medications, he reassured Harry. The bupropion would manage the acute phase of his depression, providing a biological support for Harry to recover and learn better coping strategies.

Though Harry nodded his agreement, Dr. Rostain could sense his ambivalence. He told him to think things over; medication was merely one option among many. Dr. Rostain also encouraged Harry to call his parents and clue them in. Because a big part of recovering from depression is accepting the need for support, Dr. Rostain hoped Harry's parents would provide a safe emotional place for him to come out of hiding.

Harry left the session relieved but conflicted. He felt torn about filling the prescription; wouldn't it feel weird to take a medicine that changes your very brain chemistry? Would the bupropion turn him into a stranger to himself? He redoubled his efforts to get organized and smoke less—doing his laundry for the first time in three weeks—then summoned the nerve to call his parents.

They reacted with alarm—and relief. After securing Harry's consent, the couple called Dr. Rostain and voiced their concerns. Typical of many parents upon first learning of a student's antidepressant prescription, they asked:

- How does this medication work?
- What side effects might Harry encounter? Would they be temporary or long-lasting?

- What were the antidepressant's chances of effectiveness?
- How long would Harry have to take the medication?
- Were there alternatives to taking it?

The Ballards also asked for advice in communicating with their son: "What should we say? What *shouldn't* we say? How can we best support Harry's course of therapy?"

Later that week, each parent emailed Harry. Below is his mother's message:[14]

Dear Harry,

We're glad you called. Thanks for telling us that you've been having such a hard time. The transition to college is full of new situations and new people. On top of that, I know you love running, and that your body has "goofed up" on you. I think you're blaming yourself for a lot that's out of your control.

I agree that you are typically a "people person," and thrive with friends around. It makes sense to me that a big part of your depression stems from social isolation.

Thanks for sharing your ideas about what would help. You've gotten a lot of good insights from your sessions. You asked me to send you this list of what you told me, because lists help you.

Here's what you told me you're working on in therapy:

1. Make weekly goals, and use therapy to challenge your negative thought loops.
2. Have pleasurable activities to look forward to.
3. Identify action steps that you can do to build hope and social support.
4. Ask your coach or sports doc to help you find a substitute stress-buster exercise until you can run again.

You told me that you feel worse on days that are empty, with no classes to attend or things to do. That's when you said you don't feel like getting out of bed. You have a lot of courage and guts to make yourself get up and get going even when you feel low.

Love,
Mom

Mr. Ballard didn't entirely trust himself with his email, so he asked his wife to edit it. She suggested that he delete a few "Dad-isms," such as his own clear bias against psychiatry: "You know, I've always thought that shrinks were where you went to bitch about your childhood." She also thought this could come out: "Isn't that just paying someone to listen to you complain?"

For his part, Mr. Ballard worried that therapy—or the diagnosis of depression, or any kind of "poor me excuse," for that matter—would merely give Harry "a crutch" to avoid life's challenges. For many parents like Mr. Ballard, "tough love" is the cure. However, the key to recovery is the gradual building of the necessary support and skills before removing an accommodation. It's all in the timing, as we'll discover in detail in Chapter 10.

To his credit, Mr. Ballard recognized that leading with his harder edge was not what Harry needed right now. He deleted his Dad-isms. A few days—and a few more revisions—later, he hit Send:

Hi Harry,

I'm really sorry that your semester is off to a rocky start and hope you will reach out to either Mom or me when you want or need to talk. I promise to listen if that's what you want or to try to help you problem-solve it. Just know we are here for you and want to be helpful.

If you can hear a few suggestions, please read ahead. If you'd rather not right now, no hard feelings.

Can you reach out to anyone in your suite to go to dinner with? Even if you don't have anything in particular to talk about with them, sometimes it's just better to travel in a pack.

Mom said you were concerned about your room. I know I ride you pretty hard about it when you are home. Please know I would take an hour and clean with you when we are there next.

Hang in there.

Love,
Dad

Harry felt relieved to discover that both his parents could be so understanding. Having anticipated that his mother would try to cheer him up, he was gratified when she didn't minimize his problems. He had likewise expected his dad to flip out or tell him to "man up and get off your butt." Where was that guy?

The Run to Recovery

Later, Harry would learn that Dr. Rostain had given his parents clear advice on how to support their son: be calm; be responsive, but not dismissively cheerful; don't judge; resist second-guessing or reactive critiques. Dr. Rostain confirmed the validity of Harry's emotional and cognitive paralysis and his diminished ability to get things done. The more understanding the couple could be at this stage, he told the Ballards, the more Harry would open up to them—and the quicker his recovery could be.

Mr. Ballard had always viewed his life-is-tough parenting style as a necessary counterbalance to his wife's "coddling." Now he was learning that reacting with negatives reflected his own upset—and helped his son not one bit. Judging Harry's problems only widened the emotional distance between them.

Their emails reflected an admirably responsive style of parenting. Both parents clearly demonstrated that they were listening, as they repeated what Harry had confided. This kind of "mirroring" is validating and calming to a person in distress. One definition of love is the experience of feeling known. It's easy to let someone know us when we're feeling good. But it takes enormous courage to let others, particularly parents, know us when we're vulnerable. Harry had risked letting his parents know him more fully. His parents managed their own worries, resisting the urge to make things worse by reacting anxiously: "Oh my God, you'll lose your scholarship." They didn't judge Harry for needing help. They didn't contest the diagnosis of depression. Their responses by phone and email helped Harry feel loved and understood. He no longer felt so isolated and alone.

The Ballards' emails similarly acknowledged the degree to which Harry's depressed state had interfered with his self-management. His treatment would need to recapture the motivation necessary to regain life skills such as showering daily, cleaning his room, and getting up to attend classes.

Harry's parents were divided on the antidepressant issue. While ultimately it was Harry's decision alone to make, he had asked for their input. Harry's mother told her son that she was receptive to the idea—antidepressants had helped her father vanquish a bout of depression—but Harry's father had grown up with alcoholics and worried the medication might be addictive. Unaware of his son's marijuana abuse, he unequivocally told Harry, "Look—addiction runs in our family, okay? I don't want you becoming addicted to some medicine. Popping a pill is the easy way out."

Ironically, his father's revelation convinced Harry to take the antidepressant. Dr. Rostain had assured him that bupropion was not addictive, and that most people discontinue it toward the end of their treatment. Harry was further persuaded by his desire to kick his daily marijuana habit; he hoped the medicine would help him do just that.

In the wake of these discussions, Harry started taking bupropion, whose effectiveness typically builds over the first month. He also enrolled in an eight-week mindfulness meditation program that had been recommended by Dr. Rostain. This phase of his therapy would demand learning and long-term practice. Harry found the meditation to be just as effective at alleviating his anxiety and depression as his running had been.[15] Among its key goals: to let negative thoughts pass by without getting stuck on them.

With therapy, medication, meditation, and participation in a sobriety support group sponsored by the university's athletic department, Harry began to craft new coping strategies. And the sobriety circle offered a bonus: the chance to make new friends committed to healthy behaviors.

Harry's recovery was hardly a straight path. Like so many others upon first encountering depression, he had much to learn. But he also had access to some rich resources: therapeutic support, parental compassion, sobriety goals, physical rehabilitation, and—one day in late November when the sun was shining cold and bright on the college track—a return to his beloved running.

Harry Ballard and Karin Sutton are examples of two resilient teens. They managed to seek help first, then loop in their parents after the fact. Their stories are likely to intensify the question on many a parent's mind: "What concrete steps can I take now to prepare my child for the daily challenges of college life?" See the suggestions on the next page.

HOW PARENTS CAN HELP STUDENTS

- Reduce secondary stress; be a responsive, nonreactive parent.
- Practice "roses and thorns." Ask your student to share the ups and downs of day-to-day life. Sharing disappointments counters a student's tendency toward destructive perfectionism.
- Discuss common stumbling blocks in the first six weeks (peer pressure to binge-drink) and first semester (worry about grades).
- Encourage your student to join clubs and campus activities to connect socially. These provide a better support network than partying or online connections.
- Identify coping strategies that can be continued in college, especially exercising with friends.
- Inform yourself about the campus or college website to identify key support personnel and services, such as campus tutoring, the disabilities office, college counseling, and student health.
- Destigmatize mental health concerns; separately or together, review www.halfofus.com for its list of commonly experienced feelings, among them loneliness, anxiety, depression, stress, hopelessness, or just plain feeling weird.

HOW STUDENTS CAN HELP THEMSELVES

- Continue all existing academic accommodations from high school to college. Reducing academic stress improves mood.
- Sign the HIPAA release form to let your parents more easily speak with your health care providers. (The HIPAA and FERPA privacy laws are explained in the Appendix.)
- Establish your "rules" for partying—and share your commitments with a trusted friend.
- Practice "problem" dialogues before college.
- Learn the difference between worry and anxiety, and between bad moods and depression.
- Google the TED Talk "College Students Talk About Depression."
- Designate a parent or trusted adult for "check-ins."
- Don't judge screw-ups; nobody's perfect.

8

Crisis Care

"Houston, we've had a problem here."

—ASTRONAUT JAMES A. LOVELL

Houston, we've had a problem here" has become a humorously ironic understatement to announce any kind of major difficulty. The original speaker of the line was NASA's James A. Lovell, aboard the *Apollo 13* lunar mission in 1970, informing Mission Control in Houston that an onboard oxygen tank had exploded in mid-flight.

"We came to the slow conclusion," Lovell recalled in an official NASA history years later, "that our normal supply of electricity, light, and water was lost, and we were about two hundred thousand miles from Earth." Yet thanks to some quick-witted improvisation by the crew and NASA ground controllers, and drawing on the cool of everyone involved, this story would have an improbable—and near-incredible—happy ending.[1]

Sending an adolescent out into the world, especially when some aspect of the mission goes awry, is the family version of staging a moon launch and dealing with an unplanned reentry. Years of mission engineering anticipate and guard against the expedition's known risks. The rocket fuel is expensive, and has been carefully gauged to yield a college-bound trajectory. And the exploration, though exciting, may hold great peril. In the last chapter, we saw the fine line between high functioning and crisis, in the experiences of Karin and Harry. Each encountered significant episodes of anxiety and depression during college, but were able, with therapeutic and family support, to recover while continuing their college experience.

This chapter shows what happens when crisis becomes free fall; when a teen falls out of the college orbit and the exhilaration of liftoff is replaced by the overwhelming anxiety of a failed launch. Back home, ground control scrambles to avert a crash landing. Getting everything back on course so the wayfarer can complete the mission—or steering him back to home base to redefine it—can require unprecedented feats of improvisation: parents must call upon a lifetime of nurturing and advocacy skills, all while dealing with the emotional shock of witnessing a calamity unfold.

But what distinguishes normal student angst from a full-blown mental health crisis? To help parents tell the difference, the National Alliance on Mental Health has defined the core elements of such an incident:[2]

- An unanticipated event
- No time to prepare for it
- No previous experience in how to handle it
- High emotional impact
- A threat or danger posed to self or others

A mental health crisis forces parents into triage mode, requiring them to quickly make decisions that will determine how—or even whether—a student should proceed in order to resume a college career. Although an emergency is by nature acute, its resolution will very likely be prolonged, involving choices among various treatment pathways and levels of care. Some students may experience a mix of traumatic-event-propelled combustions, from bad judgment or substance abuse to sexual assault or self-harm, yet still manage to stay enrolled. Others will run head-on into a mental health crisis that essentially derails them, sapping their ability to function academically or even at the most basic self-management levels of sleeping, eating, and bathing.

For these students, college mental health crises are often reflected in a double whammy that experts term "comorbidity": a disorder such as ADHD may be coupled with depression, or a poor form of coping such as substance abuse may actually be driven by an undiagnosed illness such as bipolar disorder. These more complex mental health problems may not be manageable within the college context. The parents of fragile youth are often in need of guidance and crisis care.

Most parents are caught unawares. The warning signs leading up to a breakdown may have been obscured by the student's lack of insight or outright denial, or veiled from parental view by HIPAA's confidentiality and privacy protections.[3] They may learn of a crisis only when a student is in imminent danger of physical harm, or after the fact when class failures emerge.

However the crisis develops, parents can play a crucial role in helping their young adult get through it. Faced with a bewildering maze of choices—including on-campus psychological accommodations, medical leave, and treatment options—how can parents make the best decisions in the brutally short time frame that is typically involved? This chapter shares the lessons learned by one mother—Dr. Hibbs—when a breaking point demanded that she safely guide her own son, Jensen, through the labyrinth of campus crisis care.[4]

A Mother's Story

Jensen, in many ways, typified talented teens who arrive on campus with a history of prior mental health treatment. Along with his archery equipment, Dungeons & Dragons books, and rock-climbing gear, he packed a psychoactive medication to manage long-standing symptoms of anxiety. That last item hardly singled him out: over the past several years, 90 percent of college counseling centers have reported an increase in students already on psychiatric meds.[5]

Jensen had thrived at his progressive high school before leaving for college. Though he'd been diagnosed with generalized anxiety disorder (GAD) at the young age of nine, the decade-long roulette wheel of diagnoses and medication trials seemed to have finally stopped spinning by his sophomore year of high school when "features of Asperger's syndrome" was added. Though I didn't know it when my son was first diagnosed, childhood GAD often predicts adult anxiety disorders; it is also associated with substance abuse, depression, autism spectrum disorders, and suicidal ideation.[6]

Jensen's crisis precipitated a year of chronic suicidal thoughts. During that time, the diagnostic picture, and therefore the appropriate medications, remained a trial-and-error work in progress. I lived the crisis forwards, and understood it backwards. Like many a conscientious mother, I thought I had prepared my son well. His crisis—a depression so severe it sent him home on medical leave the spring semester of his freshman year—taught me what I didn't know about young adult mood disorders, revealed my own biases, and required the sustenance of hope throughout.

Three years past the onset of Jensen's breakdown, he is doing well, and takes great pride in his hard-won resilience. On a hot and humid morning in July he's meeting once again with his psychiatrist, Dr. Rostain, but there's no counseling session on today's agenda; instead, Jensen is addressing a seminar with Dr. Rostain's psychiatry residents.[7]

Dr. Rostain breaks the ice by asking Jensen to describe his experience of going to college.

"I had unrealistic ideas about college that were based on popular culture," Jensen replies. "I'd meet people, go to parties, classes would be okay. While first semester was good and I made friends, had fun, and got good grades, by second semester the cracks started to show. I dealt poorly when my first-semester best friend dumped me and I withdrew socially. I used a college counselor, which helped, but not a lot—because in the end they don't really know you.

"Still, I'm not going to put everything on him. The thing is, I was talking *around* the issues; he didn't know that I was breaking down daily. I became more depressed—I was in tatters, really—and wouldn't even get up for class. I lost speed and holed up in my room."

"I didn't meet you until later, after you'd returned home," Dr. Rostain says by way of background. "How depressed were you when you left college? What was your state of mind?"

"Looking back on it now," Jensen responds, "what's kind of terrifying is that my depression began so gradually that it became the norm. My expectations for fun became 'the absence of suffering.' I knew at the time that I wasn't enjoying myself, but it wasn't until I was home on spring break that my high school friend Max told me, 'Dude, you're bad off—you gotta tell your parents.' It was pretty catastrophic, honestly. I'm lucky I made it back."

The Wonder Years

Even though I had been a practicing psychologist for twenty-five years by this point, I watched Jensen's crisis unfold while experiencing unfamiliar feelings of constant anxiety and helplessness accompanied by a heavy dose of self-reproach. *How could I have missed this coming? Why didn't I of all people see the signs?* My parental and professional roles both illuminated and distorted my understanding of my son's impending crisis. As I replayed the newsreels of his childhood in my mind, they unspooled with cherished memories and hopes. But now I saw the missed clues.

Idyllic "wonder years" preceded Jensen's first symptoms of anxiety. In common with parents the world over, I optimistically projected the arc of his imagined untroubled life far into the future. I took pride in his precocious vocabulary, his unbridled curiosity, and his eager consumption of information.

By age three, Jensen displayed an encyclopedic knowledge of dinosaurs; next came camouflaged insects. By five, he was on to poisonous plants. That was the year my father's heart condition took a serious downturn; learning this news—and the nature of Pa Hibbs's illness—Jensen urged me to tell his doctor to administer digitalis, a historically effective treatment in heart cases, derived from the poisonous foxglove plant. Those wonder years blinded me to—and scrambled my understanding of—the emerging clues.

Though Jensen's symptoms appeared singly at first, they quickly cascaded. Rather than delighting in the simple thrill of a merry-go-round, he complained that the music hurt his ears. Ditto with fireworks. By first grade, Jensen seemed fearful, tearful, and more easily overwhelmed than his classmates. In the rough and tumble of boy culture, he hated to be seen crying—"breaking down," he called it.

Still, I attempted to reassure myself, weren't these observations the exception to the very picture of a happy child—one who enjoyed play dates and was the kindest big brother imaginable?

In third grade, Jensen's symptomatic behaviors accelerated. His very slight and occasional stutter worsened markedly under the new pressure of joining advanced Spanish-speaking classmates in a mandatory Spanish-immersion class. Soon, paralysis over the prospect of making the "right" choice set in and became a hallmark feature of his anxiety. Faced with a choice between cookies and ice cream, he'd be unable to pick either. To his extracurricular activity of fencing, we added cognitive behavioral therapy (CBT) and speech therapy. And though his symptoms temporarily improved, his treatment was constantly being disrupted by an unusually high turnover rate among the child psychologists in our university health system. I had assumed, from my own clinical practice, that Jensen could remain in treatment with a valued provider. I hadn't grasped the downside of treatment within a health system whose emphasis is medical training—and clinician churn for the patient.

Lord of the Flies

Middle school is a *Lord of the Flies* fiefdom where bullying is a daily fact of life. Mocked for his stutter and teased about his frustrated "break-downs," Jensen made an easy target. Some of the bullying assumed a postmodern cast of microaggressions—minor but repeated taunting—but there were episodic physical cruelties as well. Officially, the school had a "zero tolerance" policy. Unofficially, much of the bullying flew under the radar, taking place out of teachers' eyesight at lunch or recess. And it persisted.

Compounding these social strains, the academic demands of middle school heightened Jensen's anxiety. He coped by voraciously reading mythology and fantasy material, all the while procrastinating on his assignments. Unwittingly, I fell into one of the common parental traps discussed in Chapter 7: I over-accommodated his anxiety and enabled his avoidance by helping him organize his schoolwork and meet deadlines.

Sixth grade was the first time he talked about suicide. Jensen bit his fingernails until they bled. It was time for medication.

The Pre-College Years: Struggling then Flourishing

Jensen's first round of psychoactive medications from the ages of twelve to fifteen, prescribed for his anxiety, proved ineffective. Indeed, the dosage reduction for one of them, venlafaxine, induced upwards of a weeklong bout of nausea. His psychiatrist, Dr. Amanda Aaron,[8] dismissed his GI upset as a stomach bug. Reassured, we sent Jensen and his younger brother Phillip to their favorite summer getaway—Camp Nana & Papa—the home of their paternal grandparents. But with another reduction in the dosage, Jensen became *obtunded*—medical speak for "to blunt, dull, or deaden something."

It was midnight and all was quiet, when Jensen lapsed from sleep to unconsciousness. Phillip heard wet choking sounds, then saw his brother lying on his back with thick black, green, and white vomitus running out his mouth and down his neck. Terrified, he woke his grandparents. They cleared his mouth and turned him on his side to prevent aspiration. Emergency phone tag leapt from his grandmother to me, then to Dr. Aaron and back full circle, with instructions for my in-laws to wake Jensen every half hour to check for coherent speech. Failing that, or with continual vomiting, immediate hospitalization. Through a sleepless night, Ruth and Earl kept watch. They told us not to drive the five hours. Wait and see. I slept anxiously and fitfully. I only slept at all because I had total confidence that Ruth would sit by Jensen's bedside all night, now his second mom nurse. Jensen became fully alert and hungry at 3:40 A.M. By his account, Nana Ruth fixed him the best BLT sandwich ever. With a forty-eight-hour vigil, one episode of daytime vomiting, a revised medication withdrawal plan, and follow-up hospital blood draws, Jensen was safe. A frightening chapter—and one that haunted Phillip's bedtime for years. Jensen had survived venlafaxine discontinuation syndrome, an uncommon but sometimes fatal side effect.

Gratefully, Jensen soon found the humor in it and had us laughing. With characteristic wit, he dubbed the episode "Vomit Town," and Dr. Aaron became "Dr. Quack."

BEWARE OF SIDE EFFECTS

❌ Many psychoactive medications for children and adolescents have not yet been approved by the U.S. Food and Drug Administration (FDA). Ask the physician if the medicine has FDA approval for use in children and teens. If it does not, find out beforehand what level of vigilance you should maintain before starting or stopping a medication to minimize or avoid bad side effects. In most cases, side effects appear early on and may gradually disappear. In other cases, however, side effects appear only on withdrawal. Extreme caution may be necessary, especially because precise dosage levels may not have been determined for adolescent age or weight.

With the immediate crisis past, Dr. Aaron's first task was to "wean" Jensen off venlafaxine. (Parents should know that most psychiatric drugs cannot be stopped abruptly; to avoid adverse reactions including a recurrence of depression, GI upset, or a discontinuation syndrome, their use must be tapered very gradually.) Over the next several weeks, she continuously reduced the strength of the venlafaxine dosage to zero. Realizing that she had made a serious medical error, Dr. Aaron prudently referred Jensen for a consult with her mentor, Dr. Allan Glass. Because Jensen's anxiety had not responded to the usual medications, Dr. Aaron wanted Dr. Glass to rule out bipolar disorder.

After an extensive evaluation—first with Jensen, then in shaking-the-family-tree discussions with my husband, Craig, and me—Dr. Glass dropped a bombshell: he diagnosed Jensen with "features of" late-diagnosis Asperger's syndrome, an autism spectrum disorder (ASD) that is very often accompanied by anxiety and difficulty with executive functioning.[9] Affected children and adults are considered "high functioning" when they are verbally or intellectually precocious and show no significant language or cognitive delays. Their interests often fall within a very narrow range, and their difficulties with social interactions typically result from the way they tend to misread such nonverbal cues as gestures, body stance, and facial expressions.

But what did "features" mean? As Dr. Glass explained, Jensen didn't meet the full diagnostic criteria of Asperger's. His keenly focused interests, sensory sensitivities, and social anxieties were mild enough that an entire battalion of specialists—his pediatrician, three therapists, and three psychiatrists—had overlooked the possibility of Asperger's in favor of GAD. This was due in part to the psychiatric profession's embryonic understanding of ASD in the 1990s. Over the past twenty years, neurodevelopmental medicine has greatly progressed in understanding and detecting ASD symptoms in toddlers. However, the pediatric infrastructure for diagnosing ASD in "high-functioning" children was much weaker during Jensen's childhood and early adolescence. Even today, Asperger's syndrome may remain misdiagnosed until a child or adolescent begins to encounter overlapping social and academic difficulties at both school and home.[10]

Each mental health professional who reviewed Jensen's diverse symptoms over the course of a decade—a decade that plucked my every nerve of maternal protectiveness, professional frustration, and personal helplessness—gave him an accurate diagnosis *at the time they evaluated him*. But each doctor was limited by seeing only a snapshot of Jensen's development, rather than a comprehensive picture. GAD was common, while ASD was an exotic diagnosis. In medical slang: "When you hear hoof beats, think horses, not zebras." Jensen's anxiety disorder therefore made sense—until Asperger's made *more* sense.

This zigzag path to an exact diagnosis is far more common than the medical field lets on. Transition-age diagnosis can be blurred by several factors including comorbid conditions, the lack of qualified child and adolescent psychiatrists in a geographical area, and developmental-stage problems that can be missed or over-diagnosed (such as neuro-developmental delays or ADHD). It is especially likely when multiple emotional and behavioral symptoms emerge in childhood and adolescence. The vast majority of disorders diagnosed before age fourteen are those of attention, executive functioning, and anxiety. Yet despite tremendous advances in treating brain disorders, a number of factors can camouflage the precise condition that is causing the symptoms observed during childhood and the teen years—a developmental period when the brain itself is changing so rapidly that it sometimes seems to be mischievously dodging interpretive analysis.

And Dr. Aaron's concern about the possible presence of bipolar disorder? It was forgotten and lost. Consumed by understanding an ASD diagnosis, I believed that Dr. Glass had ruled out her concern, and I forgot about it. Apparently so did she. Then, shortly after Jensen's consult with Dr. Glass, Dr. Aaron accepted an academic position out of state and transferred Jensen's treatment to a junior psychiatrist, Dr. Deborah Beltzer. Dr. Aaron's office, piled high with papers, had always resembled a temple to the absent-minded professor. With her departure, Jensen's mental health records—along with any reference to this unanswered question—got lost in the shuffle.

Following his "features of" ASD diagnosis, Jensen began a course of new medication that greatly reduced his symptoms of anxiety. As parents feeling our way from one diagnosis to another, we now understood and acknowledged that *our* first-choice, competitive high school was a bad fit. Recognizing our mistake, we transferred Jensen to *his* first-choice high school with much better social-emotional and learning support for capable, creative students. For the next three years, Jensen flourished in what he named, "high school heaven." He organized a weekly Dungeons & Dragons role-playing game (RPG) for his friends at our home. He became skilled at rock climbing and moved from the

YOU "OWN" THE RECORDS

✖ Parents have to be extremely proactive to avoid lost records. To sidestep a provider's faulty record-keeping, always ask to receive copies of all medication and diagnostic records. At the first visit, or upon a transfer of patient care, request that the doctor send you a complete copy of the prior and new records either annually or every six months.

climbing wall at the high school gym to the technically challenging peaks of Seneca Rocks, West Virginia. He became an archery instructor in order to start an archery program at his high school. And he won an academic scholarship to his first-choice college—a small liberal arts school that aligned with his academic interests and sponsored club activities in archery, rock climbing, and gaming. There were good mental health counseling and academic support services to boot.

Despite the struggles that Jensen had endured, I believed the biggest obstacles were in the rearview mirror, and that he would thrive in a college environment of social and intellectual diversity. To help him prepare for the transition ahead, I set out to learn everything I could about Asperger's. I read the literature. I attended conferences packed with apprehensive parents harboring similar concerns: How best to keep your college-bound teen on track? What were the secrets of fellow "Aspie" kids who had made it in college?

The 1990s saw a sharp rise in the number of autism diagnoses. Those children are now of college age. In 2012, a study in the journal *Pediatrics* found that fifty thousand teens "on the spectrum" turn eighteen each year, and roughly 35 percent of them attend college.[11] Stretched beyond capacity to serve neurotypical students, few colleges are equipped to provide an adequate level of social accommodations for this first generation of ASD students.

We toured two of only a handful of U.S. universities at the time with integrated ASD social supports of individual therapy, group social skills training, and built-in academic advisement. One university that Jensen applied to advertised significant support for freshman year, but the program received too few applications to open. Jensen rejected the other college outright—he didn't like its vibe. Yet his first-choice college had many available supports; with documentation, it granted him a single-room assignment.

When move-in day came in the fall, it had all the excitement of a long-awaited triumph. The happy tasks of unpacking, assembling a bookcase, buying a rug, and hanging favorite posters from home distracted us from the approaching farewells. Jensen ran into the group of guys he'd met at new-student day. Then, eager to heed the university administrators' admonitions not to be helicopter parents, we said our goodbyes.

In this hopeful moment, I felt I could finally relax my vigilance. I could let go and allow my son to get on with his life. Jensen waved us off happily. He'd already made plans with his new friends. His lunar mission was ready for liftoff.

Throughout the fall, Jensen regaled us on Skype with accounts of his social life and classes. As he'd done in high school, he hosted RPGs each weekend. Friends from around campus met in his room to play Dungeons & Dragons and Warhammer for hours of improvised character development and strategy. While Jensen joined the rock-climbing and archery clubs, the RPGs were the highlight of his week.

During Thanksgiving and the winter holidays Jensen happily shared news of friends, and celebrated with high-fives upon receipt of his grades. Reassured that he had navigated the shoals of first semester, we let down our guard. The spring semester that began so promisingly became the time that Jensen exchanged his student status for that of a "home patient."

Breakdown

Spring break provided a needed reprieve from the building stresses of the second semester. Jensen was glad to be home. During that week he kept appointments with both his hometown psychiatrist and his psychologist to discuss meds and his downshift in mood. He spent the bulk of the week hanging out with high school friends, and seemed in much better spirits. Then it was early on a Sunday afternoon in mid-March, the final day of spring break. He was packed and ready to go, but with less than an hour before it was time to head for the airport he sought me out in the den.

"Mom, Max told me I should tell you," he began hesitantly. "He said you would understand." Like most teens in trouble, Jensen had told a friend first.[12]

Concerned, I stopped typing and looked up from my work. Jensen appeared pale and sounded shaky. "Tell me what?" I asked.

"I don't think I can go back," he confided. "Every time I think of going back, I feel worse." Then he shared even more: He had missed many classes second semester. He had withdrawn socially, routinely eating alone in his room. He was scared what would happen if he returned to campus.

As steadily as I could, I asked my son, "Do you mean you're afraid you'll hurt yourself?"

"Yeah, Mom, I am. I can't help it," he explained sadly. "These thoughts, they're just there." Jensen revealed that he had tolerated the intrusion of passing suicidal thoughts for years, but had always been able to distract himself from them—until recently.

I was stunned. My mind raced, oddly torn between practical matters—checking the clock for his flight—and emotional ones: Just how fragile was my son's mood in this moment? I felt catapulted into a new reality. I struggled to find the right response, as my thoughts cascaded, frenziedly fighting for ascendance: *If he withdraws now, he'll lose the entire semester's work. Perhaps he could drop a course or two? What are the advantages of a medical leave compared with the loss of friends and the academic structure of college? Craig and I will lose thousands of dollars. And how do we know if this is spring break blues, a temporary slump, or a true breakdown? Wait, I think he has to withdraw; I'm scared to send him back. College suicide rates are 4 to 1 higher for men than women. Focus on his safety!*

I didn't want to make a mistake for which I'd never be able to forgive myself. But this would not be my decision alone. I asked Jensen to wait in the den while I told Craig what was going on and asked him to join us.

Decades before, when Craig announced his own imminent departure from college, his father had splashed a cold cup of reality on his plan: "You're not coming back here to live without a job." That threat—and his recall of dreary summer work experiences as a busboy and as a bench worker in a factory—had persuaded Craig to continue his education. So I shouldn't have been surprised that his first instinct now was to have a similar tough-love talk with his own son.

Like many parents, Craig was reflexively responding to his own biases and internalized "shoulds"—those knee-jerk reactions that often seem to compel us to act counter to our rational mind. *Shouldn't he encourage Jensen to master his fears and anxieties, just as his own father had made him do so many years ago? Tell him to gut it out?* Wondering if this was merely Jensen's old familiar anxiety talking, Craig prompted him, "Why don't you go back and just do your best? Give it another try? You only have six more weeks in the semester."

I could see Jensen waver. Was he reconsidering? *Maybe I could stick it out.* Or was he just trying to please his dad?

And so we sat there in paralyzed silence. No one—not the doctors, not our gut feelings, no expert—no one could tell us what the right decision was: Stay or exit? As a psychologist, of course, I had something of an advantage that most parents don't have when faced with a young person's deteriorating mood. Through my practice, I had seen the many manifestations of depression and could recognize the differences between the passing thoughts of suicidal ideation and the intent of a hazily formulated idea—and that's serious enough. A *plan,* however, because it envisions the specific *mechanics* of the act, represents a far more immediate danger. So even though Jensen reassured me he had no plan, I understood that his recent social isolation had precipitated a major depression—and that it was a risk factor for suicide.

In lay terms, what clinicians call "suicidality" is a Rubik's-Cube alignment of risks including access to or practice with a lethal means, opportunity, impulsivity, and being a young male. In the current crisis, my clinical head confirmed my mother's gut: I had to trust Jensen's assessment. He was the expert we needed to listen to now. Clearly the better mood we'd seen over spring break was only temporary, buoyed by the lack of academic demands and the presence of hometown friends. My fear for Jensen's safety now trumped all my prior hopes and expectations for him.

I broke the silence. "We can't send him back," I firmly told Craig. "You have to trust me on this. Let's get Jensen on his flight. I'll catch the next flight down, pack up his things, and file the formal withdrawal tomorrow." Craig paused, then nodded and said, "I'll get you a flight."

Late that night, Jensen and I scoured recycling bins on the deserted campus, dumpster diving for stray boxes in which to pack up his college life. We called out in triumph to each other whenever we scored an especially sturdy container: a mother–son bonding adventure that furnished a welcome distraction from the impending loss. We packed four suitcases, one archery case, and eighteen boxes containing books, sheets, towels, a lamp, posters, and his printer. Then we collapsed into a dreamless sleep.

Mid-morning on Monday, we met with the dean of student affairs. Explaining that Jensen was severely depressed, I handed over the documentation necessary for a medical withdrawal. To my dismay, the dean was indifferent. In a matter-of-fact tone he recited the university rules for reapplication and possible readmission a year later (a reentry, by the way, that would never occur). Jensen and I each signed papers stating we understood the legal terms and conditions of withdrawal. Twenty minutes later, my son was no longer a college student.

My flashbacks to that hopeful college tour and our Parents' Day visit to campus dissolved as I absorbed his sad reality: "Do you want to say goodbye to anyone?" I asked.

"*No*," came the adamant reply. Facebook would be the faceless messenger of his departure.

Months later Jensen would tell me, "Mom, sorry to say this, but I don't think I would have survived there."

Quietly I replied, "I know."

Suicide Risk

Who is at risk for suicide? Predicting this has long been one of the most challenging problems in mental health, but it has taken on new urgency in the twenty-first century: in a longitudinal study, U.S. suicide rates jumped 24 percent from 1999 to 2014, from 10.5 to 13 per 100,000 people.[13] Suicide is now the second leading cause of death among those ages 15 to 34.[14] Seventeen percent of high school students report having seriously considered suicide during a one-year period, while 2.7 percent made a suicide attempt that required medical treatment.[15]

Certain well-publicized factors—namely being a male with a history of depression and a recent job or relationship loss—are risk factors, but they cannot, in fact, accurately predict suicide attempts. Whereas depression is most often associated with suicidal ideation, three other conditions—anxiety, problems with impulse control, and addiction—are more strongly linked to suicide attempts.[16] Most initial suicide attempts take place within a year of the first occurrence of suicidal thoughts. For many high school and college suicides, the individual was not in treatment at the time. And there really is no typical pathway or circumstance: high-achieving students, for example, may act in a moment of panic at an impending or perceived loss of social standing. Research studies are under way at the National Institute of Mental Health and Harvard University to better predict who is at risk.

Given these uncertainties, I fell back on an age-old method—"Just ask the patient"—when confronted with my son's crisis. Many parents fear that asking young adults whether they have ever experienced suicidal thoughts might somehow "put the idea in their heads." Fortunately, I knew of several research studies showing this suggestive effect to be surprisingly rare. Given our overly "be happy" posting culture, however, too many young people have gotten the message that they should keep disturbing thoughts to themselves. Yet by the mere fact of asking about the presence of self-harming thoughts, you offer someone you love the opportunity—even the permission—to unburden themselves of suffering.

Heed the Warning Signs

The Hibbs family was very fortunate. Not only did our son have a trusted friend with the insight to counsel him wisely about his depression, but Jensen felt safe enough to tell us he couldn't return to college. All those years of positive parenting, we reflected, may have paid off at the very moment when they were needed the most. The years in which we encouraged Jensen to share his pain and disappointments; the years in which we attended psychotherapy sessions with him; the years in which we had grown from reactive to responsive parents, making the family environment emotionally safe. Of the many supports I had tried to put in place for Jensen at college—an introduction to the learning support office, therapy referrals from his hometown therapist, a family friend emergency contact—none panned out. What ultimately came to his rescue was an emotionally close relationship with his family and friends, and a familiarity with mental health treatment.

Yet I also missed many warning signs leading up to this crisis. Like too many parents of college students, I underestimated the strength of the natural support systems afforded him by parental guidance, the integrated learning services of high school, the structure of a packed academic day and social routine. In the absence of daily interactions, I had no way of knowing how bad his situation had become. I also believe I missed certain red flags because a key piece of his diagnostic puzzle was still missing in action. This would turn out to be bipolar II disorder, which revealed itself only in crisis.

My dual roles of psychologist and mother amplified my sense of responsibility and guilt for what I didn't know, the mistakes I made, and the circumstances that blindsided me. I hope the following "lessons learned" prove useful to parents in my predicament:

Lesson 1: Safety first in freshman year.

The diagnostic picture may be incomplete when you launch your student to college, and new stresses can elicit new symptoms. I therefore strongly encourage parents of an adolescent with a history of mental health concerns to consider a college near enough to make weekly visits home a practical option. Or your student might enroll as a *daily* commuter, enabling him to live at home during that critical first year of transition. This option is particularly attractive if your child arrives on campus with psychiatric medications that require close monitoring.

What I didn't know: Because Jensen left home in excellent spirits, I thought our hometown plan with Dr. Beltzer for medication review on holiday breaks, and campus counseling, as needed, would suffice.

What I learned: The medication he took in high school after his ASD diagnosis greatly relieved Jensen's anxiety, but it was not enough to "hold" him when circumstances worsened.

What you can do: Arrange monthly follow-ups with the student's current psychiatrist or a backup psychiatrist on or near campus. To find the latter, ask the college counseling center for its resource list. And unless your child can designate a trusted family member or a nearby adult as a confidant, assign yourself and your hometown as his "safety net."

Lesson 2: Kids in crisis may not realize how bad things are.

Someone in the grip of a depression or another psychiatric disorder often lacks insight into their own deteriorating mood or general level of functioning. They may be unable to let you know how bad their situation has become. Many students assume they're simply "stressed out" in response to social problems or the escalating demands of college coursework. When tests and assignment due dates ease, they may view their erosion of mood and concentration as normal when in fact it could signal an encroaching mental illness. Without accustomed feedback from family or familiar friends, problems escalate silently.

What I didn't know: I didn't know that Jensen was suffering from an undiagnosed bipolar illness that would require a different class of medication to stabilize his depression.

What I learned: Regardless of an individual's age or maturity, depression and other forms of mental illness can rob them of the ability to function on an independent level. Parents probably should not expect a student in distress to reach out on his own behalf—an especially acute challenge for teens and young adults burdened with misinformation about mental health and learning disorders.

What you can do: Let your kids know that *you* know mental illness results from impaired neural pathways in the brain, not character weakness. And don't send signals that you couldn't handle their maladjustment to college life; *tell them* point-blank that if they get in trouble *of any kind,* you want to hear about it!

Lesson 3: Denial trumps reality.

Denial can be a powerful barrier to a parent's recognition of a brewing crisis. In my case, objective reality took a backseat to the snapshot image I wanted to hold: the happy, engaged young man who was doing well in his classes, hanging out with friends, and occasionally seeing the college counselor, Mike.

What I didn't know: Hidden from view during our Skype conversations that second semester were piles of empty Chinese takeout containers, pizza boxes, and half-finished soda bottles and cans. Unwashed clothes littered the dorm-room floor.

What I learned: Due to confidentiality laws, professors and counselors are enjoined from reporting a student's class absences to his parents, and sometimes even to each other. Without a HIPAA waiver, by the same token, a college mental health center will not ordinarily inform parents or guardians when a student seeks counseling or a prescription. If a student is deemed to be a danger to himself or others, however, counselors can send him to the hospital or ask his permission to call a parent. In the absence of that permission, though, the only way counselors will contact a parent is as a last resort to safeguard public safety.

What you can do: Ask the college how much training faculty members and key advisers get in recognizing the signs of depression or other mental health problems in their students. How can they help facilitate the student getting to a mental health provider? What information are faculty members and advisers allowed to share with student health and counseling centers if they suspect a student is in trouble? What permission forms are needed to facilitate sharing?

Lesson 4: Weave a safety net.

Weeks can elapse between student need and a professional appointment at most colleges, so it's never a bad idea to gather referrals to off-campus or private-sector therapists in the college area your student is headed for.

What I didn't know: Jensen didn't understand the extent of his depression. He liked Mike, the therapist assigned to him by the counseling center, but their rapport was superficial at best. The center did not use standardized inventories to assess mood, and Mike was unaware of Jensen's deteriorating emotional state.

What I learned: Mike did not request input from Jensen's treatment providers at home or his professors on campus. Mike did make himself available for face-time individual appointments with Jensen, however—and because he enjoyed talking to Mike, Jensen perked up during their appointments.

What you can do: At or before enrollment, encourage your student to waive FERPA confidentiality and privacy protections—this empowers you to speak with campus staffers (both professors and advisers) and receive alerts from them before a course failure or crisis ensues. If your child has a mental health history, speak with the counseling center *before* he enrolls; you'll want to find out if the college requires specific waiver forms—and, if so, where they should be filed. Finally, as soon as your young person visits a mental health provider, make sure the latter has the student's signed HIPAA forms on file; this gives the clinician permission to speak to you and to your child's prior or current health providers. (Because FERPA and HIPAA privacy laws are quite complex, we explain them in detail in both Chapter 4 and the Appendix.)[17]

Lesson 5: Look into accommodations.

Any academic accommodations that may have been granted to your student in high school—extra time for test taking, for example—should be carried over into college, if possible. These were in fact available at Jensen's college, and he assured us he was committed to using the resource office as needed.

What I didn't know: Many students with executive-functioning challenges feel ashamed to ask for help and are, therefore, not prepared to advocate for themselves in college. Jensen was no exception: his self-stigma revealed itself when he remarked, "Everyone knows why you're going into that [learning support] building."

What I learned: I had not realized what an enormous shift would occur when Jensen moved from the support system at his private high school—which provided a robust infrastructure for intellectually gifted kids who struggled with learning challenges, executive functioning, organization, and ADHD—to a college environment where he would have to plead his own case to each professor for the first time. He had never "rehearsed" what such advocacy would feel like, so he was unaware of the self-stigma he would experience when it came time to request needed help at college.

What you can do:

- Train your student to become his own best advocate. Beginning in junior year of high school, have him attend Individualized Education Program (IEP) meetings at school and present his own list of requested accommodations. Once he gets to college, the student will be expected to present such requests directly to professors, even with documented accommodation needs on file.

- Before choosing a college, find out if there are mental health peer-support groups on campus. Would your student be comfortable reaching out to them in case emotional, social, or related problems arise?

- If your son or daughter has already sought therapy or medications for mental health issues, talk to them candidly about social stigmas—which are now thankfully being tackled due to the sheer number of college students openly dealing with various disorders. Peer networks designed to foster student mental health and demolish musty stereotypes are growing more robust on campuses across the country every year. Learning to reject the stigma of having a mental disorder is a lifesaving skill—and one that requires constant practice and support from others.

Lesson 6: Make full use of your support network.

A good friend of ours lived near Jensen's college town and had offered to troubleshoot if the need arose. We tried to arrange for the two to meet, but it never came about. Instead, we gave Mark's contact details to Jensen.

What I didn't know: Depression robs an individual of the ability to reach out. And kids reach out to their friends—not your friends.

What I learned: It's easy to overlook the obvious. Line up supports *before* you think you will need them, and ask your child to identify *with* you, rather than you identifying *for* him, who will be a backup contact.

What you can do: If no family member or familiar and trusted adult lives near the college of choice, consider limiting your college search to a radius of a hundred miles or so. In that case, of course, you or someone in your student's support network becomes the emergency contact. Get together with your student and that contact person before college drop-off!

Lesson 7: When social life fails, college fails.

Loneliness is often associated with aging, yet the Millennial generation and Gen Z are most likely to often feel lonely, and to feel depressed because of it.[18]

What I didn't know: Parents understandably worry about college partying, but the research on this is reassuring: social relationships are in fact a *prerequisite* for learning. Indeed, students who fail to find friends are likelier to drop out of college, either physically or emotionally.[19] Parties, hanging out, and goofing off with friends may sound counter to the mission, but they are all part of that essential social bonding. Students who transfer to another school (or who study abroad) may be extra susceptible to depression when they leave these key social-support networks behind.

Jensen had an established campus group of five or six friends, one of whom he considered his best friend. Yet first-semester best friends can prove fickle. Early second semester, the social scene had changed. Conflicting schedules and new girlfriends caused his core group of friends to drift apart. Compounding this, his first-semester best friend "dumped him" to appease a roommate who didn't like Jensen.

What I learned: Many young men do not reach out to their male friends for support. Their time together is for fun, not for the emotional unburdening that young women have the leeway—and the benefit—of seeking in their friendships. Jensen felt that his other friends did not understand the problem of being suddenly iced by his best friend. As he put it, "I guess they didn't get the memo."

What you can do: There is no easy parental patch. But through the long game of encouraging your child to share ups and downs, parents can model the reality that support helps. And when you hear the first signs of a social or roommate problem, ask your student whom he can talk to, hang out with, and have meals with.

Lesson 8: Depression almost always begins with a triggering loss.

The loss in question for Jensen was the harsh rejection by his first-semester best friend.

What I didn't know: Afterwards, when Jensen's other friends invited him to get together, he often turned them down. He'd become too depressed to engage socially. His calls home gave us only a fragment of his reality—and failed to clue us in to the depths of his distress. We encouraged him to resume rock climbing and archery. To help him reconnect with his high school friends, we paid for an online subscription to World of Warcraft. But Jensen was running on fumes and we weren't prepared for the crash landing.

What I learned: Parenting is like driving through a dense fog while constantly checking the rearview mirror for course corrections. From parenting's rearview mirror, I would come to understand what I had missed, and why. With time, I learned to forgive myself for what I didn't know.

What you can do: Pay close attention and do not normalize or minimize any loss that your child feels is significant. Lend additional support.

Crisis Crescendo

To paint a complete picture, we had gotten inklings of trouble brewing even before Jensen's spring-break declaration that he could not go back. A week before his break was scheduled to begin, he had called to tell me that he was having suicidal thoughts. He promised he had no *plan* to act on these dark urges, but frightened by his mood, we flew him home for the weekend. Naively, I thought the TLC of home and the company of high school friends would provide a needed boost.

As he walked toward me from the arrival gate, he didn't look like himself. His gait was slow, and he had put on a lot of weight in the space of just six weeks. The weight gain was a cruel paradox, for my son was disappearing into depression. I greeted him with a hug, which he passively accepted. His speech and face were unanimated. My heart sank.

Though physically present, Jensen was psychologically inaccessible and emotionally flattened. Our relationship felt strangely and sadly lost. I realized I was suffering ambiguous loss, by definition uncertain, vague, and indeterminate.[20]

With serious depression or any other mental illness, the lack of a definite time frame for a young adult's emotional recovery means parental anxiety settles into grief. Ambiguous loss can be thought of as frozen grief[21] because there is no ritual to mark the passage from emotional presence to absence. It is a loss borne alone, unseen by the outside world.

Months later, in an attempt to make sense of my own mood, I confided a few raw paragraphs to my journal:

> *My usual coping strategies—running, working, keeping busy—no longer work. I've been carried out to sea with Jensen. He's been beyond the buoy line for so long that he's tiring.*
>
> *Back on shore, the others look out to us. His brother is afraid he'll drown, and frustrated that Jensen doesn't swim back to us, as if he could. My husband protests that we have a child at sea who needs so much of my energy.*
>
> *I make the lonely swim to hold him up. I belong to and am needed in both worlds. My laps are always against the tide. Dreading going out, dreading swimming in, never at rest, feeling safe only when I'm also beyond the buoy line with Jensen. I retain the illusion that if I'm present, I can hold him up.*
>
> *My life now mimics my worst recurring memory from their childhoods. One beautiful summer's morning on an empty beach, as Craig built sand castles with Jensen, I splashed into the surf, waist-high, holding a delighted baby Phillip. A powerful wave picked me off my feet. I held Phillip over my head, with the frightened*

realization that I had risked his life. Several terrified seconds later, lived in slow-motion fear, I regained my footing and carried Phillip to shore. In flashbacks to that moment, I relive the panic that I cannot continue to hold my child above the water. He is too heavy; my arms are too weak. The wave overpowers me.

There are no lifeguards, then or now. Love is the only power keeping us afloat.

But as the crisis of spring break unfolded, I could not allow my heartache to consume the energy I needed to identify and mobilize options. Despite feeling helpless in the face of his despair, I reassured Jensen he would get better—and that I planned to do everything in my power to make sure he did. Together, Craig and I boosted his safety net, arranging for him to meet with his psychologist and psychiatrist while home, then scheduling to fly him back for weekly to bi-weekly therapy sessions for the remaining six weeks, as I still hoped at the time that he could complete the semester.

However, I also began formulating a Plan B, or, as I imagined it, the "off-ramp from college." As a precaution, I asked his psychiatrist to prepare a general letter that could be used for either course Incompletes or a medical withdrawal.

In hindsight, the question we should've spent far more energy trying to answer was this: "Is Jensen functioning independently enough to remain in college?" The answer was clearly no, yet it took Jensen's direct appeal that Sunday afternoon a fortnight later—"I can't go back"—to drive me from denial to acceptance: no longer a college student, my son's identity would now be home patient.

The Third-Floor Patient

That first week home, Jensen's relief at having left college gave way to waves of suicidal ideation. Later that first month, Jensen posted his anguish to Facebook:

> **Can you feel it? . . .**
> What if all I was before was dead, and in that instant, I was alive?
> What if it was all the five minutes after death, when the brain still functions, still reminisces and tries to make my

broken body work? Could it be this moment of "death" is
my glimpse of what is Real? No, this is what is real . . . I
think?

It burns, my chest, am I still here? Still in this mortal
realm, not yet done? It all hurts, so that must be it, I must
be alive . . . but what about dreams?

Dreams can make you hurt, make you think you are
bleeding and broken, when your body is hale and whole.

. . . nothing is real, nothing is false, but nothing
simply is.

The first treatment decision had been to remove him from the situation that had tipped him into crisis. The second, yet to be made, focused on his physical safety: Was home care even feasible for a severely
depressed young man?

Without professional input, parents cannot be expected to make informed decisions about the level of treatment (see Levels of Care,
below) their child may need. But help is available, and this decision
tree often begins with a college-affiliated first-line crisis counselor, an
emergency-room physician, or a doctor who has treated the patient
previously. In Jensen's case, I relied on his psychiatric treatment team at
home—Dr. Russ Ramsay, his CBT therapist, and Dr. Deborah Beltzer,
his psychiatrist—to make the ultimate decisions regarding hospitalization, medication, and outpatient treatment. They decided that together, they would monitor him closely while he lived at home.

They supported me in my hope that Jensen could be closely monitored as a home patient because I live "above the store," so to speak, with

LEVELS OF CARE

- Level 1: Weekly or biweekly individual psychotherapy
- Level 2: Psychiatry and medication review
- Level 3: Adjunctive group therapy (in conjunction with
  individual therapy)
- Level 4: Intensive outpatient, day hospital program
- Level 5: Hospitalization

IS IT NORMAL SLEEP OR SOMNOLENCE?

✖ The biological clock of teens and young adults favors late nights and long hours of sleep. The symptom known as somnolence, however, looks far different: it's the habit of extreme sleep, notching 14 to 16 hours at a stretch and accompanied during the waking hours by a lethargic, zombie-like state.

my husband, two sons, a dog, and a cat. On the first floor of offices, I'm family psychologist Dr. Hibbs; on floors 2 and 3, I'm B. to Craig and Mom to Jensen and Phillip. As I drew on my knowledge of mental health treatment options during Jensen's crisis, the border between my personal and professional identities drew ever thinner.

Each day that spring—and summer, fall, winter, and spring again—I shuttled between my practice downstairs and my son upstairs. Because I was scared to leave Jensen alone for more than a few hours at a time, I checked in on him throughout each of my three clinical days and more frequently still on my days off. This allayed my concerns—a bit—but I remained chronically anxious about his safety.

I would take the stairs two at a time, up two and a half flights, to his room at the end of the hall. I paused outside the door, wondering, "Has he gotten up?" Whenever I peeked in, he was tightly wrapped, mummy-like, in his sheets and comforter. *How long do I let him sleep?* I wondered. *Twelve hours . . . fourteen hours . . . **sixteen?*** His record since returning home was nineteen hours of continuous sleep. It was as if he were hibernating, waiting for the winter of his depression to pass.

Like every parent encountering a child's mental health crisis, I faced a rapidly branching decision tree:

- *Does he need to be hospitalized, or will he be safe at home?*
- *If he undergoes outpatient treatment, what kind of provider should we choose: a social worker, a psychologist, a psychiatrist, a counselor, or a family therapist?*

- *Which of the four hundred flavors of psychotherapy will be the best fit for him?*
- *If he takes a new medication, what class and dosage will be appropriate?*
- *What are their potential side effects, especially if several medicines interact?*

And like every parent, I needed help making these decisions.

During these months as a home patient, Jensen met with Dr. Ramsay weekly—and more often, if needed. Jensen also saw Dr. Beltzer every other week. Periodically, the two specialists conferred with each other. Before his crisis, I had occasionally joined Jensen in his outpatient therapy or medication appointments. In crisis, he needed me to be a therapeutic ally in all his sessions: the historian of the week, the external memory drive, reporting on his mood, sleep patterns, obstacles encountered, next goals, and strategies. His depression had checkmated cognition, energy, memory, interests, and hope.

I was exhausted—and it was only the beginning of the second week of Jensen's medical leave. Though I was the 24/7 "psych" parent on call, I asked Craig, an architect, to "spell" me by accompanying Jensen to his upcoming psychiatry appointment. We hadn't had a chance to discuss what I considered the priority: getting a more aggressive medication plan in place as soon as possible for our very depressed son. So when Dr. Beltzer prescribed nothing new, I sent this email in alarm:

March 25th

Hi Deborah,

Thanks for the overview you gave to Craig and Jensen of the different medication classes. I am writing with some urgency to get your recommendation, because Jensen can't wait two weeks for his next appointment with you to begin a medication to ease his depression. He has active suicidal ideation: "I wonder if those cars are going fast enough to hurt me? I wonder what it would be like if I threw myself off this bridge?" The only thing that stops me from hospitalizing him is his assertion that he has no intention to act on those thoughts. That and the fact that I have a home office and can check on him two or three times a day, and am home with him all day Mondays and Fridays. Even so, he spirals pretty fast. He does recover, but it takes only a small regret to send him downward.

I understand that your recommendation is to replace the Celexa (which Jensen had discontinued as per your instructions) and add Prozac or Cymbalta, and at some point withdraw the Abilify. We're all in agreement that Jensen needs an antidepressant. However, I am quite apprehensive about withdrawing the Abilify, since that is the only medication to date from which he has gotten any relief from intense anxiety and irritability. I am not qualified, nor objective enough as his mother, to pick the medication. However, I would ask that it get started sooner, and ramped up sooner, so we can see if it works.

Aside from knowing that he's in a major depression, and is also on the Aspie spectrum, I don't know if it's bipolar II like my mom, or anxiety/depression/developmental crisis mixed with Asperger's. Since there is no definitive diagnosis for bipolar II, it would seem the more conservative choice you reviewed would be Cymbalta. Having reviewed these briefly, how concerned should we be that his depression might worsen (as that seems indicated in a small number of patients under 25)? You also mentioned Strattera. Does either work faster? Does Strattera have any advantages re: concentration or energy, since his depression has vegetative features? Would the Abilify remain at the same dose?

Thank you for your recommendation. If you'd prefer to speak in person, please let me know what might work for you. Craig can pick up any prescription within the day.

Many thanks,

B. Hibbs

While most parents don't have my clinical background, the main takeaway here is in how to advocate for your child. Mental health advocacy consists of data and Q and A.

Data: a description of your observations of a child's behaviors that are most troubling to you.

Q and A: Respectfully question what you don't understand. Why this medication? What are the specific effects, including side effects as well as benefits? When should we expect to see a positive change? Answer: The treatment professional should offer a recommendation that takes into account the short- and long-term goals of symptom relief.

What I came to accept in the course of Jensen's recovery was that I couldn't be a totally objective advocate. Just like any parent whose child is in crisis, my personal fears and biases came into play as the diagnostic process unfolded.

I desperately wanted Jensen to dodge the complexity of bipolar II illness. Instead, I wanted to believe that my son was in the grip of a major—but single-episode—depression. The reason: bipolar disorder (see chart, page 206) was a mood bullet that had struck both my beloved mother and my grandmother. At a time when treatment for bipolar disorder meant institutionalization, shock treatments, or medications with severe side effects, I had witnessed years of their suffering.

After a long stretch of deep, periodic depressions, my mother was accurately diagnosed and treated with medications that permitted her to live a buoyant life: she was a highly educated career woman, a role model for her children, brave and resilient, and defiantly undefined by her illness. And now here I was, the kid kicking the backseat of the infinity loop of Jensen's diagnoses and demanding, "Are we there yet?"

We had already passed several other diagnostic checkpoints: generalized anxiety disorder at age nine, late Asperger's features at age fifteen, and major depression at age nineteen. Each diagnosis had seemed correct at the time, but I refused to accept that bipolar II disorder could be the final destination. Traumatized by my family's history of mental illness, I silently protested, *This can't be happening again. Not to my son.*

Clearly my personal fears and biases were getting in the way of what I needed most in this moment: hope. Throughout Jensen's childhood, I had always welcomed a definitive diagnosis as the path to better treatment. But as the years unspooled and we lurched from one set of treatments to the next, one class of medications to the next, I became discouraged and confused: What did Jensen really have? Did it matter? A decade on, I no longer cared what the precise diagnosis was; I just wanted my son back.

Feeling discouraged, I risked offending Dr. Beltzer, by seeking an expert consult with Dr. Rostain. The two psychiatrists soon agreed that it was in Jensen's best interests to continue treatment with Dr. Rostain.

Mission Redo

So, the first lunar mission was scrubbed. To avert a disastrous free-fall from orbit, Jensen had been obliged to jettison his independence, his student identity, his campus friends, and his feelings of self-worth. Now it was time to fail forward—and to learn. Jensen's crisis taught me what I didn't know. Lessons from crisis care would meld into lessons for parents and marriages that are needed to support a young adult's relaunch, whether from a temporary but problematic boomerang to

SIGNS AND SYMPTOMS OF BIPOLAR DISORDER[22]

Common signs of a manic state:

- Feeling extremely happy
- Talking faster than is normal
- Feeling agitated
- Overconfidence
- Decreased sleep
- Irritability
- Racing thoughts
- Acting impulsively
- Engaging in high-risk behaviors, such as reckless driving, gambling, or excessive spending

Common signs of a depressive state:

- Feeling sad or hopeless
- Irritability
- Low self-esteem
- Abandoning favorite activities
- Having difficulty concentrating or remembering
- Experiencing unusual sleep habits such as sleeping too much or too little
- Thinking about death or suicide

recovery from mental illness. Jensen's story, and those of others, follow the diverse pathways to recovery and relaunch in the next chapters.

Most important, Jensen's crisis taught me I would have to change myself to save my son. Losses—psychic, financial, aspirational—would be followed by gains. As someone who had always operated under the illusion that I could research and advocate my way out of any problems my son encountered, I now had to relinquish my tireless pursuit of problem-solving and surrender to emotional presence. I embraced mindfulness in my daily life and in parenting. Over time, I learned to accept what I could neither control nor change. In the process, I traded my narrow definition of success for a new understanding of what would enable his long-term well-being and happiness. As Jensen began the long relaunch into adulthood, I could ensure that he would not feel alone.

Finally, I turned to my mother for understanding, drawing comfort from her compassion for me and her grandson. When I was young, I took care of my mother as she weathered the depression and mood swings of bipolar illness. Now that she was old, she took care of me. I talked, I cried; she listened, cared, and remained ever hopeful. As my mother had recovered, I believed that Jensen would reclaim the ability to care about his life. Despite the many obstacles that surely lay ahead, I felt grateful that the search for strengths and resources in the family-systems model I practiced clinically would empower me to transmit renewed hope to my son and to my family.

It would be another full year before Jensen began to emerge from a depression so deep that he incised it in a single word in large block capitals on his left forearm: P R A Y.

9

Adjusting to the Boomerang Kid

Certain thoughts are prayers. There are moments when,
whatever the attitude of the body, the soul is on its knees.
—VICTOR HUGO, *LES MISÉRABLES*, 1862

You're Only as Happy as Your Unhappiest Child

The boomerang generation has landed, and parents may feel bonked on the head. Thanks to the Great Recession of 2008, more people ages 18 to 32 now live with their parents than in any other arrangement—the first time this has happened in 130 years.[1]

In many cases the boomerang touches down only temporarily, living at home after college as a way to save money for independent living. Parents and youth may embrace this arrangement as doing two goods: a chance to springboard the young adult, and a bonus time for up-close bonding after four or more years away from home. Unsurprisingly, parents are often more supportive of the boomerang kid who is making appropriate efforts to relaunch.[2]

But how should a family react when the boomerang happens not after college, but during it? When both student and parents find themselves unhappily and anxiously off the expected course? A simple "flight miscalculation" may have occasioned this return to the home planet: unprepared for the social and academic pressures of university life, a student may acknowledge being in over his head and come back to regroup. In other instances, a possibly undiagnosed psychiatric disorder such as anxiety, depression, or substance abuse may have triggered the self-imposed sabbatical.

When a mental health issue prompts the return, parents must face the fact that their prodigal is now a home patient. Parents may wonder, what life skills are needed for a successful relaunch? And when is a belly flop the same as a failure to launch? And they must grapple with a radically altered domestic dynamic: their first priority is to support their boomerang student, of course, as family dynamics exert a crucial influence on a boomerang's progression to adulthood. A positive family environment forms a "natural therapy" network, which supports a young adult's recovery and provides the best insulation against relapse. Yet parents who bear the simultaneous strain of their child's emotional and economic needs often experience stress fractures in their marriage. Without additional support, these pressures can cripple parents' resilience, defeat relaunch efforts, and make siblings feel eclipsed.

Whether your student is merely in a directionless orbit or dealing with mental health problems, this chapter details the steps you can take—on behalf of all family members concerned—to weather an unexpected return and promote a successful relaunch.

Helping a Boomerang Bounce Back

Here's a reassuring reminder for any parent who feels helpless or isolated the first time they field a distressed text message, phone call, or FaceTime request from a child on campus far away: the college environment offers a three-legged stool of support. In addition to the structure and predictability of the weekly class schedule, there's the social bolstering of friends and the psychological expertise of student support service staff.

One single mother whose son was hospitalized for a manic episode in the spring semester managed to keep her job by interacting with his counselors online during the week, then flying cross-country every weekend to spend time with him. With intensive treatment, the student recovered, completed the semester, and returned the next fall.

But what do you do when the "college as treatment center" is not a sustainable option? When a floundering student returns home, parents may feel like the legs of that support stool have been kicked out from under them. This situation can test the healthiest parent and marriage—and you should be aware that it may also draw one or both of you into self-sabotaging conflicts over your respective parenting styles.

There is no "What to expect" syllabus for parents who abruptly become mental health caregivers to their young adults. Suddenly, you must provide structure for your ex-student, who is unmoored from an educational matrix of daily activities and social life, to speak nothing of life goals. You'll double as emotional coach and life-skills manager. Yours is a cottage industry, a 24/7 on-call therapeutic support team. The job description is daunting, and the payoff—hidden as it is in a hazy future—is ill-defined. Your home patient may or may not cooperate with home rule. He may or may not comply with a medication regimen. And you can probably count on other family members to chime in with second-guessing advice and judgments.

Nor does it always take a catastrophe to land a college student back on your doorstep. Some return home through a simple combination of immaturity and what children's book author Daniel Handler would call "A Series of Unfortunate Events." Such was the case for Angelica Jones, whose successful freshman year at a public university persuaded her that she could stop taking the stimulant medication that had mitigated her ADHD since age thirteen.

Without consulting her parents or her psychiatrist, Angelica went off her medication in the fall of her sophomore year. Not long after, she was arrested for public drunkenness at a party off-campus. The college revoked her generous scholarship, and though Angelica completed the semester, she returned home for winter break determined not to resume the medicine. She was likewise loath to return to college in the spring, yet she had no solid alternative plan.

After watching her sit home for two months "doing nothing," in her parents' words, the Joneses insisted that Angelica get a job—*any* job—and save whatever money she made for future tuition costs. They asked her to sign a "tiger mom" live-at-home agreement, heavy on assuming responsibilities and consequences.[3] Angelica worked as a waitress through the summer, then returned to college in the fall. This time around, she agreed to resume her medication to better support her academics and tamp down her impulsivity. Her boomerang detour would ultimately cost the Jones family forty thousand dollars in scholarship funds—a steep price tag for a lesson in the "two-person rule" (see the following page).

As parents forge a new domestic configuration that encompasses the unexpected and floundering boomerang, they must be vigilant not to let parent burnout occur. This is one of those crux points when your young adult needs your support and teamwork the most, so take care

THE TWO-PERSON RULE

✖ In this decision-making safeguard, the student agrees to consult with two previously identified (and agreed upon) trusted adults prior to making important decisions. The designated individuals may be a parent, a mature older sibling or friend, another family member, a medical professional, or an academic adviser or mentor. This double-check on judgment provides a sturdy guide for any decision, but it is crucially important when it comes to taking (or withdrawing from) a psychoactive medication. The two-person rule can also be vital when choosing what activities to undertake when educational or job prospects are on hold.

not to let parental disagreements mushroom. Yes, you may be experiencing a form of grief at having temporarily "lost" the child you once knew and your dreams for him. But it's crucial to keep your eyes on the long-term prize: maintaining your resilience and modeling your hope in your young adult's future. Of course, that's easier said than done, as we next learn from Lou and Deidre.

Three's a Crowd: The Couple Contend with the Home Patient (and each other)

It's the witching hour, the end of a long workday, the end of the week, and the end of Nick's failed semester. Lou and Deidre Roca are headed for another argument over their son. Nick's depression has brought his college semester to a premature close. As Deidre finishes preparing dinner, she greets Lou with another problem: "I've reminded Nick twice, but he forgot to pick up the refill for his antidepressant. I'm tired of reminding him, but I'm afraid he'll run out."

Overloaded by her full-time job and worn thin by her "second shift"—monitoring Nick's moods, managing his college-return documentation, and communicating with his therapists, to say nothing of organizing their daughter's SAT prep classes, college search, and college visits—Deidre is blowing off steam. She tries to treat Nick with patience and understanding, but lately she has felt her reserves of those two precious parental resources dipping dangerously low.

Lou mixes a martini as he half-listens to Deidre deliver the daily report. He too has had a rough week at work, which may explain his stern reply: "You're doing too much, Deidre. I think you should just let Nick figure this out. He's playing you—he'll learn from screwing up."

"His medication's too important to leave to the school of hard knocks," Deidre returns fire. "If he misses a dose or two, it's not just Nick, but me who'll be picking up the pieces."

To underscore her point, Deidre reminds Lou of the string of bad luck that has brought Nick to this nadir: his girlfriend dumped him, then he had a concussion from a skateboarding accident, and soon he became depressed. "This was the semester the sky fell in on Nick," says Deidre, "and we're the ones who are supposed to be holding him up. But never mind—I'll play Atlas while you get to be the tough guy."

Drink in hand, Lou blows out of the kitchen with a parting shot: "You undermine every decision I make as a parent. Hell will freeze over before he gets through college—it's a waste of our money!"

Of all the topics that couples argue about, children (no matter how old) top the list. With their son's unexpected return to the fold, the Rocas are once again beset by conflict and, quite frankly, by deeply divisive and therefore ineffective parenting styles. Yet they must somehow summon the inner resources necessary to preserve their own health and sanity, protect their marriage, and enable Nick's younger sister to flourish. Indeed, their support will be critical to Nick's progress: his full recovery will hinge partly on his parents' capacity to function as a unified team. Hope and resilience are two resources that Team Roca can ill afford to squander right now.

Emotional Expression

Resolving any differences in your parenting styles becomes even more important when a young adult returns to the household in the throes of psychiatric illness. Family researcher George Brown was among the first to identify the many blind spots that can develop between how we *think* we parent a troubled youth and how we actually *do* connect to that person. Brown believes that a family's Emotional Expression (EE)—in this context, how supportive or unsupportive it is in treating a young adult with a mental disorder—determines the student's rebound or relapse.[4] Over the past fifty years or so, clinicians have applied the concept of EE to help improve the family environment of many people with psychiatric disorders. The goal is for parents and siblings to adopt positive ways of relating to the affected family member while reducing critical or blaming habits.

Parents can spur their young adult's recovery by expressing positive emotions. Warmth and positive regard can benefit all family relationships. Not only does their expression have a salutary effect on the student and his siblings, but it also reduces the related risk of caregiver depression.[5] In the hurly-burly of putting supports in place for a home patient, it's easy to overlook the parents' commonly experienced and heightened levels of anxiety, depression, and sense of burdened responsibility.[6] We'll return to the crucial need that parents, as caregivers, have to maintain their own mental health, in order to best help their child and family.

In the diagram (on the following page), you'll see that EE encompasses five elements that range from harmful to helpful.[7] Components with a high EE quotient are considered negative; those lower down the EE scale are deemed positive.

EMOTIONAL EXPRESSION

Harmful EE

A review of the Rocas' situation reveals some classic signs of a high EE environment:

1. Hostility. Lou blames Nick, believing that he is sufficiently in control of his illness to be able to manipulate his mother with it. This misperception of control often leads parents to classify troubling behavior as "bad"; they may therefore reflexively move to punish or chastise the affected individual. These parents often see attempts to understand underlying stresses or needs as "coddling."

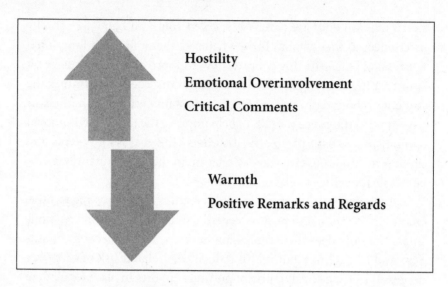

Hostility

Emotional Overinvolvement

Critical Comments

Warmth

Positive Remarks and Regards

2. Emotional overinvolvement. Add over-protectiveness to over-parenting, season with a dash of intrusiveness, and you have a surefire recipe for emotional over-involvement. Rather than blaming the child going through a rough patch, the parent typically thinks, *I'll make this sacrifice for you because I know you're helpless. You can't do it; I'll solve it for you.* Lou accuses Deidre of the over-involved sins of talking too much and doing too much, to which Nick reacts by withdrawing. Over-involvement may also take the form of pressuring the student with an emotional disability to "catch up."

3. Critical comments. Critical comments are an odd blend of hostility and over-involvement in which parents blame others: *That professor wouldn't cut you a break. I don't think your counselor is doing you any good. I'm the only one who gets you; your father/mother doesn't understand.* This odd-man-out stratagem is self-defeating on several levels: it puts a young person in a split loyalty of taking sides by pitting parent against parent or casts college staffers as "the bad guys."

Parental or familial hostility slows a young person's recovery and may even cause a relapse. Both anger and parental disengagement predict worsening of a young person's depression at follow-up. Astonishingly, a diagnosed individual living in a hostile environment may be accused of selfishness: "Look what you're putting your mother through." Many parents can't agree on what is helpful. Others must also manage a sibling's hostility.

Nick's sister, Sue, drafting off her father's anger, blasted her mother: "Why does Nick get to lie in bed all day when I still have to go to school?"

Deidre challenged her daughter's distortion with emotional support: "I know you're frustrated. You were really worried when Nick came home from college depressed. But after months, you're kinda burned out." When Sue nodded, Deidre added, "You can tell me any time you're fed up. Nick pulled the joker card this year—he's trying to get better. But let's make sure you get to see your friends and have some fun."

"Thanks, Mom," a calmer Sue replied. "It's just crummy."

The *hostility* that characterizes a harmful high EE environment is perhaps to be expected; given the circumstances, everyone is capable of a meltdown or a "worst self" moment. Yet parents must also guard against the "friendlier" pseudo-helpfulness of *emotionally over-involved* accommodations, because these inadvertently deepen dependency. And whereas the "friendly fire" of *critical comments* naturally erupts when parents feel frustrated with their partner, it's damaging for a young adult to be caught in the middle. If you find yourself or another family member exhibiting any of these three signs of high EE, take action: seek help and support. In addition to individual, couples, and family counseling, we provide names of support groups in the Appendix.

Helpful EE

The Roca family also reflects signs of lowered and helpful EE:

1. Warmth. Deidre models a reflective, validating style of parenting, even as she compassionately acknowledges Sue's anger at her brother's crisis, helping Sue achieve a more accepting perspective. Deidre defends the understandable reasons for Nick's depression as she and Lou spar.

2. Positive remarks and regards. Deidre reflects a more positive and hopeful approach towards their son, even though she is clearly exhausted on a day-to-day basis.

A helpful, low-EE family environment fosters a student's recovery through positive remarks, warmth, and appreciation. It's not just what you say, but how you say it: a responsive parenting style conveys kindness, concern, and empathy with smiles, hugs, and a caring tone.

Responsive parents take into account the unique circumstances of the moment. When their young person is going off the rails—whether with depression, anger, an anxiety attack, or problem behavior— their first instinct is to empathize, read between the lines, and identify the factors that may be contributing to the problem. They can then offer extra support. Yet most couples have a mix of emotional expression, some harmful, some helpful.

However we strive to be kind and empathic parents, any family environment is harshly tested in the crucible of a child's psychiatric illness. In the Roca family, you've seen a bright dividing line as the parents engage in a mutually reinforcing polarization between the high and low EE factions. The couple is caught in a Goldilocks dilemma.

Goldilocks and Parenting

The fable of Goldilocks prompts us to consider the dangers that may arise from extremes. In the story, one porridge is too hot, one too cold; the third, finally, is just right. Similarly, raising a child presents parents with this problem when no one gets the demands of the extreme sport of child-rearing "just right." What's the right amount of discipline? Support? Expectations? Facing too many demands and too little time on this marathon run, parents typically sort themselves into "expert" and "helper" roles. So one parent often does too much (and over-functions), while the other does too little (and under-functions). Many a marriage has foundered, unable to get it "just right."

Adding to a couple's stress and feeling of burnout is the unexpected and unwelcome emotional strain of a college student who has fallen out of orbit. Without the daily routine of classes and campus life, social isolation and hopelessness may ensue. This aimless drift can ignite a parent's deepest fears: *What's next? Will he be okay when he grows up? When will he grow up?* The young adult is going to need heaping doses of parental advocacy and guidance. But what amount of help is "just right"?

The Goldilocks dilemma encompasses the realities of dual-career families, with lingering stereotypes of the overly nurturing mother running the household and the stern, distant, breadwinning father.[8] Yet the gender stereotype holds that when a parent must become the psychiatric care manager for a troubled young adult, it is most often the mother. That was certainly the case in the Roca ménage.

Rather than making a self-inflicted choice of being over-involved, as Lou accused Deidre of being, Deidre is over-functioning—doing too much, while Lou is angrily disengaged and doing too little. The mother's higher caregiver burden often results from more contact with her child, more responsibility for the daily care that supports recovery, and an emotional coping style that leaves her more affected by her child's relapses or crises. Her "thanks"? The ubiquitous feeling of being judged by virtually everyone for her child's disorder or halting recovery.[9] This is a recipe for parental dysfunction.

Parents' Mental Health

The Role Strain of the Mental Health Caregiver

Most of what we know about chronic parental stressors comes from the lives of mothers who are the primary caregivers for children with an ongoing illness or disability: cancer, Down syndrome, or longstanding emotional or behavioral disorders.[10] These conditions may seem wildly disparate, yet they have a common impact on caregivers. Indeed, a caregiver's load is not a function of any particular diagnosis, given that many physical and psychiatric illnesses share overlapping stressors. Instead, the load varies, as the strain intensifies with the uncertainty of the diagnosis, an ambiguous projected course, and a prolonged duration of illness and disability.[11]

Parents must also gird themselves for a middle- to long-distance run, not a sprint: significant mental health problems can entail a long and gradual recovery. Depending on the diagnosis and treatment, it may take your student weeks, months—perhaps even a year or two—to get his "old self" up and running again.

Parents of a home patient must become instant experts, skilled at spotting new symptoms and adept at deciphering the meaning of moods. The primary parent-caregiver responsibilities include tabulating the daily metrics of sleep, diet, and activity levels and reporting these to mental health professionals; urging a young adult to eat, resume interests, and find a direction while managing one's own tensions and worry about the future; making sure the medication regimen is being followed; and fielding the daily psychological assessment and translating it for inquiring family members and friends.

Partners caught up in this scenario typically see their relationship subjected to excruciating pressure. Long-playing emotional demands replace the physical exhaustion of early childhood, yet there is no guaranteed maturational cure for the uncertain future of a floundering student. Here's how one father described the experience of being pressed into service as a "psychiatric care manager" for his son and called upon to develop new expertise overnight:[12]

> *I have to say that I am COMPLETELY flummoxed. Our relationship is pretty tense at times and I simply have NO idea what to DO. In my mind, it's like I am watching him drown in some kind of swirling whirlpool while I stand on the shore yards away without any means of aiding him. I feel love and sympathy for my son, coupled with a sense of utter futility.*

As if the onus of caregiving weren't heavy enough, parents of a child with serious behavioral or social-emotional problems incur a higher risk of dysfunction and are likelier to divorce[13] than those in "typical" families.[14] This pattern betrays itself, oddly enough, in a paradox called the "Down syndrome advantage."[15] These affected children, though born with physical abnormalities and below-average intelligence, rarely experience mental illness or behavioral problems. Yet even though these parents will likely shoulder the responsibility of caring for their Down syndrome child throughout their lives, their divorce rate is significantly lower than the norm—at 7.6 percent,[16] as opposed to the often cited 40 percent in the U.S. population at large.[17]

The reason for the "advantage"? Down syndrome families have numerous supportive buffers that are absent for parents of a child or young adult with a mental illness. Absent are an unequivocal diagnosis, a precise understanding of the child's developmental trajectory and prognosis, physical markers evoking social concern and sympathy for the parents, and the availability of services.[18]

Lacking these medical, social, and community buttresses, and burdened by the isolation of mental health stigma, parents functioning as mental health caregivers are bombarded by diagnostic and treatment uncertainties. They may be misdirected down therapeutic blind alleys. And they almost always feel drained by unexpected and ongoing anxieties about an unpredictable future course and outcome. What the mental health caregiver needs most, therefore, is the appreciation and support of the other parent and key supporting family members. Too often, though, parental discord undercuts this support.

Overcoming Stress Between Parents

Couples who seek treatment for their troubled college student seldom recognize the need to take care of their own relationship. While complicated enough in a first marriage, parental style differences can be exacerbated by the involuntary "in-law" relationship and tenuous bonding between a stepparent (or unrelated partner in a parental role) and a young adult. Couples, regardless of marital status, may not realize the collateral psychic damage they sustain when a household gets "blown up" to accommodate a returnee. They may not anticipate the long shadow that parenting differences cast on a relationship that has newly acquired caregiver roles. That's why we see it as a minor tragedy that most couples in significant conflict delay for an average of six years before seeking therapy for themselves.[19] The long deferment makes a successful resolution even more challenging.

And since mothers are often in the primary mental health caregiver role, how do couples compassionately support each other rather than become mired in gender stereotypes and an over-functioning/under-functioning imbalance? The mother often feels overwhelmed and exhausted, while the father feels like an outsider and grows discouraged, frustrated, or angry on observing that the mother–child bond is so close, and withdraws in response. Alone together, the couple becomes polarized.

Both partners have a responsibility to assess this feedback loop if they are to restore a healthy give-and-take to their relationship. The caregiver as expert characteristically overextends herself, then feels resentful when she needs to ask for help, while the "helper" may withhold offering that very aid because he anticipates criticism for the job he does. Rebalancing the burden of the mental health caregiver is sometimes a simple matter of frequently expressing appreciation and avoiding critiques. Or it may entail a more substantial reassignment of roles within a relationship: the over-functioning caregiver must identify what *specific* help she most needs (and which other tasks she can comfortably let go), while the under-functioning parent must identify additional responsibilities to assume—and follow through on completing them.

In either case, be aware that historical parenting differences may block the path to a healthy resolution.

That's what Lou and Deidre Roca found out—the hard way—as they attempted to juggle careers, chores, and the sudden challenge of serving as Nick's psychiatric care managers. The warning signs appeared before college. By the time Nick was fourteen, Deidre had already nicknamed her cell phone "Pavlov"; its chime alerted her to anticipate bad news. Was the principal calling to say Nick was in after-school detention for cursing in class? Was it a fellow parent complaining that Nick had thrown a pencil and hit her son in the face? The calls carried the implicit subtext of failed parenting: "Why can't you control your child? What are you doing wrong? Why can't he learn that his behavior only backfires?"

Nick was then diagnosed with ADHD, yet this better understanding of his difficulties could not keep Lou and Deidre from differing over how to parent. Whereas Lou's instinct was to let Nick experience the full consequences of his impulsive behavior, Deidre believed a softer touch was mandated—and she faulted Lou for his harsh expectations and reactive, punitive style.

Over time, these differences crystallized. Focused on Nick's behavioral problems, Lou thought of his son as "bad" and increasingly favored cracking down. Drawing on his own childhood, as many parents do, Lou believed that his stepfather's hardline style had been good for him, and that it would likewise help Nick grow up. Lou also made the mistake of expecting a clone of himself in a hard-driving, stoic son. Lou's disappointment was barely disguised in his ill-tempered reprimands of Nick. To counter this, Deidre became ever more permissive and overinvolved with her son; she could not bear to watch Nick fail—or, indeed, to experience even modest setbacks that might help him cope in the long run. Still, Lou and Deidre drew comfort from the fact that Nick had the raw brainpower to do well at college. They papered over their differences.

Once at college, Nick reluctantly owned up to poor grades his first semester. Lou fumed to Deidre that their son was "majoring in getting high and skateboarding." Then that spring, Nick's serious skateboarding accident and ensuing depression sent him home on medical leave, raising all sorts of chicken-and-egg questions in his parents' minds: Was he self-destructive and accident-prone because he was depressed? Or did his depression stem from his romantic woes and post-concussion headaches? Neither Nick nor his parents understood that even a mild concussion may damage thousands of neurons, can cause worsening ADHD symptoms, and is closely linked to an increased risk of suicide.[20,21]

Publicly, though, things were "all good." When quizzed by extended family members, the embarrassed couple played down the scale of Nick's emotional problems. The Rocas presented a convincing front, an "as if" reality: *as if* Nick were fine, *as if* the family were not overloaded by the day-to-day uncertainties. They maintained this public face even as they were growing more isolated from friends and family—and ever more stressed and depleted.

As the summer wore on and Nick's depression persisted, his parents' resilience hissed a slow leak. Nick had registered for fall classes, but by midsummer it seemed doubtful he would be ready to return in September. Having failed to look for a summer job, he slept late every morning and took little initiative to help around the house. He played online games for hours on end, despite their warnings that screen time would worsen his post-concussion headaches and prolong his recovery. And even though Nick had begun therapy and an antidepressant medication, he appeared listless and disengaged.

This summer-long "recuperation" ripped the scab off some old wounds. Deidre often found herself defending Nick to Lou, who grumbled that Nick made a lousy role model for his younger sister, and was "playing the sympathy card with his concussion, headaches, and so-called depression." "He should just get on with his life," Lou seethed aloud. "Grow up and get out."

As Nick's depression worsened, Deidre scrambled to keep up. She felt responsible to communicate with his therapists, and to keep him company to offset his isolation; she even resumed childhood reminders for her son to shower and change clothes.

For all their earlier efforts to strike a workable role balance, Deidre had become Nick's exhausted caregiver, Lou the neglected spouse. Deidre told herself that managing Nick's moods was key to his recovery. In truth, her busy over-involvement was an unconscious defense, used to allay her creeping sense of loss: What had happened to the son she once knew? Would she ever get him back? The Nick she remembered stood frozen in time in a smiling photograph on her desk.

Seeking solace, Deidre often greeted Lou with a litany of the day's worries about their son. Lou read this catalog as implicit blame that he wasn't doing enough. His defensiveness was equal parts helplessness, inadequacy, and denial that his son had a mental illness. To cope with the daily dose of discouragement, Lou worked overtime and helped more with household chores, but he also immersed himself in television and martinis. The couple was slowly losing the connection and emotional support each needed.

Widening the disconnect between the Rocas' competing parenting styles was their high EE (negative expressed emotions) regarding Nick's depression. The case notes capturing this dynamic might look something like this:

SITUATION	PARENTAL STYLE	EXPRESSED EMOTION
Nick forgets to pick up his medication	Father: strict, low warmth Mother: permissive, high warmth	Father: unforgiving, critical Mother: attentive, over-involved

Lou's hostile attitude paired with Deidre's over-involvement yielded not just harmful EE but a downward-spiraling cascade of emotional stances: when Lou asserts that Nick is responsible for his illness, Deidre defends her son and faults Lou for letting his anger create a stressful family environment. The tension in the air envelops everyone: Sue allies with her father against her "lazy" brother. Predictably, Deidre and Lou increasingly direct their frustration at each other. And Nick feels even worse about being home instead of at school like all his friends.

How to Break a Vicious Cycle

Returning to the Rocas' Friday night blow-up, it's time to send these two to "time-out." They will have to park their dispute until each is calmer. From initial salvo to full-on squabble has taken only a few minutes, and the exchange has resolved nothing. Deidre and Lou are ensnared in a cyclical pattern known as "emotional hijacking." This occurs in a split second when the brain, wired to favor survival over happiness, whiffs danger and activates the fight-or-flight response. Self-defeating behaviors often result:

Complaint: Deidre bemoans Nick's latest problem. Lou catches her distress, and reacts by accusing Deidre of doing too much, then suggesting that Nick deserves whatever consequences ensue from forgetting to take his medication. Deidre shoots back, then both shut down.

Responsibility: Feeling responsible for Deidre's overload, Lou defends

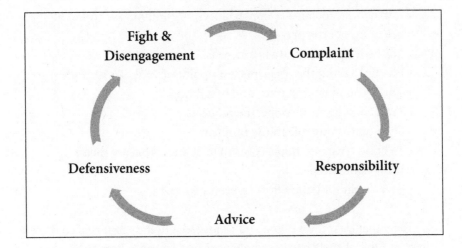

himself by giving advice. Rather than offering to take something off Deidre's plate, he tells her what she *should have done*.

Advice: It's reasonable to equate advice with problem-solving, so dispensing it can appear to be a helpful step—in theory, that is. In reality, unsolicited advice is a flight response, a coded way of saying, "Make this issue go away."

Defensiveness: Understandably, the recipient of this unsolicited counsel feels threatened—and counterattacks.

Fight and disengagement: Sensing that his good intentions have been misconstrued, the advice-giver fires back—and Round Two erupts. But there's a way to defuse this crisis: By learning to recognize the steps and triggers of this counterproductive cycle, a couple can step back from the brink of mutually assured destruction. Then, once the storm has passed, they need to take a "time in," to learn from hindsight, and resolve misunderstandings to get back on the same page.

Indeed, that's what happened when Lou and Deidre committed to developing new and healthier habits. It took a conscious effort and plenty of practice, but eventually they developed a healthier way to settle their conflicts. The following tool kit proved crucial:

9 Steps to Repair a Relationship

- Don't avoid conflict. You can't be close by sweeping things under the rug.
- Acknowledge your own mental state. If your emotional barometer reads "stormy," STOP immediately. Then proceed only when "clear."

- Learn how to have a constructive argument. Address the behavior, not the person.
- Lead with positives, then concerns.
- Practice taking the other person's point of view. To be understood, you must first offer understanding.
- Turn complaints into specific requests.
- Own up to your role in the problem.
- To build trust and hope, commit to changes that are meaningful to your partner.
- Give credit for good efforts—even your own.

To further clear the air, Lou and Deidre sought the support of couples therapy. One of their hardest challenges was learning how to disagree without launching an attack or defending with a counterattack. Dr. Hibbs suggested that the Rocas come up with a "safe" word or phrase to deploy whenever either one of them felt they were entering another cycle of emotional hijacking. They decided on "Groundhog Day"—their way of signaling, "Here we go again—let's pause and regroup."

Several years later, Lou described how the couple's sessions had helped him pivot from an angry stance to one of compassionate engagement:[22]

> I was so not prepared for my son to be a pothead and college screwup. This was not what I signed up for. I blamed Deidre for Nick's problems. Months went by when he was depressed, but I didn't tell my parents because I didn't want their advice, or to have them think that I had messed up as a dad. But I was judging my son just as I worried my parents might judge me. I didn't realize this at the time, of course—I just felt angry.
>
> Looking back on that year, I see now that I was feeling ashamed of myself, and isolated. But all my wife and son saw was my frustration. That, and my drinking. One day after too many martinis and another run-in, she told me, "I love you and want to stay married, but if you make me choose, I'm going to choose the kids."
>
> That was a wake-up call. She'd been asking me to go to a therapist with her, but until then I'd refused. I thought that when you go to a couples therapist it's the end of the line. To my surprise, the therapy helped.
>
> Dr. Hibbs reminded me that Nick still needed my involvement.

"He's your son," she said. "You held him as a baby. He still needs you." She urged me to reconnect—take him to lunch, watch movies, engage. That session was another turning point for me. I'd been a hypocrite—hassling Nick about smoking dope while I was drinking too much. I cut way back; no more after-work drinks.

Then I had my first honest conversation with Nick about substance abuse. He'd been self-medicating, just like I was. We started to be more open with each other. And then the more I engaged Nick, the better my marriage got. I stepped up emotionally, and Deidre wasn't as burdened. She was able to enforce firmer expectations for Nick because I wasn't acting like such a hard-ass. We were finally a team again.

By making these changes, Deidre and Lou were able to let go of their anger and frustration with each other, making room for the underlying sadness that each carried to sink in. Together they confronted the "ambiguous loss" of the child of their memory and dreams. By learning to sustain each other, they were better equipped to support Nick's recovery.

The "Well Child"

With their all-consuming focus on the home patient, parents can easily overlook the impact of recent events on a sibling, who may feel silent pressure to assume the role of "well child." That's something of an ironic label, for the well child is often not well at all; instead she is helping the parents by meeting an often unrecognized emotional obligation to "be okay," posing no additional burden on them.

The well child role may encompass a heightened need for academic success; or it may entail an empathic, adult-level support to a parent or siblings. The well child may also appear to be stoic or blissfully problem-free. Yet the well child role takes a heavy toll, as a sibling experiences his or her own losses too. Anger, frustration, and resentment may set in, further straining family relationships—and adding an unwanted layer of psychological complexity to the mix.

Nick's sister, Sue, felt all of those emotions and more. Initially worried, then angry that she had "lost" her older brother, she resolved not to upset her parents even more. For Sue, the well child role meant being the good student, and at home being the "easy" teen—a prematurely adult part that is exhausting to play. With time and maturity, Sue would come to understand that she needed to release herself from her well child identity bind. Three years after the concussion that precipitated Nick's emotional free fall, Sue composed a college essay about assuming the well child role for an assignment in memoir writing. Hoping it might help others, Sue offered to share an excerpt of that essay:[23]

> *I saw depression firsthand when I was sixteen. My brother spent most of the year depressed. My mother made sure he saw his therapist and psychiatrist regularly. But it was still a very long time before he functioned halfway normally again.*
>
> *At first I was very worried for him: Would he kill himself? But in that first year, my dad and I went from worried to angry. I was tired of his being sick, and frustrated by his depression. I found myself asking, 'Why didn't Nick do things differently?' Or, 'Why didn't he take charge of his life?' But I kept that to myself and I'm glad I did, because I wouldn't have wanted it to be any more difficult for him than it already was.*
>
> *Nick's therapist helped me understand that we were all experiencing something called "ambiguous loss." She explained that I also had "compassion fatigue," where you get burned out because you can't escape the constant worry over someone you care about. That helped me understand my experience and my brother's struggle better.*

As she slowly gained the perspective needed to analyze the unique perch she had occupied in the family, Sue was able to emerge from her well child chrysalis. She learned to express her needs, and to feel loved and valued even as she let go of the precociously responsible, high-achieving, and over-giving self.

At college, she would seek additional insight by joining a campus mental health support group. Among these peers, Sue found a shared sense of understanding, and embraced the upside of the well child experience: a greater level of maturity, patience, empathy, and an appreciation for her own mental health and resilience.

From Worry to Hope

Hope is definitely not the same thing as optimism. It is not the conviction that something will turn out well, but the certainty that something makes sense, regardless of how it turns out.
—VÁCLAV HAVEL, *DISTURBING THE PEACE*, 1986

As Havel asserts, hope is distinct from optimism. Optimism is a blind leap of faith that the future will be better. It's a "don't worry, be happy" unreality. Hope is earned. It is more than a feeling. Hope requires personal agency and the ability to pursue goals in the face of problems. A parent's ability to maintain and project hope is a key ingredient necessary for the home patient's improvement. This precious commodity is both balm and boon to parents and affected youth as they ride out the uncertainties of recovery. Setbacks in the boomerang's progress will occur, and to buffer this distress, consider the many forms that hope can take in our lives.[24,25] According to psychology professor and *The Power of Hope* author Anthony Scioli, hope consists of four core elements:[26]

1. *Attachment:* Maintain your trust in, and your connection to, another person.
2. *Mastery:* Your actions make a difference; you have the personal agency to make changes in your life—or another's.
3. *Survival:* Your situation is temporary, not permanent, so you are not trapped in it. It's possible to hold on to positive thoughts and feelings even as you process painful experiences.
4. *Spirituality:* There is something bigger than ourselves.

People in possession of all four of these facets are more hopeful, and therefore more resilient and helpful to another in need. So if you find yourself struggling to muster hope, try this exercise:

Exercising Your Hope Muscles
- Make a list of the people and things in your life that contribute to each of the four areas above.
- Create a visualization meditation using inspiring quotes or music.[27]

- Take time to visit a place that fills you with awe and a sense of well-being.
- To take a quiz on hopefulness, visit www.gainhope.com/hope /test_form.cfm

Hope also requires crafting a very deliberate game plan for change. This may mean abandoning unattainable goals and putting realistic ones in their place. For some parents and youth, this may mean cutting the phrase "Ivy League" out of your definition of success. For others, it may entail shooting for a technical or trade-work goal rather than lofty academic credentials. And for a third group still, it may involve pursuing radically alternative paths to independent adulthood.

It's vital to enlist the support of others to keep your hope reservoir full. Hope is contagious, so surround yourself with individuals who care about you and are willing to help you achieve your goals.

Weaving a Social Support Net

Sources of support for parents may include a partner, family members, an inner circle of close friends, or an outer circle of support groups for parents, whether in person or online. Never underestimate the healing power of this latter resource; it can buffer the inevitable feelings of isolation and social stigma that buffet the parents of "kids with issues." The National Alliance on Mental Illness (NAMI), for one, offers family-to-family educational support groups nationwide. Online chat forums can likewise be sources of comfort; you'll find these listed in the Appendix. Finally, whereas some boomerangs last longer than others, it's a certainty that every family member will be exposed to some degree of fallout. For that reason, you may wish to consider attending family (or couples) psychotherapy at some point, to deflate caregiver stress, improve coping, and build healthier relationships.

Though turning to your partner in parenting may appear to be the most logical social support, parents do not necessarily find comfort in each other—especially when a family crisis makes it clear that their beliefs, styles, and experiences diverge. Or, perhaps you may simply be piloting the parent plane solo.

Whatever its source, support essentially consists of kindness, compassion, and nonjudgmental listening. And be aware that your partner, family member, or friend may not be practiced at furnishing support, so you may have to step in and guide the exercise: "I'm not looking for advice, so please just listen for now—and please check in on me from time to time."

In the absence of such direction, your listener may succumb to "bright-siding"—a common response that minimizes concerns and the seriousness of your young adult's situation. Bright-sided comments sound like these: "I'm sure she'll feel better soon." "He probably just needs a job." "All kids go through tough times." Instead, when you're in the market for genuine empathy—don't hesitate to ask for it.

Self-Care

The chronic stress of serving as a homegrown mental health caregiver can chip away at your emotional well-being. Frequently lost in the mix is self-care—a term that may seem a cliché, but which scientific research shows to be sound. Here are three ways to make sure you get adequate doses:

1. Exercise. Regular cardiovascular exercise can be a key to maintaining both physical and emotional well-being. It has proven to be as effective as antidepressant medications for one-third of the population experiencing mild depression.[28]

2. Meditation practice can help preserve a caregiver's physical and emotional health,[29] as one father discovered when his daughter was in crisis:

> LeAnn's boyfriend called late one night to tell us she was talking about hurting herself. We asked him to call the police to take her to the emergency room, but he didn't think that was a good idea. Instead, he stayed with her while we drove from our home two hours away.
>
> Over the course of the next few months, LeAnn met with an individual therapist. My meditation practice helped me remain calm and focus on the problems to solve. I think my approach helped everyone cope better.

3. Predictable down time. Schedule time to renew your own interests. Plan to socialize with friends. Write on your calendar the occasional break from daily demands.

Acceptance

Another stepping stone on the path to a young adult's recovery is acceptance. For the parents of a young person struggling with anxiety, depression, or another mental disorder, acceptance is like a way station from grief and frustration. Without it, you feel trapped—and run the risk of burnout.

Acceptance is a process we inhabit gradually. Our initial desperate efforts to regain control can be thought of as a form of protest—one of the five classic stages of grief leading up to acceptance.[30] Accepting that certain goals are simply unattainable allows us to redirect our energy into setting new—and achievable—goals. We can then help our adolescent or young adult set new goals as well.

One mother characterized her initial approach to her son's mental illness as Sisyphean. She repeatedly pushed the boulder of his recovery uphill only to helplessly watch as it rolled down again. For her, acceptance meant that instead of endlessly searching out new doctors or having her son try new medications for the next climb, the best way to strengthen her relationship with her son was simply to enjoy small moments of fun with him.[31]

Another parent, frightened by her daughter's cutting episode, described her journey to acceptance this way:[32]

> To calm myself, I remind myself to breathe. Calming myself also relies on my ability to accept that I'm not in control. Like prayerful surrender, I relinquish control for the first time after all these years. I accept the fact that despite my love and my determination, I can't keep Tanya safe. Despite my best efforts to understand her problems, to question the doctors, to inquire about the medications, to find new resources, to imagine what might be helpful, I now fully accept the reality that I cannot control how Tanya manages her moods. I cannot govern whether she acts on the false urgency of her emotional distress. The only control I have is to remain calm—calm for Tanya, calm to teach her how to manage future events.
>
> This moment is composed of my past witnessing of all that Tanya has endured. But now there is no more problem-solving, no more advice-giving, no more anxious questions from me.

There are no more action steps. I am just listening, just being with her. I am simply being present—that's what love has come to mean.

There is no more planned trajectory. There is hope, but without the attachments of expectation, without self-soothing illusions. I am strangely at peace—still and always Tanya's advocate, ever her mother in this eternal bond.

No mere self-indulgent wallow, acceptance enables a parent to tolerate the inherent unknowns of mental illness. Acceptance includes being able to bear witness to a young adult's struggle, yet retain the dual goals of being problem-focused when appropriate and emotionally attuned when needed. It also forges a closer, more stable, and more trustworthy link between young adult and parent. In most people's eyes, that is authentic shelter from the storm.

Nor is this state of grace reserved for grownups alone. For adolescents and young adults afflicted by any kind of emotional problem, acceptance means a willingness to actively engage treatment, which may include talk therapy and psychoactive medications. Acceptance also means not judging yourself: you are not a "bad person" or a "failure" simply because you have a disease that affects the proper functioning of your brain.

Setting New Goals

By easing family tensions, cultivating social supports, practicing self-care, and accepting the reality of mental illness, Nick and his parents gradually found hope. Having worked hard to become a harmonious team, Lou and Deidre now relinquished the unrealistic goal of their son's fall return to college. Though Nick had begun to improve on a different antidepressant, the Rocas acknowledged the family's new collective reality: he (and his brain) needed more time, clearer routines, additional help managing his strong emotions, better coping for his marijuana use, and the stability of a positive home environment to solidify his recovery. In Chapter 10, we'll learn the strategies that Nick, Jensen, and other young people and their families use to reconstitute their lives in recovery and successful relaunch.

For now, Team Roca's therapy had created at least two positive outcomes:

1. Deidre and Lou recovered their hope—and with it the resilience needed to meet the needs of all family members.
2. The increased well-being of his parents and sister buoyed Nick. His relationship with his sister and father improved, encouraging him to more freely include his parents with his concerns. He now had faith that he would be heard, not lectured or rescued, which helped him tackle his own problems more directly. Several challenging obstacles still lay ahead, but the family had learned that they could face and solve the toughest problems together.

10

From Recovery to Relaunch

*And the day came when the risk to stay tight in a bud was
more painful than the risk it took to blossom.*

—ANAÏS NIN

W hen a student's struggles send him home, it's natural for parents
to worry whether the boomerang period will be a case of "up and out"
or "down and out." Despite a student's understandable but hopefully
temporary dependency, there's a very real danger of over-parenting
in this situation. Parents may sympathetically change their own behaviors to help the young adult avoid anxiety or alleviate stress. This
family accommodation style can result in a stack of "Get out of jail free"
cards that spare the young person such maturity tasks as household
chores, studies, or looking for a job, deepening their emotional and
financial dependence on parents.[1] Boomerang then becomes "failure to
launch."

If boomerang has become practically an affectionate term, why does
failure to launch (FTL) connote a lazy, entitled young bum with over-
indulgent parents? Boomerang suggests a temporary state, while FTL
portends the young adult who never develops the skills that are vital
for success in relaunch and life. The FTL phenomenon now appears to
be spreading across the industrialized world. In Italy, these self-isolating,
highly dependent adult children are known as *bamboccioni,* or "big
babies." In England they go by KIPPERS (Kids in Parents' Pockets
Eroding Retirement Savings) or NEETs (Not in Employment, Educa-

tion, or Training). More ominously, perhaps, is the Japanese word for these young hermits: *hikikomori,* a term that denotes pulling inward or being confined.[2]

Back in the United States, meanwhile, Millennial and Gen Z men are faring worse than women, with more at home, and for longer time periods. (This is especially true for non–college graduates.) Parents of these stalled adults spend at least eight hours a week caring for them, according to the Bureau of Labor Statistics.[3] Whereas "failure" suggests the end of a process, many young adults are not defeated by their setbacks but merely recovering from them. We therefore prefer "faltering launch," a term coined by psychologist Eli Lebowitz.[4,5]

The parents of these youth share common complaints: college dropout, work avoidance, need for financial support, computer/Internet addiction, and a day-for-night sleep inversion.[6]

Students undergoing a faltering launch not only must contend with whatever problem sidelined them—anything from a learning disability to executive functioning challenges, to mood or substance disorders—but they also endure the insidious comparisons to their successful peers or siblings. Perhaps most devastating is the comparison to the "theoretical" self. That is the self before an orbital malfunction, the self that "should be" caught up. Together, these challenges and blows to self-confidence and self-reliance create a higher hurdle in recovery.

In this chapter, we present a range of strategies and tactics designed to ignite and propel a sputtering takeoff. You'll learn recovery interventions to avoid the trap of overprotection and reduced family accommodations, to implement the "Ulysses contract" (a self-binding "deal" between parent and young adult), and discover how to mobilize youth marooned in their childhood bedrooms. You'll encounter some real-life scenarios in which recovery was a quick turnaround. Yet even when all hands are summoned on deck, a minority of young adults may need long or intensive outpatient mental health treatment before they can make the slow U-turn of an ocean liner, steaming in the wrong direction for months. Still others will require psychiatric hospitalization, typically triggered by a suicide attempt, a psychotic break, a life-threatening eating disorder, or the need for rapid treatment to stabilize mood. In each case, parental guidance and expectations must be flexible enough to take a temporary setback in stride, yet sturdy enough to weather the debilitating effects of a young adult's more complicated mental illness. We'll return to Nick and Jensen as their parents illustrate the zigzagging and resourceful pathways towards recovery and relaunch. But for a more commonly experienced floundering scenario, we begin with Wanda, whose parenting by accommodation has backfired.

The Trap of Protection

Wanda is a single mother worried that she has contributed too much to her only child's pre-collegiate academic success. Now, with her nineteen-year-old daughter, Liz, on the verge of dropping out of her small liberal arts college, Wanda has resolved to take preventive action. Liz had returned from her freshman year at college with a 2.5 GPA and two Incompletes; finishing each one would entail the production of a fifteen-page research paper. Wanda secretly dreaded that Liz might parlay the Incompletes into a permanent boomerang. Liz shows all the features of anxiety-driven procrastination, but is thankfully free of the severe symptoms of an anxiety disorder.

"I was the emotional ER this weekend," Wanda confides. "Now summer is here, and I have no idea what Liz is going to do." It's an annual quandary, faced by 75 percent of American families: How do you keep your adolescent constructively engaged, possibly even productively employed, during the long summer vacation?[7] Already the summer was four weeks old, and though Liz waitressed on weekends, she had shown no inclination to dive back into her coursework.

Prompting Liz to finish her schoolwork was an age-old behavioral rut for Wanda: "How are you coming on that paper? Don't wait 'til the last minute to study for that exam. You'll feel better if you get a little work done every night." In the run-up to college, Wanda had feared easing up, lest her daughter's well-documented procrastination netted lower grades.

Though that's a legitimate concern, it has tilted the balance from protection to dependency. Wanda may not recognize it quite yet, but she has enabled Liz's procrastination. Liz entered college unprepared for organizing and completing the long-range assignments typical of a liberal arts course load. Now, from the privacy of her bedroom—where she has reassured her mother she is working on her Incompletes—Liz spends hours each day chatting online with friends, binge-watching *Game of Thrones,* and posting to social media.

Exasperated by the lack of results, Wanda has changed tactics, moving from cajoling to hectoring to exploding. Liz's responses have run the gamut too, from dissolving in tears—"Can't you see how stressed out I am?"—to angrily erupting, "Leave me alone! Maybe I'm just not cut out for college!" This emotional range—from tearfully overwhelmed to heatedly defiant, verging on occasionally threatening—typifies the defense of and resistance to change of anxiety-driven procrastination. Finally, Wanda suggested that Liz talk to a tutor or a therapist. Liz countered testily, "I'm fine—*you're* the one who needs help! You're always pushing me!" Liz's closed-mindedness to needing help betrayed her immaturity.

All of which left Wanda to wonder: How long should she—how long should *any* parent, for that matter—allow a kid to drift?

The Trap of Family Accommodations

Troubled that neither indulgence nor prodding had budged Liz, Wanda sought counseling for herself. As she described her futile attempts to change her daughter's behavior, Wanda underscored her bind with a rhetorical question: "What am I supposed to do? Stay home from work to make sure she finishes her Incompletes?" Wanda also vented her exhaustion and resentment that Liz still relied on her to do the laundry, grocery shopping, household cleaning, and cooking, much as she had done for her as a child.

Dr. Hibbs recognized the classic signs of *family accommodation*—a mutually reinforcing style that entraps parent and faltering young adult in a tangled web of diminished expectations.[8]

There is no bulletproof prescription for parenting the young adult who drops out of college, or graduates but stalls out in his room playing video games, or returns home on mental health leave. Shifting the balance away from parental adaptation and toward increased responsibilities for the young adult, however, points the way to some promising treatment interventions.

In applying this model to families, we ask parents to focus on *self-change*. As parents gradually decrease family accommodations, there is often a commensurate uptick in the faltering student's capacity to function independently. It's a step-back/step-up dance.

"Let's make a plan to reduce the accommodations that are

reinforcing Liz's dependence on you," Dr. Hibbs suggested. "Why not 'strike while the iron is cold,' by calmly introducing an idea that lets Liz save face? Let Liz know you agree with her that you've been too involved with her coursework—and that you intend to back off. Tell her you trust her to make the decision that's right for her, whether that's finishing her Incompletes or supporting herself in her own apartment. As for that mountain of household responsibilities, how about avoiding a head-on approach, which Liz would predictably resist, in favor of letting some of them slide, and see what she picks up?

Acting on these suggestions, Wanda was able to exchange her former goal—"helping" Liz complete her coursework—for a new one: letting Liz struggle and possibly fail. Yes, Liz was willful, but not blind; she was almost certain to assume some of the responsibilities herself.

Over the course of the next few weeks, Wanda admitted to having been too helpful. "I thought my nudges and reminders in high school were helping you," she told her daughter. "I was wrong then, and I'm doing the same thing now. I promise I won't do it anymore."

Without declaring any change in domestic duties, Wanda decided to be more transparent about needing help around the house. When Liz asked, "What time's dinner?" Wanda replied, "I haven't prepared anything—rough day at work—but whatever you want to cook would be great."

Wanda stayed resolute in the face of what she knew would be her daughter's resistance to the implicit message to grow up. Sure enough, Liz went on an unannounced strike for a few days—barely speaking to her mother or doing any chores—but Wanda was prepared for the pushback: she simply maintained a pleasant demeanor while continuing to refrain from cooking meals, grocery shopping, or doing laundry.

Liz got the message. Her pique turned to acceptance of the new reality. Liz owned up to her childlike reliance on her mother and began helping out in the kitchen. Wanda showed her appreciation with specific thanks for each chore undertaken, which in turned helped cement her daughter's shift in behavior.

Other course corrections came from Liz alone. The absence of her mother's prompts made her feel more intrinsic pressure to complete her coursework, so Liz reinstated a calendar system she had used in high school. She set weekly deadlines to finish her Incompletes and made an intake appointment with her college's learning support office for the fall semester.

BETTER COPING

❌ Better coping can be thought of as another highly useful tool you have the opportunity to add to a young adult's "recovery skill set." But banish the notion that it automatically results from harnessing willpower. Instead, lasting change demands that an individual recognize—and own up to—problem behavior, then devise a concrete plan of action to change it. The change steps (which may seem only incremental at first) include:

- Recognition of the problematic coping behavior.
- Awareness of triggers that precede the behavior.
- Insight into a habit's emotional logic.
- Motivation and commitment to replace the default coping behavior with a healthier, more effective strategy.
- The skills to change.
- The resilience to recover from a relapse.

By stepping back from the water's edge, Wanda helped Liz cross the Rubicon into young adulthood. And as Liz felt the current begin to tug at her legs, she abandoned the avoidant and dependent behaviors before they could pull her under. Having learned to shoulder a more age-appropriate load of personal responsibilities, Liz was able to salvage her two Incompletes. She was back in college by the fall.

The Parent–Child Deal

Unconditional parental love is an unspoken bargain: in exchange for love, an education, and the fulfillment of his material needs, my child will return my love by meeting my age-appropriate expectations for maturity leading to independence. And whether a child is two years old or twenty, the trick for parents is to find incentives to encourage a child to invest in his own personal growth and future goals. But then along comes a mental illness to bankrupt the deal. Amid the dependencies, distractions, and destructive urges that often ensue, parents may need to employ extraordinary interventions to motivate and re-engage their faltering young adult.

These will test not just your patience but your creativity. And your courage: parents who fear pushing a fragile young adult will be understandably reluctant to saddle them with challenges that appear insurmountable. The danger, of course, is that family accommodations once deemed necessary to support a "sick child" can become entrenched, reinforcing a young adult's dependency—and thus his impairment. Variously resentful, anxious, or simply depleted, parents may sporadically agitate for change, only to lose their resolve upon meeting forceful resistance.

Yet parental determination and resourcefulness, as we're about to see, often underpin a young adult's recovery.

Irritability and Aggression as Symptoms of Depression

Lou and Deidre Roca—the parents of Nick, who had crashed his skateboard before a depressed crash-landing home—had exhausted their storehouse of strategies to spark their son's interest in life. His computer became his best friend, and video games—specifically MMORPGs, or massive multiplayer online role-playing games—his sole occupation. As he became more isolated, his mood darkened.

At first his parents saw Nick's online gaming as just the time sink of a depressed mood. They took comfort in the fact that he wasn't so isolated when playing games online with his high school friends. After all, he had played online games since middle school. Deidre and Lou had been concerned back then, but they found reassurance in the sounds of (virtual) laughter and loud camaraderie that filled the house as Nick and his friends joined forces in playing World of Warcraft (WoW) and other popular games. They also took comfort in the news of gaming's supposed benefits, such as problem-solving and social skills.[9]

Yet connecting online—whether via interactive computer games, social media, or texting—does nothing to alleviate a depressed mood. Loneliness and a lack of family or peer connection "is riskier to health and survival than cigarette smoking or obesity,"[10] reports developmental psychologist Susan Pinker. There's simply no substitute, it turns out, for face-to-face interaction with family and friends.

Later, Nick's irritable depression temporarily cost him his real-time friends, driving him deeper into isolation and social retreat. Now his gaming habit seemed to exacerbate those trends, occupying both his days and his nights. And though Nick tried not to take direct aim at family or friends, he felt out of control: "I would become enraged and couldn't get out of that mood for hours. When a driver cut me off, I'd scream and curse and totally lose it. I couldn't control my anger. I could get triggered by a stupid political argument on the Internet, or a wrong word choice; maybe someone looked at me funny. When fight-or-flight got set off, I'd get furious, then fume; the rest of the day would be ruined. Once it set in, I couldn't shake it."

With Lou's patience wearing thin, he repeatedly lectured his sullen son. Deidre, thinking he was unable to cope, simply felt sorry for Nick. Neither his father's punitiveness nor his mother's hand-wringing altered his behavior, though a gleam of light could be seen in his defensive preface to any mention of his gaming: "I know you hate it, but . . ."

"I don't hate your games," his mother responded. "I just worry you're using gaming to avoid doing something social in real time."

"But everyone else has a life," Nick fired back. "My high school friends are in college or have real jobs. I don't have a girlfriend. This is all I've got. I know I'm just a drag on everyone—a total waste of space." Nick's feelings of alienation and of being a burden to his family, so evident in those self-abnegating remarks, signaled a heightened suicide risk.[11] Regrettably, Deidre and Lou even argued about this. Deidre was worried that Nick might feel so much a burden to them that he might attempt suicide. Lou dismissed his son's remarks as a pity party. See the list on p. 241 for a few examples of assessing suicide risk.[12]

Each yes raises the level of risk, but there are many more factors than a parent can expect himself to know, or have the expertise to evaluate. Family social support could counter this risk, but Nick's parents were divided on what that support might mean.

Lou and Deidre's initial efforts to banish Nick's depression focused on the poor coping embodied in his day-for-night online play. Their brief effort backfired one frightening evening when Lou threatened to confiscate Nick's computer. The two got into a shouting match that culminated with Nick's giving his father a hard shove, then running out of the house.

NEVER DOWNPLAY A SUICIDE RISK

- Suicidal thoughts occur in about a third of depressed individuals. Parents should seek professional help to assess the level of risk.
- Personal and family history provide important clues: Have there been suicide attempts by the young person or significant others in his or her life?
- Does the young person have a detailed plan?
- Has the young person given away prized possessions?
- Does the young person lack the understanding and support of a significant other?
- Does the young person feel alone, or a burden to others?
- Does the young person display poor impulse control?

Hours later, Nick showed up distraught and apologetic, saying, "I'm a worthless disappointment. You'd be better off without me." Deidre tried to reassure her son; Lou barely glanced his way.

Conceding that neither Deidre's empathy nor Lou's tough love had worked, they entered treatment with Dr. Hibbs to develop more effective parenting skills. They would begin by modifying both Lou's authoritarian approach and Deidre's sympathetic protection.

Nick, too, sought treatment, individually with Dr. Rostain. Periodically, both therapists and family met to compare notes. Based on what they had learned over the course of a few months, the therapy team suggested a course of *behavioral activation*—a treatment for depression that focuses on scheduling incremental activity.[13]

That's where behavioral activation comes in, beginning with pleasurable pursuits and gradually introducing avoided ones. This "outside in" eight-session therapy leads to improvement in the participant's mood through promoting greater engagement in enjoyable and functional activities. Using values clarification, activity monitoring, and scheduling, the individual's mood, confidence, and competence are boosted.

But what activity would Nick choose to add? It had to be something he enjoyed doing, so he proposed skateboarding. His parents had

THREE GOLDEN RULES OF PARENTING

✖ Defeatism is an occupational hazard for parents when a young adult's mental illness is severe and accompanied by stubborn resistance to change. By heeding three golden rules of parenting, however, you can overcome your sense of helplessness—and set the one you love on the road to recovery:

- **Offer unconditional support.** Make it clear you will be there to support the person through his recovery, no matter what.
- **Suspend judgments.** Now is not the time to pass sentence on your young adult. Consider undertaking the therapeutic writing exercise in which a parent records happy memories of several moments when they most cherished their child—as a baby or toddler, perhaps, or just last week when you laughed together at that YouTube video. Reconnecting in this way to a young adult you may feel you've "lost" can redouble your commitment to "getting him back."
- **Set limits.** To decrease marital polarization, each parent must move toward the middle. Expectations that have been set too high by one parent may need to be dialed back, while the permissiveness of a second may need to be cinched up a notch. The goal is to closely align each partner's understanding of what it means to provide clear and compassionate parenting.

dissuaded Nick from skateboarding since his accident, but now they agreed that its social benefits outweighed their concerns. Soon Nick was logging less time in his room than at the skate park nearby. There he made a contact with a fellow skater that led to a part-time job at the local skate shop. Nick relished the camaraderie and often went skating with his coworkers after hours.

With this toehold in recovery, it was time to confront gaming again—this time with a powerfully collaborative intervention.

BEHAVIORAL ACTIVATION

✖ Decades ago, when psychologist Charles Ferster first proposed his "learned theory of depression," he simultaneously suggested something called *behavioral activation* as a way to treat it.[14] When an individual becomes depressed, Ferster theorized, they may seize on unproductive or repetitive activities as a way to avoid or mitigate negative thoughts or feelings. Invariably, passivity results. The adapted graphic image below by psychologist Rachel Leonard reflects how negative events lead to depressed response and then avoidance patterns.[15]

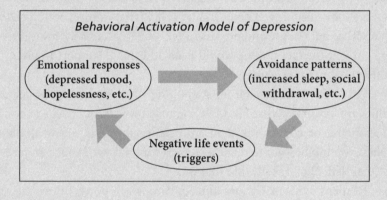

Behavioral Activation Model of Depression

Emotional responses (depressed mood, hopelessness, etc.) → Avoidance patterns (increased sleep, social withdrawal, etc.)

Negative life events (triggers)

The "Ulysses Contract"

At a family therapy session, Dr. Rostain intervened. "Nick, you're going to have to manage your gaming. It's a *nonchemical addiction*." Though unfamiliar to Deidre and Lou, the term refers to the wide range of substances or activities that can cause a dependency: not just chemical culprits such as drugs, nicotine, and alcohol, but also nonchemical malefactors such as shopping, gambling, pornography, junk food, and online gaming. Each one of these has a stimulant effect on the brain, unleashing a rush of the neurotransmitters norepinephrine, whose job it is to mobilize the mind and body for action, and dopamine, which is directly involved in activating the reward circuits.

That stimulant sequence may solve a short-term mood problem, but the brain quickly accommodates the upsurge, then craves more norepinephrine and dopamine—demanding, in effect, another "hit" to sustain its elevated mood. That's precisely what was happening in Nick's brain: gaming lit up his "reward switchboard," but constant stimulation disrupted his sleep and sapped his motivation to move forward in life.

Nick would eventually acknowledge that his gaming was a problem, but like every addict he first tried bargaining to keep his habit. "Okay, I'll limit my gaming to after-dinner hours," he reassured his parents. "Okay, I'll get off the computer at midnight."

This early bargaining phase is actually a positive development—the dawn of an addict's acknowledgment that he's out of control. (If you had control, after all, you wouldn't bargain—you'd change.) Bargaining represents the crumbling of denial. When Nick's bargaining period ended in nothing but relapse and promise after broken promise, he was forced to confront the fact that he would need additional support in order to resist the lure of his games.

With Nick now inhabiting something of a psychiatric no-man's-land—no longer denying his addiction to gaming but not yet successful at reducing or controlling it—Dr. Rostain suggested a new strategy: "Nick, you might want to make a Ulysses contract with your parents."

Puzzled, Nick asked what that was.

"Homer's story of Ulysses and the Sirens is a powerful narrative," Dr. Rostain explained, "because it crystallizes the idea that your ability to manage yourself is not uniform. Certain settings, situations, or temptations will simply swamp your better judgment. There's a part of you that knows yourself, but it can get overwhelmed by another part of you that's swept away in the moment.

"Like Ulysses, you need to find a way to resist your particular temptations. For Ulysses, it was the song of the Sirens, so hypnotically beautiful it caused sailors to steer their craft toward its source and shipwreck on the rocks. So Ulysses made a pact with his sailors: they would plug their ears with beeswax, then lash him to the mast. That way he could hear the Sirens' singing but resist their spell.

"Tools like the Ulysses contract allow young adults to envision 'temptation scenarios' they are likely to face in real life, picture the risks, then come up with resistance tactics ahead of time," explained Dr. Rostain.

Intrigued, Nick agreed to enter a Ulysses contract to support his goal of reining in his online gaming. He and his parents came up with—and signed—the following document:[16]

Nick's Ulysses Pact

> The goal of this contract is to support my recovery from depression. The intent is to provide an agreed consequence should I not adhere to measures of self-directed structure and organization in my work and self-care.
>
> I've done a really good job and made progress by taking meds, keeping therapy appointments, helping more around the house and getting a part-time job at the skate shop.
>
> My goals are: to balance online usage (particularly WoW) in order to increase my opportunities and preference for meeting people, and having a healthier lifestyle with daily exercise.
>
> During the week I commit to:
>
> 1. Work before play. No game-based computer activity until after dinner, ending by midnight. Start the day with activity, not passivity.
>
> 2. Maintain personal self-care. This includes a regular sleep routine: waking up on my own and getting to work on time.
>
> 3. Manage my earnings. Save up to move out.
>
> 4. Resist slips by talking to my doctors and parents.
>
> Consequences if relapse:
>
> First occurrence: My computer will have parental time controls.
>
> Second occurrence: I may ask to borrow a parent's computer to check email or Facebook while mine is held for 24 hours for each infraction. I may not install games on another computer.

Lou and Deidre had learned that a war of wills is a losing proposition—behaviorally speaking, a kid can hold his breath longer than any parent can—and that young adults are much likelier to abide by decisions when they themselves are the ones making the choices and fielding the consequences. Nothing about parenting a faltering young adult is certain, however, so they waited anxiously to see if the Ulysses pact would hold.

Nick made a good effort the first month, even though he lost his computer for a few days when he broke the deal. This time, however, there was no blowup. Another month elapsed, his parents on tenter-hooks the entire time, when one evening he casually announced, "Oh, I quit the games yesterday."

What had happened was this: After one particularly frustrating game, Nick had signed off in a "rage quit" for a week, complaining that his group was overrun with newbies and so the games were no longer as entertaining. The week's respite gave him the perspective necessary to reassess his online involvement. At week's end, he returned online, only to find his old games "trash . . . not challenging . . . not worth my money."

Lou and Deidre were greatly relieved that the Ulysses contract had worked—and hopeful it might come in handy in any future situations that required a formal mechanism for managing risk.

Nick was progressing from depressed college straggler to a young adult with direction. He described his recovery as a very gradual turn: "I became aware of the before/after difference only as my depression lifted," he recalled months later. "It wasn't like shaking a magic stick or taking a miracle pill and presto-shazam, you're all better. But I felt a gradual gain in confidence through pushing myself bit by bit out of my comfort zone. I began to show up for my life again."

Over time, Lou and Deidre accepted the absurdity of wanting a college degree for their son more than he wanted one for himself. With a new sense of purpose and hope, Nick thought he might want to run a skate shop one day. For now, however, he was content with his job and the new friends he was making. With additional work hours came more income, eventually enabling Nick to move into an apartment with a few roommates. Relaunch had occurred.

While Wanda prevented Liz's floundering launch with a reduction in family accommodations, Nick and his parents had a higher bar to clear. His moderate but persistent depression brewed in the mental cauldron of bad luck, bad timing, bad habits, and parental polariza-tion. As you've seen, it took patience, treatment, and some degree of courageous change on the part of parent and child alike.

Next, we pick up where we left off in Chapter 8. We conclude with the experiences that Dr. Hibbs narrates from Jensen's life-threatening crisis to recovery. Individually, together as a family, and under the care of Dr. Rostain, they overcame many obstacles that are corralled here as object lessons, hoping they will prove useful to others on this long-distance run.

"Sometimes I think we want this more than he does."

From Breakdown to Breakthrough

All journeys have secret destinations of which the traveler is unaware.

—MARTIN BUBER

Just as you can't run a marathon the day after heart surgery, recovery from a serious mental illness is counted in months, sometimes years. There are no mile markers on this run, no best personal time, no cheering crowd at the finish line, itself a mirage that only becomes a reality in hindsight.

With midnight approaching, Jensen and I are still in the basement of our home, swamped by Hurricane Irene. We're a two-person bucket brigade, scooping up water and using cardboard boxes as sponges. I open the last sturdy box that once held a large skillet, but quickly close the lid and return the carton to its shelf.

"What's in that?" Jensen quizzes.

"Oh, just some kitchen stuff I put away," I say. "We can't use the box."

Time collapses. It's two and a half years ago and I'm hiding Jensen's two pristine, ornamental knives, vestiges of his childhood interest in medieval weaponry. Hidden for him, safe from his depression. The knives are so well hidden, almost forgotten, that the shock of seeing them again creates a tightness in my chest and releases the physical memory of endless months of anxiety, exhaustion, and sadness. Just as I did then, I conceal my experience to protect my son.

Jensen accepts my vague explanation just before he shoos me out of the cellar. "Mom, go to bed," he says. "I'll take over." Now he's the solo human sump pump, toting five gallons of Irene with each run, sixty feet from the broken pump at the far corner of the basement to the toilet.

I greet him again at 5:30 the next morning, as he emerges shirtless, pants rolled up, sweating but smiling.

"Jensen, you're my hero," I say. "Have you been up all night?"

"No," he says, "but I couldn't sleep much because I was worried about the basement flooding."

"Me, too. I'm up now—you go back to bed."

I silently marvel that he's back. I have my thoughtful, helpful son back.

For Jensen, the return to good mental health and independence from major depression in his bipolar type II illness was a stop-and-start process that consumed roughly three years. Recovery's long time frame was due in part to the nature of bipolar illness, which is highly treatable, yet can be difficult to diagnose and medicate. Those years introduced five psychoactive medications, his wake-up/cope/go-to-sleep pharmacy. He added the self-medications of mood boosting cigarettes, energy drinks, and junk food. By the end of depression's grip, he was down to one medication and had cleaned up the litter of the acquired bad habits.

Recovery challenges young adults to re-create a routine for independent life and relaunch. Jensen weathered two college exits before shifting from a B.A. in creative writing to an associate's degree in applied science and technology, which in turn led to a full-time biomedical technology job. His successful relaunch included moving out, time with friends, and later, a loving partner.

Jensen's hard-won lessons of recovery apply to parent and child alike. They include: maintaining hope and empathy, supporting behavior change with better coping, an active treatment plan, and building self-acceptance. We begin with perhaps the most important of all—hope.

Lesson 1: Don't lose hope.

There is no tincture of time cure for a significant mental illness. There is treatment, best comprised of diagnosis, medication, talk therapy, and family support. There will be blind alleys you run down, consults you seek, medications tried and rejected, and accommodations made when needed and withdrawn to encourage growth. You will time-travel backwards with the regret of what you didn't know. Try not to linger there. Instead, be present, and know that your support will make a difference. While you may temporarily feel hopeless, it's crucial to prevent that from becoming a permanent state of helplessness. Your hope, your care, your advocacy are crucial to your child's recovery. During the early stages of your child's recovery, there may be little recognition or gratitude for your efforts. Don't take it personally. It's part of the illness.

One student who didn't want to have his parents visit college when he was depressed much later acknowledged this in a note:[17] "Thank you for teaching me that needing help is okay. And thank you for being there when I needed that help; and giving me space when I couldn't receive it."

The crisis that precipitated Jensen's return home mixed relief tinged with anger at his life and despair about himself. Longing for the pseudo-adult life of a college student, Jensen hated being at home the first spring and summer of his medical leave. He balked at our attempts to impose rules and resisted accepting even minimal responsibilities. He was alternately angry at his life and despairing about himself. He "coped" by sleeping his life away, mothballing constructive routines.

Jensen generously shared the following narrative of those early months when recovery seemed unimaginable.

"When I went home for spring break from my first college," Jensen recalled in a 2014 interview with Dr. Rostain and his psychiatry residents, "I realized how terrified I was of going back. My dad wanted me to finish the semester, but I was suicidal, so my mom put her foot down and I came home. To give you an idea of how anxious I was, when my mom's flight was late [to withdraw me from college and retrieve my belongings], I was convinced she had tricked me into going back alone.

"I was a shell of myself for a long time. For the next two years, I was pretty much a mess. I took up smoking cigarettes and was soon up to a pack and a half a day. Which was remarkable," he interjected humorously, "because until then my experimentation with drugs had been limited to prescription antidepressants."

"I understand this was a really rough time for you," Dr. Rostain interjected, "during which you had an ongoing visceral and graphic preoccupation with suicidal thoughts. Your mother has told me you would go on walks with her and talk about stepping in front of a car."

"Yeah," said Jensen, "I was never going to die by my own hand, but jump on the train tracks or step in front of a bus. I'd be at PATCO [regional rail] in New Jersey late at night and have to call my dad to come pick me up because I didn't trust myself not to jump."

During these frightening few months, Jensen never used suicide as a threat or an instrument of emotional blackmail; instead he was dispassionately describing an impulse that sometimes felt overwhelming to him. Early on, a parent or a friend accompanied him whenever he left the house.

Gradually, as his mood improved, Jensen began walking around the neighborhood unaccompanied, then the city. The goal was to protect him from harm while promoting his independent functioning. In this spirit, Craig and I encouraged him to participate in outside activities; he agreed to call on occasions when he felt in danger of harming himself. When he called, his dad drove to pick him up.

During this time, I consistently maintained that he would recover. I reassured him, time and again, "My mother recovered from her terrible depression. I know that you will get better too."

He regarded me sadly, as if he must tell a naïf that there is no Santa Claus, and replied, "I know you believe that."

He was hanging on to the hope and love that we, his parents, maintained.

Lesson 2: Blend empathy with structure.
Severe depression had robbed Jensen of his initiative and interests. His earlier aspirations—accrued through decades of encouragement,

the gratification of accomplishments, and the company of friends—no longer motivated him.

Five months into his medical leave, Jensen's severest depressive symptoms were beginning to show a slight improvement, though his medications were still being adjusted. Accordingly, we focused on the behavioral-activation strategy of adding pleasurable activities (see page 243). Jensen invited friends over for a weekly game of Dungeons & Dragons. He agreed to resume archery. He took daily walks. But when Craig or I mentioned adding some structure to his daily routine—a local class, a volunteer activity, a part-time job—we encountered a firestorm of resistance. Despite his pushback, we held firm.

For Jensen, like many college students recovering from a treatable but major mood disorder, the combination of anxiety, negative comparisons with peers, and ensuing social isolation create seemingly insurmountable obstacles to relaunch. Parents must therefore quell their apprehension in response to their child's depression, anxiety, panic, or avoidance, and be aware that too much protectiveness can lower the odds of full recovery. The goal is to foster independence by gradual exposure to increased demands, while simultaneously resisting the young adult's default to avoidance. Through slow, steady, and systematic exposure to perceived stress-inducing situations, individuals learn that the reality they encounter isn't as overwhelming as what they imagined it would be.

A Mother's Tough-Love Moment

Reducing the level of family accommodations for a faltering young adult with suicidal thinking is a treacherous and nerve-racking process. Because Jensen had loved school in the past, Craig and I were adamant that he sign up for two classes at the local community college. We were hoping they might reignite his interest.

The first morning of class arrived with a downpour—and an outpouring of anxiety. He was terrified to go. Though it was only a thirty-minute walk, I decided to drive him—in part to make sure he went, in part to relieve my fear he might step into traffic.

Along the way, Jensen tried bargaining with me. "Don't make me go. I'll get a job. I'll clean the house. I'll do something else. I don't think I'm cut out for college."

I tried reasoning. "Jensen, I know you're worried about going back into a classroom. But you didn't leave college for academic reasons—you did well the first semester and kept your scholarship. And you've enjoyed school before."

"No," he countered, "I was failing second semester."

I tried conciliation. "I know. You were so depressed that you weren't going to classes. But that's not on your transcript, because you withdrew for medical reasons."

"Please don't make me go to class," he implored.

I tried insistence. "Jensen, you need some *structure* in your days."

"I hate that word!" The failure of bargaining had brought on an anxiety attack. "Please don't make me go," he tearfully pleaded. "I'm scared to go back—it's too painful."

I observed myself from a distance: the very caricature of the "tough love" mother, implacable in the face of her child's pleas. Except that I had never been one of those parents. Instead, I had always been guided by psychological best practices: providing positive incentives, having the children take part in making choices (so they wouldn't reject parental suggestions out of hand), using logical negative consequences, never resorting to physical discipline, and being compassionate.

In fact, I saw now, I had been too understanding. Too protective. Too accommodating.

Determined to help Jensen break through this latest crisis of anxious dependency, I suddenly intuited that the mother he needed in this moment had to lend a firm hand, not a sympathetic ear.

But I knew my resolve could last only a few more blocks. As I stared through the insistent metronome of the windshield wipers at the slow-moving traffic ahead, disgorging students one by one at the entryway, I consciously slowed my cadence, even though my heart was racing. "Jensen, I need you to go into the classroom," I told him. "Take a clonazepam—it will help you calm down in about fifteen minutes. Get the medicine out of your backpack, and take it now."

Slowly, he took the pill out of his backpack and swallowed it. Then, I continued. "I think what you're experiencing is post-traumatic stress—this is the first time you've gone back into a college classroom. If you decide to drop the class later on, that's okay—but you'll never know that unless you go in there and sit down."

Mercifully, we finally arrived at the drop-off. But Jensen stayed glued to his seat. At barely half his size, I firmly pushed his left shoulder, telling him sternly to get out of the car. Dutifully he opened the car door, heaved himself out, and trudged up the steps among the swarm of students. I watched him pass through the door as I pulled away, my tough-love facade melting in a puddle of sadness, exhaustion, and worry.

Jensen walked home later that morning and rather cheerfully reported that he planned to drop the early-morning architectural history class. Philosophy, though, he would keep—he liked the professor. For Jensen and me on this day, at least, an emotional storm had ebbed into relief.

Lesson 3: Boredom can lead to purpose.

The View from Inside the Storm

My parents had me go back to community college. The next year I enrolled in my second four-year college. I was a commuter student for a year, then lived on campus. But I had no real interest in my classes. I could always persuade a friend to hang out or play Magic or Halo.

Not surprisingly, I began failing my classes—my meds were still all screwed up, and so was my sleep. By the end of that year I left college again. It didn't help that three different English teachers had told me I didn't need a college degree to become a creative writer, so I just got to thinking, "Fuck—why am I even here?" It felt like none of it—the classes, the whole college idea—really mattered. I didn't know what to do to make life worthwhile.
—Jensen

Jensen's second exit from college wasn't impulsive, but it certainly wasn't a masterpiece of careful planning. His risk-taking had abated and his self-control had improved, but a mild depression persisted, draining his conscientiousness, self-management, and initiative-taking. There followed a very worrisome interregnum of a few months when no one—neither Jensen, his parents, nor his therapy team—knew what to do next.

This period of Jensen's recovery was a time of self-imposed educational exile—characterized, at least at first, by boredom. An Internet-free family vacation, with its lack of distractions, evolved from "What am I going to do?" ennui to a powerful goad to creativity. Within two weeks, Jensen wrote a seventy-page modern fantasy novella, "The Rogue

Inquisitor." He also realized he wanted a pathway to a job—one with benefits and no possibility of being outsourced. This was significant progress.

After considering out-of-state college options to reduce his home dependency, we set up vocational testing, which revealed Jensen's high technical aptitude. Accepting that the dreaded specter of "structure" with a purpose was preferable to boredom, he completed a six-month internship at a computer-repair shop, then enrolled in a two-year program in biomedical technology at an urban community college.

Jensen was slowly *reinvesting himself* in his life again. One semester he proudly made the dean's list—then kept it up for all the following three semesters. Though still vulnerable to setbacks, he was learning to view obstacles as nutshells of necessary changes.

Lesson 4: Better coping is the goal.

Concurrent with Jensen's educational and vocational exploration was the search for better coping strategies. Good behavioral habits are often lost to a prolonged mood disorder, so rebuilding them is essential to recovery. The first step in this process is to list strategies and goals. Not only does this give the young person a target to aim at, it heightens their self-awareness. On Jensen's list, for example, were several dos— a good sleep routine, daily self-management—and a number of don'ts, among them avoidance, impulsivity, and negative self-talk.

Working with Dr. Ramsay, his CBT psychologist, and with his parents as home-team support, Jensen outlined and implemented a range of behavioral strategies designed to achieve a successful educational outcome and support a stable mood.

Lesson 5: Better living through chemistry.

At depression's nadir, five psychoactive medications were the neurochemical darts hurled at Jensen's suicidal thoughts, lethargy, anxiety, and sleep disturbance. Yet the first four medications in this "cocktail" missed the bull's-eye of symptom relief.

With the introduction of the fifth medication, a new class of mood stabilizer, I prayed for two things. One, that the lamotrigine would work, and two, that it wouldn't kill him—I still couldn't forget his traumatic withdrawal from venlafaxine, years before. I knew that lamotrigine can produce a lethal rash known as Stevens–Johnson syndrome. Typically, the rash appears very early in treatment and the

BEHAVIORAL STRATEGIES FOR BETTER MENTAL HEALTH

Tips to Improve Mood
- Take your medicine.
- Do your work; it will make you feel better about yourself.
- Don't avoid or procrastinate.
- When you question your judgment, use the two-person rule: Bounce your thinking off a parent and a trusted friend.
- Get at least thirty minutes of aerobic exercise every day.
- Adopt good sleep habits.

Tips for a Good Bedtime Routine
- The bedroom is for sleeping, not gaming.
- Go to bed at roughly the same time each day; be equally consistent about your wake-up routine.
- Stop computer use at least thirty minutes before bedtime. Leave all electronic devices outside the bedroom.
- If you wake up during the night, read a book to help you fall asleep again.

How to Cope When You Feel Really Distressed
- Most problems are temporary and can be solved.
- Talking things out usually helps.
- Write down the names of some people you can call for help.
- Commit to a plan to resist harmful actions when you're upset.
- Take steps to banish a lousy mood:
  - Listen to soothing music.
  - Take a walk.
  - Watch cartoons or a funny show.

Tips to Maintain Good Study Habits
- Challenge perfectionist thinking. Needing help is not the same thing as failing. Unless you've done something 10,000 times, you're still just practicing.

(continued)

- Don't start the day online.
- Start your work early in the day—it's a procrastination killer.
- Don't go online when you're studying.
- Assume everything will take twice as long as you think it will.
- Make use of support services at college.

medication is discontinued. Still, nothing had been typical about Jensen's treatment. Within two weeks of starting lamotrigine, Jensen developed a small red rash on his upper arm. Because it hadn't spread to his face, trunk, or other areas, Dr. Rostain expertly slowed the increase, but continued the medication. I held my breath. A month passed; the lamotrigine crept to a therapeutic dose. Finally, for the first time in a year, Jensen was no longer suicidal.

Jensen emailed:

Dear Dr. Rostain,

This is Jensen, and I wanted to let you know what is going on with me. While the suicidal ideation has vanished, my depression is still very prominent. I have trouble waking up, I am irritable, tired, and I don't get pleasure out of day-to-day life.

At a higher dose still, the depression began to lose its stranglehold. Not every young adult complies with taking medications, and some simply refuse to take them on the regular basis they require. Jensen went along with the plan, he later reported, because he didn't care enough to resist. Later on, as his depression lifted, he was too frightened to drop any medication, even one that was causing significant weight gain. He was more afraid of a relapse.

Lesson 6: Kicking bad habits.

While waiting for a medication regimen that worked, Jensen unfortunately developed a pack-and-a-half cigarette habit. U.S. adults with mood and anxiety disorders consume a staggering 40 percent of all cigarettes sold in the country.[18] One reason why: cigarettes deliver a powerful but deadly over-the-counter psychoactive agent, whose action is context dependent. Smoking can be used to relax, or it can be used as a stimulant.

Jensen, like most smokers, knew the habit was bad for his health, but that knowledge didn't automatically confer the commitment to stop consuming a highly addictive substance that temporarily makes you feel good.

Craig and I were distressed at Jensen's smoking, which was sabotaging his health. Yet in the self-change model we had decided to adopt, we understood and accepted the reality that Jensen would only be able to tackle health hazards when he was no longer depressed.

Sure enough, as his mood improved toward the second year of his recovery, Jensen resolved to quit smoking. We enthusiastically supported his effort, throwing nicotine gum and then regular chewing gum his way. With each passing day, week, and month that he didn't smoke, we congratulated him. There were no reproaches for relapses, only encouragement to identify and booby-trap his triggers.

One of those triggers was hunger.

One evening at a restaurant, waiting for the food to arrive, Jensen announced he was having a "nic fit" and left the table in an agitated rush. I waited a few minutes before following him outside, where I found him pacing back and forth and muttering irritably, "I never should've agreed to stop smoking—this is awful." Knowing better than to argue the benefits of his decision, I simply conceded how hard it is to quit. We walked along the road in silence until Jensen felt calmer, then returned to a cold dinner.

Seated at a table nearby was a family with a profoundly disabled child of about eight years old. The tableau gave me a powerful dose of perspective: for all the uncertainties attending Jensen's recovery, his condition was, after all, treatable.

Over the course of several months Jensen kicked his pack-and-a-half habit. He reinforced his resolve by watching frightening American Cancer Society anti-smoking clips. In one, an esophageal cancer patient with a tracheotomy spoke in a mechanical voice: "Don't smoke." He listened.

Jensen targeted junk food next. "Before the medicines worked," he reflected much later, "I was eating nothing but very flavorful foods—sweet, savory, salty, spicy—and I'd have to be stuffed before I would stop. And I was using Mountain Dew to regulate my energy levels, so I was drinking the stuff like water."

His weight gain, and the metabolic catalyst of the combination of his medications, had resulted in a prediabetic condition. Now, finally, Jensen agreed to gradually reduce the medications from five to three to one. He concurrently vowed to eat a healthier diet. This involved a simple shift in tactics—he changed his walking route to bypass the neighborhood 7-Eleven—and gained the serendipitous recruitment of a strategic partner in his father, who'd been looking for ways to improve his diet too. Jensen took up more vigorous exercise and, over the course of several months, returned to his normal weight and a healthy blood sugar level.

Lesson 7: Don't be afraid to hold your child accountable.

Early in his recovery, Jensen, characteristically too honest for his own good, developed the bad habit of lying to avoid our disapproval. Perhaps the most blatant fabrication involved a class he described in detail: the studies, the assignments, what he liked and didn't like about the professor, the time and day of the class. Then he came clean. After attending a few class meetings, he decided that the local bookstore held more interest. That's where he could be found during the hours that would account for the class and travel time. Skipping classes, a habit that took root during the spring semester leading up to medical leave, slipped easily into hiding the fact, then lying. Despite my nonjudgmental demeanor, he said he was afraid to tell me he skipped, then ashamed to tell me he lied, then too late for me to help. He showed remorse, threw dust on himself, *mea culpa*, and then repeated the pattern the next semester.

In order to break this habit, Jensen needed to understand his own emotional logic. We talked, he talked in therapy, he reflected. Jensen's light bulb came on: "I get into negative thinking and an almost phobic fear of going back to college classes [since his crisis and medical leave]. I'm scared to try and fail—so not trying and therefore not failing seems better at the time." This vicious cycle repeated itself even as its noose tightened. Then, reluctantly, but with obvious remorse, he would fess up.

Earlier in his recovery we were afraid to hold him accountable for his actions. This problem couldn't be solved when he felt suicidal, the ultimate expression of "I don't care." Then, Jensen spiraled down into self-loathing when his habit of avoidance, or skip-hide and lie, walloped him. He became mired in a self-defeating stance: *I'm awful and undeserving.* "You're wasting your money on me. I shouldn't even go to college." No parental scolding or display of disappointment was necessary. He'd already subjected himself to far worse.

Later, and less depressed, he seemed to care, but also seemed unable to muster the magical ingredients necessary for change.

Over time, as we watched Jensen weather the many harrowing stages of a deep depression, we had far more confidence in our son. He no longer required our protection but our prompting to take ownership of his behavior. Not holding a young adult accountable sends a stealth message that he's too fragile to handle real-world consequences. As I encourage other parents in similar straits to do at an appropriate time, we later asked Jensen to come up with a solution for another skipped class.

Craig said, "You owe it to us to repay a portion of that tuition money."

"I feel sick about that," Jensen replied. "I'm so sorry."

"That's a good sign," I said kindly. "Remembering how bad you feel now will help you resist the urge to lie again. What do you think you can do to feel better?"

The three of us sat quietly, the air thrumming with tension, while Jensen gathered his thoughts. "I feel just awful," Jensen lamented again. But soon he resolved. "I'll have to earn the money to pay for the class I skipped. I made a mistake, but now I can make it up."

"That will really help you," we offered.

Jensen incrementally paid off the debt with money he earned at university-run psychology experiments. Crucially, he had learned the psychic benefits of lightening one's emotional load, and would therefore be much likelier to hold himself accountable in the future.

This was real progress. Jensen was judging himself less harshly than he had in the past, and focusing on the behavioral traits he could change going forward. With accountability had come self-acceptance.

Lesson 8: Self-acceptance.

Self-acceptance is that breakthrough experience, sometimes a lifetime in the making, when we finally grasp and embrace our quirks, our limits, and our strengths. It supplies much-needed insulation from life's inevitable shocks, but it can be hard to achieve, whether you've struggled with perfectionism, or mental health related stigma, or both.

A sense of humor is an encouraging sign of self-acceptance, as Jensen made clear during a final appearance before Dr. Rostain's psychiatry residents. Several years had passed since his freshman meltdown, and Jensen had gained enough perspective on the experience to describe the end of an odyssey.

"How would you describe to others what we call neuro-atypical?" Dr. Rostain asked him.

"I don't typically use phrases like 'I'm aspie' or 'I have bipolar disorder,'" Jensen replied. "Instead, I tend to play it off as a joke. Here's the CliffsNotes version: 'I'm anxious and not good at reading you, so I often can't tell whether you're joking or not.' But I try not to announce it. I use the police sketch rather than the photograph. Anxiety explains a lot of behavior, and I think more and more people now understand that. While reading strangers is harder, with family and friends, I often know what they're feeling before they do."

Dr. Rostain: "Did the experience change your parents?"

"Well, my mother's a therapist, so that's in the win column," said Jensen. "She could be an avenging angel when things went wrong in middle school or high school. And my dad has come to recognize his own OCD-style issues and flaws. He was much less aware of how he came across when I was younger—he's become much more understanding. I mean, I wouldn't be here without them."

Jensen, too, has arrived at an understanding. Of all the things he may accomplish in his life, he reports, he'll never be prouder of anything more than beating his depression: "It's pretty great now, knowing what's wrong with my brain, and knowing how to cope with it. I'm not depressed; I'm finally on the right medication; I'm engaged; I have friends and a good job. I used to think I wasn't normal. Now I think I'm just shy of normal—but I've also come to see that no one's *completely* normal."

Recovery: Yours, Mine, Ours

A young adult's passage from mental illness to recovery and relaunch requires transformational change and profound self-acceptance on the part of both generations. For some, an extended time at home without real-world pressures is an effective strategy. For others, it creates a dependency trap. Each individual's pathway will be unique.

Yet certain features are common to every recovery. A faltering launch is a Hydra-headed mix of circumstances, biology, and self-management. We all need to be aware that the undertow of a heightened childlike reliance on parents creates obstacles to independence. Customarily age-appropriate expectations can seem overwhelming to someone in the throes of a serious mental health issue, precipitating an anxious cycle of avoidance and family accommodations. But when parents realize they can make changes that sympathetically acknowledge their young adult's struggle without capitulating to it, the vicious cycle breaks and recovery begins.

A parent's embrace of this challenge requires accepting what you can and cannot control while broadening your family's earlier definitions of success. Putting something in the win column, as Jensen might phrase it, no longer demands an exclusively linear trajectory. The future—yours, mine, ours—holds not a lesser life, but simply a different one than first imagined.

11

Recasting the Safety Net

It takes a village to raise a child.

—AFRICAN PROVERB

As you've no doubt gathered by now—perhaps from these pages, perhaps from your own personal experience—launching a young person into the world of higher education is a baton toss that requires some deft footwork. But it's not just you and your teen out there on the track: standing on the sidelines—and ready to step in at the first sign of a stumble or a fall—are the college administrators who double as race officials in your student's marathon. Working together, you can take steps to help guarantee that your student completes what can be a grueling course, in physically and emotionally sound condition.

Given the risks and challenges covered in prior chapters—and given the tendency of college students to magnify the academic demands placed upon them—it makes sense to educate yourself about the full array of a college's available supports as your young adult transitions into this new environment. Parents and students alike can benefit from having a clear road map of the college's resources (which you're paying for, after all)—resources that promote the psychological health and well-being of your child and, of course, intervene when problems arise.

This chapter peels back the lid on a typical administrator's thinking: what forces guide her in allocating a university's precious resources among its student health, mental health, and other support services?

This is hardly the dry arithmetic problem it may sound like, for colleges need parents and students to partner with them by understanding their institutional limits and utilizing the supports they are able to offer. In the pages that follow we'll also take a look at the current most widely accepted public-health-policy model for promoting wellness and resilience, preventing problems such as suicide and sexual assaults, and identifying students in distress and getting them help. We'll introduce you to important organizations that are taking the lead on improving the safety net, such as the Jed Foundation, the Association for University and College Counseling Center Directors, and the student advocacy group Active Minds.

College counseling centers have a newly central role to play in strengthening the student safety net; we'll examine the challenges they face in doing so. We'll also consider the role that students, parents, and other family members can play in two crucial areas: challenging negative stereotypes about mental health and encouraging students who need help to get it.

Some controversial legal and ethical issues drive the manner in which a modern college approaches a student who is experiencing difficulties. We'll pry those apart, as well as scrutinize the outsize role that campus security and student discipline may be called upon to play in the life of a troubled college student. Finally—and in the spirit of realism, not alarmism—we'll recommend how to prepare yourself and your young person to weather a crisis.

Let's start with a look at existing college safety nets and how they work.

Weaving Safety Nets for All

Over the past several decades, as their roles and functions have evolved, colleges and universities have created administrative divisions of student affairs with a mandate to oversee all aspects of student life other than curricular and academic advising. Depending on the institution's size and resources, student-affairs divisions may have responsibility for:

- residential life (both housing and supervision by resident advisors [RAs])

- student activities such as student government, athletic teams, student organizations, and Greek-letter institutions
- chaplaincy
- student support centers for minorities, women, and LGBTQ students
- student conduct (otherwise known as the disciplinary system)
- student center operations
- new-student orientation and parent/family programs
- student disability center
- health, mental health, and crisis intervention services
- other student support services such as career advising, and financial advising

In addition to supervising delivery of these services, the director of a student-affairs division—usually a vice provost or a dean—must coordinate with other administrators to ensure that their combined efforts advance the institution's basic mission and allocate resources to serve the needs of all students.

The strength of any college's safety net hinges on three factors:

1. The degree to which the institution accepts the notion of *in loco parentis*—literally, "in the place of a parent"—by guiding students through their college experience
2. The availability of institutional resources
3. The interpretation of federal and state laws when it comes to enforcing FERPA, the ADA, HIPAA, and Title IX, as well as statutes for handling safety threats (violence, suicide) and for dealing with alcohol or substance use on or near campus

The startling recent rise in campus sexual assaults, shootings, and other safety concerns has prompted a sea change in the way colleges go about identifying at-risk students, whether the peril in question is a grave public-health threat or the far less grievous prospect of an imminent class failure. The new order of the day is for colleges and universities not just to sponsor violence-prevention and crisis-response programs but to actively monitor their impact.

And as *The Stressed Years of Their Lives* has illustrated, the student safety net on college campuses nationwide is being fortified every day to catch much less visible—some would say much more insidious—falls.

With the dawning awareness that social isolation, alcohol and substance abuse, and mental illness are not just saboteurs of academic performance but instigators of dropout, there's a new sense of urgency about promoting the psychological health, well-being, and resilience of students. In practice, the aim is to reduce stigmas surrounding mental illness and developmental disabilities and to provide easy and immediate access to health and mental health services.

Though most parents and administrators agree that it's up to the institution to weave this safety net, the composition of its strands and the fineness of its mesh vary wildly from one campus to the next. It can be an eye-opener for parents to get a sense of how college administrators and support-services personnel approach the task of vouchsafing students' emotional and physical safety. By familiarizing yourself with the resources available at the school and in the surrounding community—and by *actively* collaborating as much as possible with "key helpers" such as academic advisers, RAs, and chaplains—you can help ensure that a student's nascent difficulty in coping with or succeeding at college gets addressed before it becomes a crisis or a tragedy.

But what about the obligations of those ultimate consumers of educational services, college students themselves? Just as parents do, institutions of higher learning have reasonable expectations of what students will bring to the table: they expect them to care for themselves both physically and mentally; to avoid taking unnecessary risks; to behave in accordance with codes of student conduct; to maintain passing grades; to contribute to campus life in a positive way; and to surface any difficulties they are having with a member of the faculty or staff.

If you get the sense your undergrad hasn't quite grasped every facet of this message, be aware that most colleges expect parents to encourage their students to adhere to these principles, and to notify the appropriate personnel of any serious concerns they have in a timely fashion. Does that sound like hectoring? Au contraire: both the school and the "parental units" are united in their concerns. Both parties are keenly interested in seeing the younger set learn, grow, mature, and gain skills in both cognitive and noncognitive domains; both parties hope students will make the most of what the campus has to offer; and both wish to avert harm at all costs.

Intriguingly, the difficulties created by over-parenting have tossed two related problems in administrators' laps. One is how the institution can evade the very same trap itself—that is, how can it avoid shouldering an overly large burden of responsibilities for the student? The other is how to craft a reasonable set of policies and practices that foster greater responsibility-taking by students. This is no small feat for a student population unpracticed at handling unexpected reverses.

How Does It All Connect?

How can administrators, professors, and campus staff work together to create a safety net that encourages students to care for themselves while guaranteeing that resources are allocated appropriately? The model used by many colleges draws heavily on the work of the Jed Foundation (JED), which has taken a leading role in promoting emotional health and curtailing campus suicides.

Donna and Phil Satow created the foundation following the 1998 suicide of their youngest son, Jed. For schools, students, parents, and countless others, JED has become a treasured source of information in the years since then. As shown in the model below, the foundation endorses a public-health approach to the challenge of suicide prevention.

JED Campus is a foundation offshoot designed to "guide schools through a collaborative process of program and policy development with customized support to build upon existing student mental health, substance abuse, and suicide-prevention efforts."[1] Any college or university can become a member of the JED Campus program by agreeing to participate in a self-assessment at the start and end of the four-year program. Participation includes a visit by a team of Jed Foundation experts to provide technical assistance.

JED Campus comprises several components, led by a module customized to help schools "anticipate and evaluate clinical and programming needs, examine how they deploy both personnel and financial resources to address challenges, and evaluate programming effectiveness. Policies, systems, and strategic planning demonstrate that the school takes these issues seriously and addresses them in a thoughtful, pragmatic, and formal way."[2]

Another key aspect of JED Campus addresses life skills—topics such as managing friendships and relationships, solving problems, making decisions, coping with stress, and finding life purpose and identity. Another factor, dubbed "connectedness," underscores the disproportionately large bearing that social relationships have on college success and mental health:

> *Research has shown that loneliness and isolation are significant risk factors for mental health problems or suicidal behavior. Therefore, supportive social relationships and feeling connected to campus, family, and friends can help lower risk. Efforts to facilitate social connectedness should go beyond simply encouraging students to get involved on campus. For example, some campuses have developed smaller "living and learning communities" where students have the option to live with other students who share their major or interests. Some campuses also have dedicated space in their student unions for students to meet and socialize together.*

"Only 10 percent of students ever get seen by a college counselor," notes Victor Schwartz, the foundation's medical director. "Way more of them have symptoms or illnesses, but aren't being seen—they need other kinds of support. All colleges must face up to this key question: What is the best way to *connect* students—to one another, to supportive social networks, and to student support services? We know for a fact that resiliency, life skills, and connectedness are the most important coping factors for preventing mental illness."

Dr. Schwartz applies the JED framework when evaluating any campus, trying to ascertain how well the school provides "an organized, integrated approach to student services that helps kids with fundamental life skills such as conflict resolution, communication, and stress management." The JED Campus assessment team then looks for ways in which the model might help foster a campus culture that is positive, inclusive, and respectful of diversity.

"We want to be sure all institutions of higher learning address all facets of campus mental health promotion," adds Dr. Schwartz. "We'd like them to demonstrate that they understand the importance of prevention, community outreach, stigma reduction, screening, rapid response, teamwork, student engagement, and communication with families."

To achieve these goals, however, many schools may need to fundamentally transform their campus culture. The Jed Foundation also recognizes that parents can play a critical role in advocating for positive changes in campus culture, and it directs parents to learn more about how their child's college handles mental health issues through prevention, outreach, and intervention.

Can a Task Force Change a Cultural Mindset?

Early in 2014, the University of Pennsylvania was shaken to its core by the suicides of two students within the span of just a few weeks. Coming on the heels of two other suicides the semester before, these highly publicized tragedies galvanized the university community: Was something wrong with Penn? Why had this spate of deaths occurred? To answer these tough questions and more, Penn President Amy Gutmann and Provost Vincent Price convened the Task Force on Student Psychological Health and Welfare.

The Task Force was authorized to "examine the challenges confronting students that can affect their psychological health and well-being; review and assess the efficacy of Penn resources for helping students manage psychological problems, stress, or situational crises; and make recommendations related to programs, policies, and practices designed to improve the quality and safety of student life." To this end, the working group invited student representatives—along with interested faculty, key professional staff, and experts in the field—to come up with a blueprint for addressing the mental health issues that obviously weighed so heavily on Penn students (and, by extension, all university students). In keeping with the JED Campus framework, the Task Force conducted an exhaustive inventory of the university's programs for enhancing student psychological health and welfare. Directors of student support services were interviewed. Public meetings were held with student leaders and campus group participants, and with interested faculty and staff. Data from annual student surveys of campus life were carefully reviewed. And emails from interested constituencies were read and analyzed.

One year to the day after the Task Force was convened, it issued these recommendations:[3]

1. Communicating at every level of the student experience about the importance of mental health and well-being to student success;
2. Making information about available resources and supports for student mental health and wellness across the University easily accessible;
3. Educating and training faculty, staff, students, parents, and families about fostering mental health and responding to students who need help;
4. Optimizing the resources devoted to Counseling and Psychological Services (CAPS) to meet the needs of students as efforts continue to engage the entire community in sustaining and improving the psychological health and well-being of Penn students.

Beyond these strategic goals, the report sharply criticized the prevailing culture at Penn, which prizes "destructive perfectionism" and fosters the so-called "Penn face"—an inauthentic veneer of projected happiness masking profound insecurity, unhappiness, and alienation. The report urged students to speak candidly with another person about their pain and suffering when it occurred; to reject the notion that being perfect is the sole road to being happy; to find alternative paths to success should the initial ones be untenable; and to overcome the stigma of getting help for stress, distress, and signs of mental illness or substance misuse.

Innovations endorsed by the Task Force included:

- expansion of CAPS staff and service hours to meet student needs
- introduction of a single phone number (the HELP line) to serve as an entry point for those seeking assistance with health or mental health challenges
- expansion of "gatekeeper training" (created at Penn and known as I CARE)

Since the report's release, progress has come on several fronts: CAPS service hours and locations have been expanded and wait times for appointments have been significantly reduced. New initiatives have been launched to promote wellness, including more classes in stress management and fitness and a web-based wellness app. Larger numbers of students, faculty, and staff have been trained under the I CARE program. Perhaps even more impressively, students have been staging public "speak out" sessions where they detail their own experiences with learning differences, developmental challenges, anxiety, depression, substance misuse, and trauma. And Penn has established a Division of Student Wellness Services, headed by a chief wellness officer, to integrate efforts across the university so as to promote student psychological health and well-being.

To be sure, even these vital first steps have not eliminated a culture of perfectionism and cutthroat competition at Penn and similar top-rated universities. It will take a lot more sustained effort on the part of administrators, faculty, students, and even parents to change these aspects of contemporary college life. Penn history professor Jonathan Zimmerman suggests that institutions of higher learning could reduce the sources of excessive stress that push many students over the edge, with three fundamental changes:[4] The three changes would admit qualified students by lottery; require open access to all extracurricular activities; and ban corporate recruiting on campuses. Some might protest that these measures take the competitive edge off. Yet, as we've seen, that edge cuts both ways.

Campus Counseling

The college safety net must support campus culture as it is, which has necessitated a rapid expansion of mental health services. In Chapter 1 and throughout the book, we've alerted you to this challenge and what may be involved in assessing your student's need for such services. Below, we summarize the purpose, role expansion, resources, and strain on this important fiber in the net.

Campus counseling centers were originally set up to offer short-term assistance to students struggling to adapt to school, handle social stress, or manage transient adjustment disorders. With the remarkable recent increase of mental health needs among college students, however, the role of these centers has expanded to include:

1. Educating students to promote health and prevent mental health problems
2. Training faculty members, staff ("gatekeepers"), and peer helpers
3. Coordinating with residential life staff, academic advisers, campus security, student disability services, student center directors, and athletic coaches

The need is high, and many counseling centers are under-resourced—"stretched to capacity," as a recent report in *The Chronicle of Higher Education* characterized their plight.[5]

Each year, the Association for University and College Counseling Center Directors (AUCCCD) surveys its members about every detail of providing counseling and mental health services to college students across the United States. The 2016 canvass gathered responses from 621 centers representing close to 7 million students, or one-third of total higher-education enrollment, and revealed the following:

- The vast majority of directors reported an ongoing, steady rise in the number of students arriving on campus already on psychiatric medication. The 27 percent already on psychiatric medication in 2016 was up from 20 percent in 2003, 17 percent in 2000, and just 9 percent in 1994.
- 25 percent of center clients reported suicidal ideation, up from 20 percent in 2014.
- 12 percent of center clients were admitted for psychiatric hospitalization.
- The vast majority of center directors reported a higher number of students with severe psychological problems. Distinct increases were seen in problems with anxiety, medication issues, clinical

depression, learning disabilities, campus sexual assault, problems stemming from earlier sexual abuse or self-injury, and crises requiring immediate response.

In response to the rising need for services, and in keeping with the framework suggested by the JED Campus initiative, counseling center directors have moved to expand their outreach in five ways:

1. Training faculty and others to respond helpfully to students in difficulty
2. Making appropriate referrals
3. Expanding external referral networks
4. Serving on interdisciplinary committees aimed at identifying troubled students much earlier
5. Offering web-based psychoeducational assistance

Other innovative approaches noted in the *Chronicle* distribute high-demand resources by:

1. Rationing counseling sessions (capping number or frequency)
2. Shifting from individual counseling to groups (especially short-term groups)
3. Walk-in sessions
4. "Stepped care" triage approaches that assign most students to online care (mostly self-help)
5. Assigning students with more severe, chronic, or intransigent cases to more intensive treatment, often through referrals to community providers

This off-campus referral option is not as straightforward as it seems. Dr. William Alexander, the former CAPS director at Penn, describes referrals as an inevitable mixed blessing: "In many communities, it's hard to find affordable and accessible resources for students, especially those who are uninsured or underinsured. We've hired a care coordinator to assist in this task, but not all counseling centers can afford such a service. It's not uncommon for students and families to be told to find services on their own."

A related thorny issue for college counseling centers is just how much psychiatric care, including medication management, they are able to afford: psychiatrists are more expensive than psychologists or social workers, and universities are reluctant to take on the burden of managing long-term mental health problems in their counseling centers. Unfortunately, the number of psychiatrists specializing in the care of college students may be thin on the ground in the surrounding community, further complicating the student's or family's search for one.

This is not to say that today's counseling center has abdicated its traditional—and honorable—mission: helping students get through tough times, work out important relationship issues, and cope with unexpected academic setbacks or changes of interest. Indeed, the recent trend toward cases of greater acuity and chronicity may have eclipsed the counseling center's actual broad usefulness in the eyes of many parents, who increasingly have come to view the center as a treatment venue for students with longstanding mental illnesses. This tension has been difficult

QUESTIONS TO RAISE WITH
STUDENT AFFAIRS PERSONNEL

- How does the school monitor student adjustment to college?
- What first-line support services are available to students who are having difficulty?
- What are the school's policies and practices regarding alcohol and illicit substance use?
- How does the school communicate with parents when concerns arise?
- How can parents convey their concerns to school personnel? Whom should they contact?
- What does the school do when students are not willing to go for help?
- What happens if a student needs additional help beyond what is offered by the school?
- Does the school participate in the JED Campus, Active Minds, or NAMI on Campus programs? What are the priorities for improvement that the school has selected to work on?

for directors of campus mental health centers to reconcile. Regrettably, says Dr. Alexander, parents "no longer see the counseling center as a place to go for handling stress or academic problems, but that's what it's there for—and that's why its services are underwritten by student fees."

What If Your Child Is Seeking Out Counseling at School?

Especially for parents who hadn't expected any problems of this nature to arise, it can be hard to adjust to the knowledge that their young person is using campus mental health services. But in view of the statistics—roughly 1 in 3 college students will face a mental health challenge that could benefit from treatment—Dr. Alexander believes that "parents must accept the likelihood of their young adult experiencing depression or indulging in substance misuse."

As explained in Chapter 4, for this very reason, we believe parents should discuss privacy concerns and laws with their teen *before* college entry. That includes discussing your wish to help in an emergency, and asking your teen to sign both an advance medical care directive and HIPAA waiver, so that you will be able to participate in their care. Assuming you put these safeguards in place, and your teen confides he is seeking counseling, what next?

First off, respect their privacy. This sends an important message to your young person that you trust his judgment about needing help, and that you are eager to be helpful in whatever way he thinks would be most helpful. You should look at the counseling center's website to learn more about their services, including the range of resources available, the orientation and training of center staff, and their policies regarding sharing information with parents or others, which are usually guided by HIPAA regulations. If you have specific questions, it might be helpful to call the counseling center and ask to speak to the director.

According to Dr. Alexander, parents have a role to play, and their inquiries should be welcomed: "It's great when parents call to find out what's going on," he says. "They've been doing this for years, and we should embrace it. The attitude of the counseling center staff should be 'family friendly'—that is, open to parents' input.

"Yet parents must also recognize that their student is at a new stage in life, and approach the counselor with that mindset. They might do well to say something like, 'Listen, I understand my student is an adult—I'm just trying to help him or her succeed in college. Can you help me figure out how to help him or her?' That makes a collaborative relationship more likely to emerge among therapist, student, and family."

If your young adult agrees to it, direct phone contact with the mental health provider can be very helpful in clarifying family medical and psychiatric history, information about the student's past mental health issues and current stressors, and insights into family dynamics that might be impacting on the current situation. An open channel of communication will make it easier for you to understand the goals and approaches to treatment that are being utilized, and it will enable your child's provider to turn to you if treatment barriers arise or if it appears that additional mental health resources will be required.[6]

And in case of a crisis, remember: parents are always free to share concerns and facts with a health provider and there are no privacy laws

---

QUESTIONS TO RAISE REGARDING CAMPUS COUNSELING SERVICES

- What types of services are offered by the counseling center?
- Where are the services located? What are their hours? How long is the wait list?
- Who staffs the counseling center? What is their usual case load?
- What is the involvement of parents in treatment planning and delivery of care?
- Do counselors/therapists/mental health providers ever communicate with parents?
- Are there limits to the services and/or number of sessions offered?
- What happens if a student needs more help?
- Who should parents contact if there are concerns about how the student is doing?
- What are the school's medical leave policies for mental health or substance use problems that are hindering academic performance or adjustment to school?

barring the doctor or therapist from receiving your input. Similarly, your input may be essential to effective treatment if your teen lacks insight into the severity of an emerging mental health problem. Students and parents are often unaware that mental health concerns are protected under the same antidiscrimination laws that cover physical or learning disabilities.[7]

Full Hearts, Active Minds

When Alison Malmon was a freshman at the University of Pennsylvania in 2000, her older brother, Brian, a student at Columbia University, committed suicide. For three years Brian had been suffering from schizoaffective disorder, a chronic mental illness, and it ultimately took his life.

Searching for a way to make sense of her reactions to the tragedy, Malmon realized that many students were dealing with mental health issues—in themselves, or in close family members or friends—but lacked a ready source of peer support. This led her to create a student organization, the first of its kind in the country, to combat the stigma of mental illness and to provide a safe place for students to talk openly with one another about the challenges of dealing with these issues.

After graduating in 2003, Malmon tabled her original scholastic ambition—to pursue graduate studies in psychology, her undergraduate major—in favor of moving to Washington, D.C., to found Active Minds. It is now the nation's largest mental health advocacy group for college students. With some 400 chapters comprising more than 12,000 active members, Active Minds provides the resources needed to conduct campus-based workshops, lectures, and awareness campaigns aimed at reducing the social stigma of mental illness. The group also spreads the word about the realities of living with a mental health issue and works to strengthen the campus safety net for students.

Malmon believes students must take leadership roles in creating "communities of concern" that support, encourage, and empathize with people whose issues threaten to marginalize or isolate them. Her biggest epiphany to date? Witnessing the passion and dedication of student leaders across the country: "I've been truly inspired by the openness, enthusiasm, and compassion of this generation," says Malmon. "They really want to change society in the direction of inclusiveness and democratic ideals. For them, mental health is the social justice issue of their time. They believe in ending stigma once and for all, and in showing people with mental health issues true solidarity. They understand the risks all young people face when they leave home and move to a new place, and they work hard to make people feel welcome and connected. They see the pain and suffering that depression, anxiety, and eating disorders inflict on young lives—and on those of their friends and families. And they understand the importance of advocating for more mental health resources, including suicide-prevention efforts, to reinforce the safety net for everyone."

The group's outreach efforts help to dismantle the walls of silence that often enshroud students in distress. In order for real change to occur, students with mental health challenges must feel welcomed on campus; they must receive an unequivocal message that they are respected members of the student community, and that the university administration genuinely cares about them. Making campuses less stigmatizing for students with mental disorders is one of the major goals of Active Minds and the Jed Foundation, and it is a cause that parents of vulnerable students should vigorously support.

And if their student confronts a hidebound stigma when dealing with a mental health issue, what can parents do? Malmon doesn't hesitate to answer the question: "*Listen* to the upsetting things your child is telling you." (If that's too hard to do, parents may need to find support for themselves.)

"Second, parents should be open and honest about their own mental health issues. This is so important for the student—it sends a message that there's nothing to be ashamed of. It builds trust and opens channels of communication.

"Third, support your student's decision to seek mental health care—and be willing to participate in it when needed."

Catch Them Before They Fall

Before your teen heads to college, parents should educate themselves about how the college handles a student in a developing or full-blown crisis. This means asking about the school's safety and security policies, crisis care coordination, and notification protocols. Educating yourself beforehand is absolutely critical to becoming an effective partner to the college in an emergency scenario. Below we discuss how these issues are addressed at the University of Pennsylvania, and what that means for parents in such a context.

Maureen Rush, vice president for public safety at the University of Pennsylvania, believes that keeping campuses safe requires all parties concerned to pool whatever information they glean in the course of their daily rounds. It's her job to make sure Penn's police officers and public-safety staff are trained and equipped to respond to every conceivable campus emergency, and that they know how to quickly communicate the essentials of a crisis to students, families, faculty, and staff.

When Rush served on the Task Force for Student Psychological Health and Welfare, she brought the perspective of someone who has had to respond to the report of a student threatening suicide. And more than once she has had to console a parent worried sick by a student's ominous silence of several days.

Penn's HELP Line—one of the most effective tools the university has developed to promote campus safety, especially where mental health issues are concerned—was Rush's idea. It provides a single point of contact for everyone to find help whenever it is needed. If a call comes into the line from a distressed student expressing thoughts of harming himself, for example, the call is instantly routed to a CAPS team member who can assess the crisis. If the threat is immediate, the operator keeps the student on the line while a police officer is dispatched to her location. Every member of the HELP Line's response team has been trained in communication techniques that provide "emotional first aid" to anyone experiencing a mental health emergency.

Rush describes what happens next: "When police arrive at the student's location, they try to talk to them in a calm and supportive way. If the student continues to express suicidal ideas or plans, they will do their best to persuade them to accept an escort to the ER. Most of the time, luckily, this strategy succeeds and the student accepts the help. The next step is to notify the Student Intervention Services [SIS] team—they work with students who are the most at-risk—and the student's RA. (SIS is often made aware of the emerging crisis before the police arrive, in which case they can be on hand to support the transfer to care.) Unless the student specifically agrees to it, parents are not routinely notified during these initial steps."

Parents frequently get angry on learning they were not told immediately, Rush concedes, but this part of the protocol is designed to protect the student's privacy. Rush says she understands their reaction—then quickly points out that parents need to inform themselves about the school's safety and security policies and, wherever possible, to cooperate with members of the crisis-response team.

"Campus security is a 24/7 service," says Rush. "We and the local hospitals are the point of contact for any emergency that arises in the middle of the night. Parents need to ask themselves, 'Who will be around if my kid needs someone at 3 A.M.?' (And they should be able to answer that question.) It's also a good idea for parents to know ahead of time what steps they should take in an emergency. I think collaboration and communication is always the best strategy."

Ideally a college will possess enough resources that it can perform a "warm handoff"—a transition conducted in person between two members of a health care team—from a campus or off-campus location to emergency medical care. A model for this continuity-of-care team would keep tabs on the student and help with either hospital admission or discharge, as well as communication with the family. If the student has already been seen in the counseling center, their therapist would be notified and included in the crisis-management process.

These linkages among a college's police force, student-support staffers, and mental health clinicians are crucial to making students with acute mental health issues and their families feel supported. Colleges are all over the map in terms of how many staffers they can marshal to handle a student in crisis, but as Rush observes from experience, "Forewarned is forearmed."

"Okay, People—Party's Over!"

Campus security serves three primary safety functions: quelling Animal House–style drunken revelries; responding to safety risks; and, when needed, alerting the medical response team. While each college or university has a code of student conduct, many students and parents treat this document as mere window dressing. Again, forewarned is forearmed—take time to discuss these policies with your teen at the start of each semester. Without this understanding, we've seen parents and students shocked to be kicked out of housing, put on suspension, and instructed to seek counseling.

QUESTIONS TO RAISE REGARDING CRISIS INTERVENTION SERVICES

- Is there a Crisis Response Team on the campus? If so, who is on it? If not, who are first responders when a crisis arises?
- How are crises handled?
  - Injury
  - Alcohol/substance use
  - Mental health
  - Safety violation
- Where are students taken if they are involved in a life-threatening situation?
- What are the school's policies regarding notifying parents when there is a crisis? Who is responsible for this communication?
- Who should parents contact if they learn of a crisis involving their student?

As with suicide risks, student privacy concerns dictate that parents will not be apprised immediately about this type of occurrence. Students whose alcohol poisoning lands them in a hospital bed have to face at least one strain of music: upon recovery, they may find themselves written up, talking to a dean or RA, or possibly even being remanded to a campus drug- or alcohol-intervention program.

Conflict by Peaceful Means

With robust college safety nets in place, there should be nothing but smooth cooperation ahead between school officials on one side and students and parents on the other.

Right?

Well, *theoretically,* maybe. But in reality, conflict situations arise even in the best of circumstances. The stickiest of these are disputes over dismissals and involuntary leaves of absence, mandatory mental health evaluations, "threat assessments" arrived at by committee vote, disciplinary issues, and "reasonable accommodations" for students with disabilities. Here again, it's important to familiarize yourself with the school's policy manual for its procedures for handling conflicts in these domains. The bulk of these policies explain the institutional response when students are falling short of academic standards, struggling to get along with others, or showing signs of being too ill or disabled to benefit from being in school. Parents and students need to be proactive about addressing serious problems as soon as they arise, because the longer you wait, the more likely it is that the school will take steps to resolve them.

Not all the power resides in the hands of the institution, however. For example, a school cannot arbitrarily remove a student with a troubling mental illness from a dormitory unless it can show that he represents a "direct threat" to the safety of himself or others. In several recent cases where universities attempted to impose mandatory leaves because a student was exhibiting suicidal intentions or behaviors, the schools were found to have violated the student's rights because they had failed to conduct a comprehensive evaluation of the student's condition.[8] Except in cases where a serious mental illness obviously mandates an immediate departure from campus, this due-process requirement protects students from coercive action.

Disciplinary proceedings may be triggered whenever a student's behavior appears to violate the school's code of conduct. On most college campuses, the office of student conduct carries out an impartial investigation of the misconduct claim. It's natural for parents to be alarmed when they learn their student is being investigated and to react in a protective fashion when their student is facing a disciplinary procedure.

It's equally vital that parents understand their role: to be simultaneously supportive of their young person and respectful of the school's obligation to carry out an inquiry and issue a ruling. Any parental attempts to intervene in these proceedings will usually be rebuffed as overreach.

As former Penn student conduct director Michele Goldfarb observes, it's not a productive approach:

> On a number of occasions over the years, parents have attempted—often aggressively—to intervene when they thought their child was "in trouble" with the university's disciplinary system.

> *Frequently these interventions occurred when a student was facing discipline and consequences for allegations of academic dishonesty. In response to these parental contacts, our approach was to emphasize the goals of the disciplinary process—that is to say, its educational, proactive, and restorative dimensions for the student. Our hope was to get the parents on board and have them understand we wanted their student to reflect deeply about how they ill-advisedly went down this road, what factors led them there, and—most important—what steps they could take to avoid ending up there again in the future.*

Another important arena for parents to take a similarly proactive and balanced approach pertains to academic accommodations. Reasonable accommodations, according to disability discrimination lawyer Karen Bower and JED's Dr. Schwartz, are "modifications to policies, procedures, and rules that are designed to provide students who have disabilities with an equal opportunity to meet academic and technical standards so that they remain and succeed in school. Schools must modify academic and other requirements as necessary to ensure that they do not discriminate or have the effect of discrimination on the basis of handicap. However, a school need not make changes that would fundamentally alter its operations, alter the essential nature of its program, waive essential academic and technical requirements or standards, or cause it an undue financial burden."[9] What this means in practice is that parents and students should discuss instructional modifications with the college long before your student arrives on campus, to be sure that they are appropriately implemented and that your student is taking advantage of them.

But even with accommodations in place, students with learning difficulties often find it difficult to meet the academic or technical standards of their institution of higher learning. It's therefore critical for students and parents to approach this challenge together, discussing whether tweaks in course load or living arrangements might make all the difference.

And when students exhaust every other option, the best answer may be to take a leave of absence, especially to address any mental health issues hindering learning. As a best practice, schools need to institute liberal voluntary-leave policies so that students can take a leave without major consequences, such as financial hardship, loss of health care coverage, or stringent reapplication requirements. Regrettably, in certain circumstances, colleges enforce mandatory or involuntary leave policies in ways that have raised ethical concerns and legal challenges. Parents should inform themselves about these rules and policies and discuss them with their teen before college begins.

Finally, students who take a leave need an exit-planning process that should include parents and student support services (i.e. advisers, deans, counselors). This planning needs to address the potential social stigma and loss of campus friends and social support associated with taking a leave. This approach minimizes the chances that a student who needs to take time off resists doing so until their mental health deteriorates to a crisis point. Conversations about preparing for a leave, about what will happen during the leave, and about how and when reentry to college can be expected should take place as the leave is being planned. Ideally, parents should be included as early as possible in the process in order to facilitate the transition out of school.

Facing the Future with Hope

Parents, take heart: colleges across the country are waking up to the needs of students with mental health issues, mindset barriers, and learning challenges. In contrast to polarizing societal trends, a "culture of acceptance" is taking root that will eventually embrace the diversity of the student body and welcome all students who are different. This flourishing culture dedicates itself to enhancing diversity, promoting inclusion, and offering real help to students who need it. A number of model programs are emerging that promise to amplify the effectiveness of mental health promotion, suicide prevention, and mental illness interventions.

Looking for a clear sign of the times? Just consider the widespread acceptance of the stress-reduction, resiliency, mindfulness, and well-being programs now being offered to students as routine components of their college experience. Another positive development: the explosion of online resources for students, parents, faculty, and staff keen to learn more about the mental health challenges of young adults.

If you'll permit us one final metaphor, a groundswell is sweeping that old "sink or swim" philosophy of college survival out to sea. Rising like a new tide in its place is our fresh understanding of the complex neurobiological changes occurring during adolescence and young adulthood, as well as our more nuanced sociocultural appreciation of the diverse needs and vulnerabilities of young people.

Best—and least stressful—of all, "parents as partners" is becoming a genuine mantra of higher education.

Appendix

INTERNET RESOURCES

Authors' website: thestressedyearsoftheirlives.com

Finding an Effective Provider
Firsthand Referrals

If your family has joined any of the many support groups for parents dealing with mental illness during your child's illness, seek firsthand referrals and experience from other parents.

You may also seek information from the local branch of the National Alliance on Mental Illness (NAMI), the largest grassroots mental health organization dedicated to helping those affected by mental illness. NAMI's local branches in a state or region often retain lists of providers recommended by those families who are members of NAMI, and make this available to all inquirers. NAMI also offers advice on a range of issues on mental health and legal issues via the NAMI HELPLINE: https://www.nami.org/Find-Support/NAMI-HelpLine/NAMI-HelpLine-Top-Ten-FAQs, Monday through Friday, and a Crisis Text Line 24/7 for families in crisis: https://www.crisistextline.org

Professional Organizations

The websites of the major professional organizations that deal with mental health issues provide information on the particular profession, provide assistance with finding a therapist, and provide information on mental health problems.

American Academy of Child and Adolescent Psychiatry, provider finder. https://www.aacap.org/AACAP/Families_and_Youth/Resources/CAP_Finder.aspx

American Association for Marriage and Family Therapy. http://www.aamft.org/iMIS15/AAMFT/

American Psychiatric Association. https://www.psychiatry.org

American Psychological Association. http://www.apa.org

National Association of Social Workers. https://www.socialworkers.org

SAMHSA's Behavioral Health Treatment Services Locator provides referrals to low cost and sliding scale mental health care, substance abuse, and dual diagnosis treatment. Phone 800-662-4357 to learn more about treatment and services.

For many more resources, see NAMI's list of top HELPLINE resources, http://www.nami.org/Find-Support/NAMI-HelpLine/Top-25-HelpLine-Resources

Resources for Mental Disorders

Anxiety and Depression Association of America. www.adaa.org/

National Institute of Mental Health. www.nimh.nih.gov/

National Institute on Alcohol Abuse and Alcoholism. www.niaaa.nih.gov/

National Institute on Drug Abuse. www.drugabuse.gov and www.nida.nih.gov

U.S. Department of Health & Human Services:

- Eating Disorders Treatment and Reviews: This site contains the largest database on reviews for treatment centers, from both consumers and professionals. http://www.edtreatmentreview.com
- Mentalhealth.gov home page: https://www.mentalhealth.gov/ For young people: https://www.mentalhealth.gov/talk/young-people/
- National Registry of Evidence-Based Programs and Practices (NREPP) is a searchable database of mental health and substance abuse interventions to help the public find programs and practices that may best meet their needs and learn how to implement them in their communities. All interventions in the registry have been independently assessed and rated for quality of research and readiness for dissemination. http://www.samhsa.gov/nrepp
- Office of Adolescent Health: http://www.hhs.gov/ash/oah/adolescent-health-topics/mental-health/
- The Substance Abuse and Mental Health Services Administration (SAMHSA) provides the Behavioral Health Treatment Services Locator, an online, map-based program visitors can use to find facilities in their vicinity. https://findtreatment.samhsa.gov/

Critical Resources and Helplines
Mental Health Support and Suicide Prevention

The American Foundation for Suicide Prevention provides referrals to support groups, mental health professionals, resources on loss, and suicide prevention information. Phone: 1-888-333-2377. https://afsp.org

NAMI Crisis Text Line. Text NAMI or START to 741–741. The Crisis Text Line will connect a family with a trained crisis counselor to receive free, 24/7 crisis support via text message. https://www.crisistextline.org

National Suicide Prevention Lifeline at 1-800-273-TALK and http://suicidepreventionlifeline.org. Calls made to this 24-hour hotline are routed to the caller's nearest crisis center.

YouMatter is a National Suicide Prevention Lifeline site for young adults, complete with a blog where visitors can share problems and receive support. http://www.youmatter.suicidepreventionlifeline.org

Other Crisis Helplines

Clay Center for Young Healthy Minds: Beyond Sexual Assault. https://www.mghclaycenter.org/parenting-concerns/teenagers/alis-story/

National Eating Disorders Association Helpline. 1-800-931-2237, free texting and chat. https://www.nationaleatingdisorders.org/help-support

National Sexual Assault Hotline. 1-800-656-HOPE, free instant messaging. https://www.rainn.org

Stomp Out Bullying—Chat Line: http://www.stompoutbullying.org/information-and-resources/helpchat-line/

The Trevor Project—Saving Young LGBTQ Lives. 1-866-488-7386 or text: 1-202-304-1200 https://www.thetrevorproject.org/#sm.0000hyxo9ax0nee5sdo1o4iorv55t

What's Your Grief? https://whatsyourgrief.com/

Campus Supports

Active Minds is an important voice for mental health advocacy at high schools and campuses nationwide. It develops and supports student-run mental health endeavors to create communities of support and reduce stigma. This nonprofit organization works to increase students' awareness of mental health issues, provide information and resources regarding mental health and mental illness, encourage students to seek help as soon as it is needed, and serves as a liaison between students and the mental health community. http://www.activeminds.org/about

Jed Foundation (JED) is a national nonprofit that exists to protect emotional health and prevent suicide for our nation's teens and young adults. JED partners with high schools and colleges to strengthen their mental health, substance abuse, and suicide prevention programs and systems. JED's mission is to equip teens and young adults with the skills and knowledge to help themselves and each other. JED encourages community awareness, understanding, and action for young adult mental health.

The Jed Foundation. https://www.jedfoundation.org/who-we-are/. Also on Facebook at https://www.facebook.com/JedFoundation/ and Instagram at https://www.instagram.com/jedfoundation

Questions to Ask Counseling Center Staff

Source: Kadison, R., and DiGeronimo, T.F. *College of the Overwhelmed: The Campus Mental Health Crisis and What to Do About It.* (San Francisco: Jossey-Bass, 2004), 206–207.

- What are the counseling resources? Is there a separate fee?
- Are there limits on the number of counseling sessions per student?
- Is there a psychiatrist available to prescribe medication if necessary?
- What is the staff-to-student ratio for counselors?
- How long is the waiting list in November and March?
- Does the school have an infirmary where students who need brief or extended care can stay when hospitalization isn't required?
- Who should a student call if there is an emergency in the dormitory?
- Can my child's medication be monitored. Is there a separate fee?
- In what circumstances would a student be referred to a health provider or hospital outside the college community?
- What local facilities does the college refer students to?
- What kinds of mental health services outside the college community will the school insurance cover?
- Have the faculty, staff, and residential staff been trained to identify and properly refer students struggling with mental health issues?
- How does a student contact the counseling service center to make an appointment?
- What are your guidelines on confidentiality? Under what circumstances would I be contacted?

What if a Youth Needs Hospitalization?

Specific questions to ask your doctor: "Questions to Ask Before Psychiatric Hospitalization of Your Child or Adolescent" is available at http://www.aacap.org/AACAP/Families_and_Youth/Facts_for_Families/FFF-Guide/11-Questions-To-Ask-Before-Psychiatric-Hospitalization-Of-Your-Child-Or-Adolescent-032.aspx

Recovery from Psychosis

First episode psychosis. https://www.nimh.nih.gov/news/science-news/2016/team-based-treatment-for-first-episode-psychosis-found-to-be-high-value.shtml

National Institute of Mental Health. https://www.nimh.nih.gov/index
.shtml

Recovery After Initial Schizophrenia Episode (RAISE). https://www
.nimh.nih.gov/health/topics/schizophrenia/raise/index.shtml

APPS
Android and iPhone Apps for Mood Disorders

Apps recommended by the APA (2014): PTSD Coach. https://itunes.apple
.com/us/app/ptsd-coach/id430646302?mt=8

Bipolar disorder: Healthline.com lists the best iPhone and Android apps
for bipolar disorder, including apps to monitor sleep, medication, and mood
over time, and apps to explain the diagnosis. For the complete list, see "The
Best Bipolar Disorder Apps of 2017" at http://www.healthline.com/health
/bipolar-disorder/top-iphone-android-apps#1

Breathe 2 Relax: Breathing techniques to relieve stress. https://itunes.apple
.com/us/app/breathe2relax/id425720246

CBT*ABC way: Cognitive-behavioral therapy apps in Spanish and English,
iTunes, $6.99. TikalBayTek. http://www.tikalbaytek.com

Headspace: A meditation app that helps people begin and establish a meditation practice. https://www.headspace.com

PRIME (Personalized Real-time Intervention for Motivation Enhance-
ment): A Facebook-like mobile app that connects members to a circle of peers
and professional clinicians who can assist as needed. Its goal is to inspire
young people (ages 14–30) who have recently been diagnosed with schizophrenia to increase social connection to reduce depression and symptoms.
May be adapted to others at risk for other mental disorders. https://itunes.apple
.com/us/app/ucsf-prime/id1031402495?mt=8

ReliefLink: An app developed by Emory University for suicide prevention
and more general support for improving mental health. iTunes, free. https://
itunes.apple.com/us/app/relieflink/id721474553?mt=8

Step Away: Mobile intervention for alcohol addiction. iTunes, $4.99.
http://stepaway.biz

What's My M3: This app offers a free 3-minute checklist and assessment for several mental health problems. Better monitoring of mood and mental health can be an important tool. https://whatsmym3.com

Online Peer Support & Therapy

7 Cups. https://www.7cups.com
Instant support through text and online with trained peer listeners, licensed therapists, and peer support for a variety of problems. Demographic is primarily Millennials.

Mindstrong Health. https://mindstronghealth.com
Former NIMH director Dr. Tom Insel is involved in smartphone-based behavioral healthcare to intervene preventatively in the treatment of a range of behavioral health disorders.

Parenting Resources, Preparing for and Supporting the College Transition

Active Minds, The Issue: Student Mental Health. http://www.activeminds.org/issues-a-resources/the-issue

The Clay Center for Young Healthy Minds is a website that educates families about mental health issues across the lifespan. Includes tips and videos on parenting concerns when teens leave home. http://www.mghclaycenter.org/parenting-concerns/teenagers/when-kids-leave-home

InfoAboutKids is an ongoing collaboration of the Consortium for Science-Based Information on Children, Youth and Families. The site covers a wide array of developmental issues, from the purely physiological to brain development and emotional and mental health issues. The site also offers a compilation of other resources for parents, caregivers, and professionals. http://infoaboutkids.org/about-us

The Jed Foundation provides Transition Year, an online education center with comprehensive information to help parents and students review choices for college, transition, and emotional issues, and for those students transitioning with diagnosed mental health conditions. The guide was designed with input from authorities on college mental health. Transition Year, Parent Edition. http://transitionyear.org/parent/intro.php

SADD: Students Against Destructive Decisions (formerly Students Against Drunk Driving). A leading organization committed to saving students' lives by focusing on substance abuse, depression, bullying, body image, and more. https://www.sadd.org

SpeakUp!: A wealth of information and listings ranging from stress and substance abuse to relationships and mental health in the transition years. SpeakUp! facilitates conversations between youth, educators, and parents on student-selected behavioral health topics. https://speakup.org

Evidence-Based Education on Mental Health and Interventions

Mental Health First Aid (http://www.mentalhealthfirstaid.org/cs/about /research/) is a peer-reviewed, international, and evidence-based program; an 8-hour course that teaches lay people how to identify, understand, and respond to signs of mental illnesses and substance use disorders. A search tool helps people locate courses near their location. https://www.mentalhealth firstaid.org/cs/take-a-course/find-a-course/

Mental Health First Aid USA also is listed on the Substance Abuse and Mental Health Services Administration's National Registry of Evidence-based Programs and Practices (NREPP). http://nrepp.samhsa.gov/02_about .aspx.

The NREPP is an important resource as well, listing over 70 evidence-based programs with reliable information on mental health and substance abuse interventions. New program profiles are continually being added, so the registry is always growing. See https://nrepp.samhsa.gov/landing.aspx to access the latest updates.

Understanding and Overcoming Stigma
Research

The National Academies of Science, Engineering, and Medicine in 2016 delivered to the Substance Abuse and Mental Health Services Administration a study outlining six recommendations urging them and other government agencies to focus more on reducing stigma. The report found that currently, U.S. public and private anti-stigma efforts are "largely uncoordinated and poorly evaluated."

The key recommendations are:

- The federal Department of Health & Human Services should take the lead on stigma-reduction initiatives.
- Research should explore how to design and test communications programs and large-scale surveys tracking people's beliefs.
- Leaders should gather input on initiatives from people who have experienced mental illness.

- Efforts should include grassroots work since research shows personal contact is more effective than education alone.
- Efforts should also include peer support services since evidence suggests that people who use these services are more likely to access other kinds of mental health care.

National Academies of Sciences, Engineering, and Medicine. 2016. *Ending Discrimination Against People with Mental and Substance Abuse Disorders: The Evidence for Stigma Change.* Washington, DC: The National Academies Press. https://doi.org/10.17226/23442

- http://www.nap.edu/catalog/23442/ending-discrimination-against -people-with-mental-and-substance-use-disorders

Resources for Families and Students for Fighting Stigma

Active Minds, National Day Without Stigma: Many universities have a chapter on their campus, and if not, students can apply to start one. Through campus-wide events and national programs, Active Minds aims to remove the stigma that surrounds mental health issues, and create a comfortable environment for an open conversation about mental health issues on campuses nationwide. Their mission is to empower students to speak openly about mental health in order to educate others and encourage help-seeking. http://activeminds.org /our-programming/awareness-campaigns/national-day-without-stigma

Autism Speaks. Reducing stigma through global awareness and advocacy to increase research and access to care and support for affected individuals and their families. https://www.autismspeaks.org

The Jed Foundation, About Us. https://www.jedfoundation.org/who-we -are/. Also on Facebook at https://www.facebook.com/JedFoundation/ and Instagram at https://www.instagram.com/jedfoundation/

The NAMI StigmaFree campaign urges individuals, companies, organizations, and campuses to create an American culture in which the stigma that is often associated with mental health conditions is ended and replaced by hope and support for recovery. See more at: https://www.nami.org/Press -Media/Press-Releases/2015/National-Alliance-on-Mental-Illness-Launches -Stigm

Privacy Laws Affecting Information Privacy and Medical Care of Teens, College Students, and Young Adults

There are two critical laws affecting the privacy of medical and education records: the Health Insurance Portability and Accountability Act (HIPAA)

Privacy Rule related to the use and disclosure of information, and the Family Educational Rights and Privacy Act (FERPA).

HIPAA is intended to protect the privacy of a medical patient's identifiable health records, including electronic health care transactions. It gives patients the right to inspect their own medical records and request amendments to medical records. This law also restricts release of confidential communication with the patient or the patient's medical records. To be in compliance with HIPAA, students' health information also must be protected.

FERPA, on the other hand, provides protection of students' educational records and is specific to education institutions that receive federal funds. FERPA also applies when a student studies abroad. Simply being his or her parent won't allow you to sign tax returns or leases for the coming year on his behalf.

Clearly worded summaries of how HIPAA and FERPA affect students and families can be found on the website of the American School Counselor Association (ASCA), https://www.schoolcounselor.org/magazine/blogs/july-august-2010/hipaa-or-ferpa-or-not, and the World Privacy Forum. https://www.world privacyforum.org/2015/02/student-privacy-101-health-privacy-in-schools-what-law-applies/

Given that schools may have sensitive health information—or request that information from students and parents—it is important for families to understand which law covers health record privacy for school records. The answer is often complex, because both laws can apply to this information. In some cases, no privacy law applies to the health records. Basically:

- HIPAA, the Health Information Portability and Accountability Act, applies to some school health records some of the time. More generally, it prohibits sharing of medical information subject to patient consent outside the school records context once a student comes of legal age.
- FERPA, the Family Educational Rights and Privacy Act, applies to most school health records most of the time.
- No privacy law applies to some private school health records some of the time.

The Association of State and Territorial Health Officials (ASTHO) provides more detailed information about the interaction of these laws, and a chart providing a snapshot of the rights, duties, and limitations imposed by FERPA and HIPAA. See the ASTHO Public Health Access to Student Health Data Issue Brief [http://www.astho.org/Programs/Preparedness/Public-Health-Emergency-Law/Public-Health-and-Schools-Toolkit/Public-Health-Access-to-Student-Health-Data/] and the text of the federal laws and regulations for more detailed information.

ASTHO is the national nonprofit organization representing public health agencies in the United States, the U.S. Territories, and the District of Columbia, and the over 100,000 public health professionals these agencies employ.

Advance Directives for a Young Adult

The eighteenth birthday has many implications, but one of the most important—and most often overlooked—is that parents no longer have any inherent legal authority over the student. While medical professionals have discretion to share information without the patient's permission, some who are risk averse will not. So, in an emergency, telling medical professionals that you are someone's parent will not allow you to make medical decisions for them. And if a student goes abroad, simply being his parent won't allow you to sign tax returns or leases for the coming year on his behalf.

There is a simple solution. *Before* age 18, parents should help every young adult either download and sign free forms, or consult with an attorney and have three important documents drafted for him or her: a durable power of attorney, a health care proxy, and a HIPAA authorization. These documents allow a young adult to decide who should have the power to make which decisions for him if needed, and will provide both the student and the parents with a great deal of peace of mind.

To record his medical preferences, your teen will need to complete written documents called advance directive forms. There are two types of advance directives, and it's important to have both:

- A living will spells out what types of medical treatment a person wants at the end of life if he's unable to speak for himself. It tells medical professionals a person's wishes regarding specific decisions, such as whether to accept mechanical ventilation.
- A health care power of attorney appoints someone to make health care decisions—and not just decisions regarding life-prolonging treatments—on one's behalf. The appointed health care agent (also called an attorney-in-fact or proxy) becomes the patient's spokesman and advocate on a range of medical treatments the patient sets out in the document. Of course, the health care agent makes decisions only when the patient can't communicate on his own. This type of document is sometimes referred to as a health care proxy, appointment of a health care agent, or durable power of attorney for health care. It is different from a regular durable power of attorney, which typically covers only financial matters.

If your child has a history of a mental disorder, you may also want to ask about a psychiatric advance directive (PAD). This legal document permits a second party to act on your child's behalf if he becomes acutely ill and unable to make decisions about treatment. The PAD is written by your loved one when they are currently "competent." It details the individual's preferences for treatment should they become unable to make such decisions due to their mental health condition.

For more information on advance planning, see NAMI's website on crisis planning at http://www.nami.org/Find-Support/Family-Members-and -Caregivers/Being-Prepared-for-a-Crisis#sthash.94I5iwsr.dpuf and the AARP fact page, How to Prepare With Your Adult Child for Emergencies, at http:// www.aarp.org/home-family/friends-family/info-2016/how-to-prepare-with -your-adult-child-for-emergencies-mq.html.

Notes

1. Fault Lines in the World of Today's Youth

1. The book's true-to-life vignettes are composites, with the exception of Jensen's story. All names are pseudonyms, and all identifying information has been changed. This format protects the confidential nature of the individuals, while illustrating a variety of experiences, problems, and solutions.

2. Rampell, Catherine. "It Takes a B.A. to Find a Job as a File Clerk." *New York Times.* http://www.nytimes.com/2013/02/20/business/college-degree-required-by-increasing-number-of-companies.html.

3. Stress in America survey. American Psychological Association. February 2014. http://www.apapracticecentral.org/update/2014/02-13/teen-stress.aspx http://www.pewresearch.org/fact-tank/2016/06/08/increase-in-living-with-parents-driven-by-those-ages-25-34-non-college-grads.

4. Ibid.

5. Ibid.

6. The National Sleep Foundation recommends adolescents get eight to ten hours of sleep. https://sleepfoundation.org/media-center/press-release/national-sleep-foundation-recommends-new-sleep-times.

7. The generations by approximate (and overlapping) birth years are: Millennials (or Gen Y), 1980–2000 (Harvard Center); Generation Z (or iGen), mid-1990s–2010 (Sarah Brown, *The Chronicle of Higher Education*).

8. Jackson, D. "Just to Sit and Listen." *Chronicle of Higher Education,* January 26, 2018.

9. Wilson, R. "An Epidemic of Anguish." *Chronicle of Higher Education,* August 31, 2015.

10. Liu, C. H., Stevens, C., Wong, S. H. M., Yasui, M., and Chen, J. A. "The Prevalence and Predictors of Mental Health Diagnoses and Suicide Among U.S. College Students: Implications for Addressing Disparities in Service Use." *Depression and Anxiety* (2018): 1–10. https://doi.org/10.1002/da.22830.

11. Healthy Campus Objectives. ACHA.org. AI-1.3, AI-1.4. 2014. https://www.acha.org/HealthyCampus/Objectives/Student_Objectives/Healthy

Campus/Student_Objectives.aspx?hkey=a9f191de-243b-41c6-b913-c012 961ecab9.

12. Undergraduate student reference group. Executive summary. Fall 2017. http://www.acha-ncha.org/docs/NCHAII_FALL_2017_REFERENCE _GROUP_EXECUTIVE_SUMMARY_UNDERGRADS_ONLY.pdf.

13. Copeland, W. "Mental Health in Young Adulthood." Presentation at IOM/NRC Workshop on Improving the Health, Safety and Well-being of Young Adults, Washington, D.C., 2013. https://www.ncbi.nlm.nih.gov /pubmed/24872982.

14. Davis, M. "Young Adult Mental Health." Presentation at IOM/NRC Workshop on Improving the Health, Safety, and Well-Being of Young Adults, 2013. Washington, D.C., 2013. Accessed September 27, 2014. https://www.ncbi.nlm.nih.gov/pubmed/13677456.

15. Active Minds. "The Issue: Student Mental Health." http://www.activeminds .org/issues-a-resources/the-issue. Accessed November 16, 2016.

16. Pedrelli, P., Nyer, M., Yeung, A., Zulauf, C., and Wilens, T. "College Students: Mental Health Problems and Treatment Considerations." http:// www.ncbi.nlm.nih.gov/pmc/articles/PMC4527955/.

17. Center for Collegiate Mental Health. 2015. Penn State Reports.

18. Heller, Nathan. "Letter from Oberlin: The Big Uneasy: What's Roiling the Liberal-Arts Campus?" New Yorker, May 30, 2016, 57.

19. Field, Kelly. "Mental Health: Stretched to Capacity." Chronicle of Higher Education LXII, no. 22 (2016): A9.

20. Copeland, W., Shanahan, L., Costello, E. J., and Angold, A. "Cumulative Prevalence of Psychiatric Disorders by Young Adulthood: A Prospective Cohort Analysis from the Great Smoky Mountains Study." Journal of the American Academy of Child and Adolescent Psychiatry 50, no. 3 (2011): 252–261. https://www.ncbi.nlm.nih.gov/pubmed/21334565.

21. Center for Behavioral Health Statistics and Quality. The NSDUH Report: Major Depressive Episode among Full-Time College Students and Other Young Adults, Aged 18 to 22. Rockville, MD: Substance Abuse and Mental Health Services Administration, 2012.

22. National Alliance on Mental Illness. "College Students Speak: Survey Report on Mental Health." 2012. Retrieved from http://www.nami.org /collegereport.

23. Bangasser, D. A., et al. "Sex Differences in Corticotropin-Releasing Factor Receptor Signaling and Trafficking: Potential Role in Female Vulnerability to Stress-Related Psychopathology." Molecular Psychiatry 15, no. 9 (2010): 877, 896–904. https://www.sciencenews.org/article/his -stress-not-her-stress. https://www.sciencenews.org/article/his-stress-not -her-stress.

24. Bangasser, D., and Valentino, R. J. "Sex Differences in Stress-Related Psychiatric Disorders: Neurobiological Perspectives." 2014. https://www.ncbi.nlm.nih.gov/pmc/articles/PMC4087049/.

25. Mintz, Steven. *Huck's Raft: A History of American Childhood.* Cambridge, MA: Harvard University Press, 2004, 6.

26. Ibid., ix.

27. Ibid.

28. Ibid.

29. http://www.famousquotegallery.com/u-s-president-quotes.

30. https://www.ourdocuments.gov/doc.php. June 22, 1944. P.L. 78-346,58 Stat.284.

31. "A Nation at Risk: The Imperative for Education Reform." http://www2.ed.gov/pubs/NatAtRisk/index.html.

32. Mintz, *Huck's Raft, 383.*

33. "Film Team." Race to Nowhere. http://www.racetonowhere.com/film-team.

34. Bruni, Frank. "Rethinking College Admissions." *New York Times,* January 20, 2016, A25. http://www.nytimes.com/2016/01/20/opinion/rethinking-college-admissions.html.

35. Abeles, Vicki. *Beyond Measure: Rescuing an Overscheduled, Overtested, Underestimated Generation.* New York: Simon & Schuster. 15.

36. Goyal, Nikhil. "Solutions for Stressed-Out High-School Students." *Wall Street Journal,* February 12, 2016, C3. http://www.wsj.com/articles/solutions-for-stressed-out-high-school-students-1455301683.

37. FOMO is defined as "a pervasive apprehension that others might be having rewarding experiences from which one is absent." Przybylski, A. K., Murayama, K., DeHaan, C. R., and Gladwell, V. 2013. "Motivational, Emotional and Behavioral Correlates of Fear of Missing Out." *Computers in Human Behavior* 29, no. 4 (2013): 1841–1848. http://dx.doi.org/1-.1016/j.chb.2013.02.014.

38. Fagan, K. "Split Image." http://espn.go.com/espn/feature/story/_/id/12833146/instagram-account-university-pennsylvania-runner-showed-only-part-story.

39. Twenge, Jean M. *iGen.* New York: Simson & Schuster, 2017.

40. Arnett, J. J. *Emerging Adulthood: The Winding Road from the Late Teens Through the Twenties.* New York: Oxford University Press, 2004.

41. Arnett, J. J. *New Horizons in Emerging Adulthood: Early Adulthood in a Family Context.* Edited by A. Booth and N. Crouter. New York: Springer, 2012.

42. Arnett, J. J., and Fischel, E. *Getting to 30: A Parent's Guide to the 20-something Years.* New York: Workman Press, 2014.

43. Mintz, *Huck's Raft,* 383.

44. DeSilver, D. "Increase in Living with Parents Driven by Those Ages 25–34, Non-College Grads." http://www.pewresearch.org/fact-tank/2016/06/08/increase-in-living-with-parents-driven-by-those-ages-25-34-non-college-grads.

45. The generations by birth year are: Boomers: 1946–64 (Census Bureau), then, roughly, Gen X: 1965 to about 1980–1984 (Harvard Center).

46. Bump, Philip. "Here Is When Each Generation Begins and Ends, According to Facts." *Atlantic,* March 25, 2014. https://www.theatlantic.com/national/archive/2014   /03/here-is-when-each-generation-begins-and-ends-according-to-facts/359589/.

47. Pew Research Center. "Social and Demographic Trends." 2015. Retrieved from http://www.pewsocialtrends.org/2015/12/17/1-the-american-family-today/.

48. Ibid.

49. "President Obama & Marilynne Robinson: A Conversation in Iowa." *New York Review of Books,* November 5, 2015, 4–6.

50. Nagaoka, J., Farrington, C. A., Ehrlich, S. B., and Heath, R. D. "Foundations for Young Adult Success: A Developmental Framework." U Chicago Consortium on School Research. June 2015.

51. Lebowitz, Eli, and Omer, H. *Treating Childhood and Adolescent Anxiety: A Guide for Caregivers.* Hoboken, NJ: Wiley, 2013.

52. Psychology professor Wendy Grolnick identified these factors underlying parental protection. Grolnick, W. S., and Pomerantz, E.M. "Issues and Challenges in Studying Parental Control: Towards a New Conceptualization." *Child Development Perspectives* 3 (2009): 165–170.

53. Gottlieb, Lori. "How to Land Your Kid in Therapy." *Atlantic,* July/August 2011.

54. New, Jake. "Lives Cut Short." Inside Higher Ed. September 19, 2014. https://www.insidehighered.com/news/2014/09/19/freshman-deaths-show-risks-transitioning-college-life.

55. William Deresiewicz. *Excellent Sheep: The Miseducation of the American Elite, and the Way to a Beautiful Life.* New York: Free Press, 2015.

56. Lythcott-Haims, Julie. *How to Raise an Adult: Break Free of the Overparenting Trap and Prepare Your Kids for Success.* New York: Henry Holt, 2015.

57. Ibid., 94.

58. http://jenni.uchicago.edu/papers/Heckman_Rubinstein_AER_2001_91_2.pdf.

2. Before You Go: Social-Emotional PREP

1. Zimmerman, Jonathan. "Welcome, Freshmen. Look at Me When I Talk to You." *Chronicle of Higher Education,* 2016. http://www.chronicle.com /article/Welcome-Freshmen-Look-at-Me/237751.

2. Mischel, W. *The Marshmallow Test: Mastering Self-Control.* New York: Little, Brown, 2014.

3. Duckworth, A., and Steinberg, L. "Unpacking Self Control." *Child Developmental Perspectives* 9 (2015), 32–37.

4. Duckworth, A. L., and Seligman, M. E. D. "Self-Discipline Outdoes IQ in Predicting Academic Performance of Adolescents." *Psychological Science* 16 (2005): 939–944.

5. Brach, T. *Radical Acceptance: Embracing Your Life with the Heart of a Buddha.* New York: Random House, 2004.

3. Welcome to Campus: Overcoming Mindset Barriers to Success

1. Graduation from college is declining for every category of student: part-time, full-time, older, and traditional. According to the National Student Clearinghouse, a scant 53 percent of students who entered college in the fall of 2009 had earned a degree by May 2015. Completion rates fell most sharply at four-year colleges, where the dropout rate was a sobering 33 percent. Higher college enrollment is offset by the sobering reality that the United States has the lowest rate of college completion in the developed world.

2. Kuh, G. D., Kinzie, J., Buckley, J. A., Bridges, B. K., and Hayek, J. C. *What Matters to Student Success: A Review of the Literature.* 2006. 57. https:// nces.ed.gov/npec/pdf/Kuh_Team_Report.pdf.

3. Bean, J., and Bean, J. P. "Dropouts and Turnover: The Synthesis and Test of a Causal Model of Student Attrition." *Research in Higher Education* 12, no. 2 (1980): 155–187.

4. Chambliss, D., and Takas, C. *How College Works.* Cambridge, MA: Harvard University Press, 2014.

5. Ibid., 4.

6. Sacerdotal, B. "Peer Effects with Random Assignments: Results for Dartmouth Roommates." *Quarterly Journal of Economics* 116, no. 2 (2001): 681–704.

7. Chambliss and Takacs, *How College Works,* 2.

8. Bartlett, Tom. "When a Theory Goes Viral." *Chronicle Review,* May 21, 2017. http://www.chronicle.com/article/The-Intersectionality-Wars/240095.

9. Ohio State University. Suicide Prevention. https://suicideprevention.osu .edu/prevention-information/special-populations/minority-students/.

10. LGBT Youth. https://www.cdc.gov/lgbthealth/youth.htm.

11. Yeager, D., and Walton, G. "Social/Psychological Interventions in Education: They're Not Magic." *Review of Educational Research* 81, no. 2 (2011): 267–301. https://www.yc.edu/v5content/student-services/docs/successdocs/drtinto/Social-PsychologicalInterventionsinEducation.pdf. 2011.

12. Chambliss and Takas, *How College Works,* 4.

13. National Student Clearinghouse Signature Report. *National Postsecondary Enrollment Trends: Before, During and After the Great Recession.* 2011. http://pas.indiana.edu/pdf/National%20Postsecondary%20Enrollment%20Trends.pdf.

14. Tough, P. "Who Gets to Graduate?" *New York Times,* May 18, 2014. http://www.nytimes.com/2014/05/18/magazine/who-gets-to-graduate.html.

15. Bennett, J. "Learning to Fail." *New York Times,* June 25, 2017. https://www.nytimes.com/2017/06/24/fashion/fear-of-failure.html.

16. Resilience Consortium. https://resilienceconsortium.bsc.harvard.edu.

17. Bennett, "Learning to Fail." http://www.nytimes.com/2016/09/30/health/teenagers-stress-coping-skills.html.

18. Counseling and Mental Health Center, University of Texas. https://www.cmhc.utexas.edu/thrive/index.html.

19. College students of African American or Asian ethnicity are much less likely to ask for help.

20. Tough, "Who Gets to Graduate?"

21. Hamblin, J. "Why Succeeding Against the Odds Can Make You Sick." *New York Times,* January 27, 2017. https://www.nytimes.com/2017/01/27/opinion/sunday/why-succeeding-against-the-odds-can-make-you-sick.html.

22. Mujadid, M., et al. "Socioeconomic Position, John Henryism, and Incidence of Acute Myocardial Infarction in Finnish Men." *Social Science and Medicine* 173 (2017): 54–62. http://www.sciencedirect.com/science/article/pii/S0277953616306530?np=y.

23. Reinhard, Jessica, and McGrath, Marie C. "First-Generation College Students: Common Risk Factors and Strategies for Success." *Pennsylvania Psychologist* 77, no. 8: 24–25.

24. Brody, G., Yu, T., Miller, G., and Chen, E. "Resilience in Adolescence, Health and Psychosocial Outcomes." *Pediatrics* 138, no. 6 (2016). https://pediatrics.aappublications.org/content/138/6/e20161042.

25. Ibid.

26. Yeager and Walton, "Social/Psychological Interventions."

27. Lubrano, Alfred. "The 'Imposter' Syndrome of First-Generation Penn Students: Uneasy Among Privileged, Distanced from Family." *Inquirer.*

http://www.philly.com/philly/news/university-of-pennsylvania-working
-class-college-education-freshmen-family-20171004.html.

28. "The Indentured Class." http://www.scpr.org/events/2015/09/30/1769
/the-indentured-class-the-social-costs-of-student-d/.

29. Dagher, V. "Millennials Saving More for Children's College Than Older
Generations." *Wall Street Journal,* October 1, 2016. http://www.wsj.com
/articles/us-parents-are-saving-more-money-for-children's-college
-1475028003.

30. Hoover, Eric. "The Long Last Miles to College." *Chronicle of Higher Education* LXIV, no. 7 (2017): A14–A18.

31. Canada, Mark. "How the Provost Can Help Students Succeed?" *Chronicle of Higher Education,* LXIV, no. 7 (2017): A25.

32. Lehmann, Chris, interviewed September 26, 2016, Science Leadership
Academy, Philadelphia, PA.

33. Tough, "Who Gets to Graduate?"

34. Yeager, D.S., et al. "Teaching a Lay Theory Before College Narrows Achievement Gaps at Scale." *Proceedings of the National Academy of Sciences of the United States of America* 113, no. 24 (2016). https://www.ncbi.nlm
.nih.gov/pmc/articles/PMC4914175/.

35. Rubinstein, N. "Depression the Leading Cause of College Dropout."
2011. http://www.goodtherapy.org/blog/depression-leading-cause-college
-drop-out/.

36. Johnston, Angus. "Student Protests, Then and Now." *Chronicle of Higher Education,* December 11, 2015. https://www.chronicle.com/article/Student
-Protests-ThenNow/234542?key=pvkpng0aAW9y_gsvqxH0dC7G
-3fCeh6TlsXQH_kGaBdLYVJ1dzhpTmZjLUlvZlgtOU9f SVZaTXd3M-
kxRc2RHeTdNMkc4MkJUUl93.

37. Wexler, Ellen. "How Mental-Health Care Entered the Debate Over Racial Inequality." *Chronicle of Higher Education* LXII, no. 13 (2015): 10.

38. Rostain, Anthony L. "Stigma Reduction and Help Seeking on Campus—
Selective Review of the Literature."

39. Czyz, E. K., Horwitz, A. G., Eisenberg, D., Kramer, A., and King, C. A.
"Self-Reported Barriers to Professional Helpseeking Among College
Students at Elevated Risk for Suicide." *Journal of American College Health*
61, no. 7 (2013): 398–406. doi:10.1080/07448481.2013.820731.

40. Eisenberg, D., Hunt, J., and Speer, N. "Help Seeking for Mental Health
on College Campuses: Review of Evidence and Next Steps for Research
and Practice." *Harvard Review of Psychiatry* 20, no. 4 (2012): 222–32. doi
:10.3109/10673229.2012.712839.

41. Eisenberg, D., and Lipson, S. K. "The Healthy Minds Study." 2015–2016
Data report. http://www.healthyminds.org/system/resources/.

42. Ibid.

43. This is a composite vignette in which the mother's description is not a quote.

44. Selingo, J. "Giving Young People an Alternative to College." *New York Times*, June 23, 2016. http://www.nytimes.com/2016/06/23/education /giving-young-people-an-alternative-to-college.html.

4. What to Expect When Johnny's Got Issues

1. NAMI. "Finding A Mental Health Professional." http://www.nami.org /Find-Support/Living-with-a-Mental-Health-Condition/Finding-a -Mental-Health-Professional.

2. Paus, T., Keshavan, M., and Giedd, J. N. "Why Do Many Psychiatric Disorders Emerge During Adolescence?" *Nature Reviews Neuroscience* 9, no. 12 (2008): 947–957.

3. http://depts.washington.edu/mhreport/facts_violence.php.

4. Beck, Melinda. "Confusing Medical Ailments with Mental Illness." *Wall Street Journal*, August 9, 2011. http://www.wsj.com/articles/SB10001424 053111904480904576496271983911668.

5. NAMI StigmaFree campaign. https://www.nami.org/Press-Media/Press -Releases/2015/National-Alliance-on-Mental-Illness-Launches-Stigm. Retrieved November 16, 2016.

6. Denizet-Lewis, Benoit. "Why Are More American Teenagers Than Ever Suffering from Severe Anxiety?" *New York Times*, October 11, 201. https:// www.nytimes.com/2017/10/11/magazine/why-are-more-american -teenagers-than-ever-suffering-from-severe-anxiety.html.

7. Gopnik, Alison. *The Gardener and the Carpenter: What the new science of child development tells us about the relationship between parents and children*. New York: Farrar, Strauss and Giroux, 2016.

8. Baldwin, A. L. "Socialization and the Parent-Child Relationship." *Child Development* 19 (1948): 127–136.

9. Power, Thomas. "Parenting Dimensions and Styles: A Brief History and Recommendations for Future Research." *Childhood Obesity*, Suppl 1 (2013): S14–S21. doi:10.1089/chi.2013.0034. http://www.ncbi.nlm.nih.gov /pmc/articles/PMC3746212/.

10. Maccoby, E., and Martin, J. "Socialization in the Context of the Family: Parent-Child Interaction." In *Handbook of Child Psychology*, edited by P. H. Mussen. New York: Wiley, 1983. 1–101.

11. Baumrind, Diana. "Current Patterns of Parental Authority." *Development Psychology Monograph* 4, no. 1, pt. 2 (1971): 1–103.

12. Baumrind, D. "Patterns of Parental Authority and Adolescent Autonomy." *New Directions for Child and Adolescent Development*, no. 108 (2005): 61.

13. Ibid., 62.

14. Mandara, J. "The Typological Approach in Child and Family Psychology: A Review of Theory, Methods, and Research." *Clinical Child and Family Psychology Review* 6 (2003): 129–146. https://docslide.com.br/documents/the-typological-approach-in-child-and-family-psychology-a-review-of-theory.h.

15. Fulwiler, M. "What Kind of Parent Are You?" Gottman Institute. 2014. https://www.gottman.com/blog/what-style-of-parent-are-you/.

16. Gottman, John. "An Introduction to Emotion Coaching." https://www.gottman.com/blog/an-introduction-to-emotion-coaching/.

17. Ibid.

18. Hooley, J. M., and Teasdale, J. D. "Predictors of Relapse in Unipolar Depressives: Expressed Emotion, Marital Distress, and Perceived Criticism." *Journal of Abnormal Psychiatry* 98 (1989): 229–235.

19. Though the Hopkins' vignette is a composite, this is quoted with permission from a particular individual.

20. "While the average net price of college education as a percentage of family income has risen moderately for the top 75 percent of the socioeconomic spectrum, it has skyrocketed for the bottom quartile, who paid 44.6 percent of their income for a degree in 1990, versus 84 percent today." Foroohar, R. "How the Financing of Colleges May Lead to Disaster!" *New York Review of Books,* October 2016, 28–30.

21. Weir, Kirsten. "Brighter Futures for Anxious Kids." *Monitor on Psychology* (2017): 51–55.

22. Merikangas, K. R., He, J.-P., Burstein, M., Swanson, S. A., Avenevoli, S., Cui, L., Benjet, C., Georgiades, K., and Swendsen, J. "Lifetime Prevalence of Mental Disorders in US Adolescents: Results from the National Comorbidity Study-Adolescent Supplement (NCS-A)." *Journal of the American Academy of Child and Adolescent Psychiatry* 49, no. 10 (2010): 980–989. Published online July 31, 2010. doi:10.1016/j.jaac.2010.05.017.

23. Halldorsdottir, T., Ollendick, T. H., Ginsburg, G., Sherrill, J., Kendall, P. C., Walkup, J., and Piacentini, J. "Treatment Outcomes in Anxious Youth with and without Comorbid ADHD in the CAMS." *Journal of Clinical Child & Adolescent Psychology* 44 (2015): 985–991. http://dx.doi.org/10.1080/15374416.2014.952008.

24. Ginsburg, G., Drake, K., Tein, J.-Y., Teetsel, R., and Riddle, M. "Preventing Onset of Anxiety Disorders in Offspring of Anxious Parents: A Randomized Controlled Trial of a Family-Based Intervention." *American Journal of Psychiatry* 172, no. 12 (2015): 1207–1214. http://dx.doi.org/10.1176/appi.ajp.2015.14091178.

25. Hamblin, J. "Why Succeeding Against the Odds Can Make You Sick." *New York Times,* January 27, 2017. https://www.nytimes.com/2017/01/27/opinion/sunday/why-succeeding-against-the-odds-can-make-you-sick.html.

26. Thapar, A., and Cooper, M. "Attention Deficit Hyperactivity Disorder." *Lancet Clinic,* September 16, 2015. http://dx.doi.org/10.1016/S0140 -6736(15)00238-X.

5. How to Plan—and How to Follow Through

1. Lezak, M. D. *Neuropsychological Assessment,* 3rd ed. New York: Oxford University Press, 1995.
2. Barkley, R. A. *ADHD and the Nature of Self-Control.* New York: Guilford, 1997.
3. Barkley, R. A. *Executive Functions: What They Are, What They Do, How They Evolved.* New York: Guilford, 2012.
4. Noreika, V., Falter, C. M., and Rubia, K. "Timing Deficits in Attention-Deficit/Hyperactivity Disorder (ADHD): Evidence from Neurocognitive and Neuroimaging Studies." *Neuropsychologia* 51 (2013): 235–266. doi:10.1016/j.neuropsychologia.2012.09.036.
5. TO COME.
6. Prevatt, F. "Coaching for College Students with ADHD." *Current Psychiatry Reports* 18 (2016): 110. doi:10.1007/s11920-016-0751-9.
7. Steel, P. "The Nature of Procrastination: A Meta-Analytic and Theoretical Review of Quintessential Self-Regulatory Failure." *Psychological Bulletin* 133 (2007): 65–94.
8. Ramsay, J. R. "The Relevance of Cognitive Distortions in the Psychosocial Treatment of Adult ADHD." *Professional Psychology Research and Practice* 48 (2017): 62–69.
9. Gawrilow, C., and Gollwitzer, P. M. "Implementation Intentions Facilitate Response Inhibition in Children with ADHD." *Cognitive Therapy and Research* 32 (2008): 261–280.
   Web Resources:
   http://www.drthomasebrown.com/assessment-tools/
   https://edgefoundation.org/

6. Risky Business: The Adolescent Brain

1. Seaman, Barrett. *Binge: What Your College Student Won't Tell You.* New York: John Wiley and Sons, 2005. Quoted in Minding the Campus essay: "Collegians Legally Drinking at 18?" September 2, 2008. http://www .mindingthecampus.org/2008/09/collegians_legally_drinking _ at/#more-9198.
2. Arnsten, A., and Rubia, K. "Neurobiological Circuits Regulating Attention, Cognitive Control, Motivation, and Emotion: Disruptions in Neurodevelopmental Psychiatric Disorders." *Journal of the American Academy of Child and Adolescent Psychiatry* 51 (2012): 356–367.

3. Steinberg, L. "A Social Neuroscience Perspective on Adolescent Risk-Taking." *Development Review* 28 (2008): 78–106.

4. Chein, J., Albert, D., O'Brien, L., Uckert, K., and Steinberg L. "Peers Increase Adolescent Risk Taking by Enhancing Activity in the Brain's Reward Circuitry." *Developmental Science* 12 (2010): F1–10. doi:10.1111/j.1467-7687.2010.01035.x.

5. Chambliss, D., and Takas, C. *How College Works*. Cambridge, MA: Harvard University Press, 2014. 95–96.

6. Fischer, C., and Hoover, B. "River of Booze: Inside One College Town's Uneasy Embrace of Drinking." *Chronicle of Higher Education*, December 2014, 1–9.

7. McMurtie, B. "Why Colleges Haven't Stopped Students from Drinking." *Chronicle of Higher Education*, December 2014, 10–15.

8. Carrick, A. K. "Drinking to Blackout." *New York Times*, September 19, 2016. http://www.nytimes.com/2016/09/19/opinion/drinking-to-blackout.html.

9. Ibid.

10. Wechsler, H., Kuh, G., and Davenport, A. E. "Fraternities, Sororities and Binge Drinking: Results from a National Study of American Colleges." *NASPA* 46, no.3 (2009): 395–416.

11. Armstrong, E. A., Hamilton, L., and Sweeney, B. "Sexual Assault on Campus: A Multilevel, Integrative Approach to Party Rape." *Social Problems* 53 (2006): 483–499.

12. Rasmussen, N. *On Speed: The Many Lives of Amphetamine*. New York: NYU Press, 2008.

13. *Facing Addiction in America: The Surgeon General's Report of Alcohol, Drugs and Health*. https://addiction.surgeongeneral.gov/surgeon-generals-report.pdf.

14. Benson, K., Flory, K., Humphreys, K. L., and Lee, S. L. "Misuse of Stimulant Medication Among College Students: A Comprehensive Review and Meta-Analysis." *Clinical Child and Family Psychology Review* 18 (2015): 50–76.

15. DeSantis, A., Noar, S. M., and Webb, E. A. "Nonmedical ADHD Stimulant Use in Fraternities." *Journal of Studies on Alcohol and Drugs* 70 (2009): 952–954.

16. Garnier, L. M., Arria, A. M., et al. "Sharing and Selling of Prescription Medications in a College Student Sample." *Journal of Clinical Psychiatry* 71 (2010): 262–269.

17. Schwartz, C. "Generation Adderall." *New York Times*, October 16, 2016. http://www.nytimes.com/2016/10/16/magazine/generation-adderall-addiction.html.

18. Talbot, M. "Brain Gain." *New Yorker,* April 27, 2009. http://www.newyorker
    .com/magazine/2009/04/27/brain-gain.

19. "Facing Addiction in America: The Surgeon General's Report on Alco-
    hol, Drugs, and Health." U.S. Department of Health and Human Ser-
    vices. 2016. https://addiction.surgeongeneral.gov.

20. American Psychiatric Association. *Diagnostic and Statistical Manual of
    Mental Disorders, Fifth Edition (DSM-5).* Washington, D.C.: American
    Psychiatric Publishing, 2013.

21. Prochaska, J. O., DiClemente, C. C., and Norcross, J. C. "In Search of
    How People Change: Applications to the Addictive Behaviors." *Ameri-
    can Psychologist* 47 (1992): 1102–1114. PMID: 1329589.

7. Anxiety and Depression

1. Center for Collegiate Mental Health. Annual Report, January 15, 2018,
   https://ccmh.psu.edu/files/2019/01/2018-Annual-Report-1-15-2018
   -12m2sn0.pdf

2. Ibid.

3. Ibid.

4. Twenge, J. "Time Period and Birth Cohort Differences in Depressive
   Symptoms in the U.S., 1982–2013." *Social Indicators Research* vol. 121,
   no. 2 (2014): 437–454. doi:10.1007/s11205-014-0647-1.

5. National comorbidity survey. https://www.hcp.med.harvard.edu/ncs/.

6. Borchard, T. "Sanity Break." Everydayhealth.com. September 3, 2013.

7. American Academy of Child and Adolescent Psychiatry. "The Anxious
   Child." Retrieved November 15, 2016. http://www.aacap.org/AACAP
   /Families_and_Youth/Facts_for_Families/FFF-Guide/The-Anxious
   -Child-047.aspx.

8. Center for Collegiate Mental Health Annual Report, 2018, Ibid.

9. Nock, M. K., Teper, R., and Hollander, M. "Psychological Treatment of
   Self-Injury Among Adolescents." *Journal of Clinical Psychology* 63
   (2007): 1081–1089.

10. Ibid.

11. Quoted with permission, and using a pseudonym to protect confidenti-
    ality.

12. Academy of Child and Adolescent Psychiatry. "Facts and Families,
    Depression in Children and Teens." Retrieved November 15, 2016.
    http://www.aacap.org/AACAP/Families and Youth/Facts for Families/
    FFF-Guide/The Depressed-Child-004.aspx.

13. Wong, Y. Joel. *Journal of Counseling Psychology* (2016). http://www.apa
    .org/news/press/releases/2016/11/sexism-harmful.aspx.

14. Although "Harry" is a composite vignette, these are actual emails,
    quoted with permission, from a college student and his parents.

15. *The Carlat Report Psychiatry, Meditation,* ed. Glen Spielmans. February 2014: 6.

8. Crisis Care
1. Rothman, L. "See a 1970 Explanation of What Happened to Apollo 13." *Time.* April 11, 2015.
2. National Alliance of Mental Health, 2008.
3. A reminder, HIPAA governs confidentiality between students and counseling professionals, and can bar the school from sharing medical records with parents. See chapter 4 and the appendix for a more complete explanation of this law.
4. "A mother's story" is told in the first-person voice.
5. http://www.collegecounseling.org/wp-content/uploads/NCCCS2014 v2.pdf and http://www.collegecounseling.org/wp-content/uploads/Survey -2013-4-yr-Directors-1.pdf, 1, 11.
6. Franklin, Martin. "Understanding Anxiety in Children with Autism Spectrum Disorders." Presentation at the Center for Autism Research, University of Pennsylvania, November 8, 2012. http://www.wsj.com/articles/as -suicide-rates-rise-scientists-find-new-warning-signs-1465235288.
7. Advanced clinical medical education is greatly enhanced by the real-life opportunities for "learning from the patient." Jensen generously agreed to participate in this process and permit excerpted quotes here.
8. The names and identifying information of all family members as well as treating providers are changed to protect confidentiality.
9. Asperger's syndrome was collapsed into the diagnostic category of autism spectrum disorders in the *DSM-5* in 2013. Colloquially, high-functioning autism is still referred to as Asperger's, "on the bubble," or "on the spectrum."
10. Ibid.
11. Shattuck, P., Narendorf, S., Cooper, B., Sterzing, P., Wagner, M., and Taylor, J. "Postsecondary Education and Employment Among Youth with an Autism Spectrum Disorder." *Pediatrics* 129, no. 6 (2012): 1042–1049. https://www.ncbi.nlm.nih.gov/pmc/articles/PMC3362908/.
12. According to the campus mental health organization Active Minds, 67 percent of students tell a friend they are feeling suicidal before telling anyone else. http://www.activeminds.org/issues-a-resources/the-issue.
13. Curtin, Sally C., Warner, Margaret, and Hedegaaard, Holly. http://www .cdc.gov/nchs/data/databriefs/db241.pdf.
14. Ibid.
15. Kann, L., Kinchen, S., Shanklin, S. L., et al. "Youth Risk Behavior Surveillance—United States, 2013." *Morbidity and Mortality Weekly Report* 63 (2014): 1–168. http://www.nabi.nlm.nib.gov/pubmed/24918634.

16. Petersen, Andrea. "As Suicide Rates Rise, Scientists Find New Warning Signs." *Wall Street Journal*, June 7, 2016. http://www.wsj.com/articles/as-suicide-rates-rise-scientists-find-new-warning-signs-1465235288.

17. See more at http://www.nami.org/About-NAMI/NAMI-News/Understanding-What-HIPAA-Means-for-Mental-Illness#sthash.zbyoVqgH.dpuf.

18. Gil, Natalie. "Loneliness: A Silent Plague That Is Hurting Young People Most." *Guardian*, July 20, 2014. http://www.theguardian.com/lifeandstyle/2014/jul/20/loneliness-britains-silent-plague-hurts-young-people-most.

19. Chambliss, Dan, and Takacs, Christopher. *How College Works.* Cambridge, MA: Harvard University Press, 2014.

20. Boss, Pauline. *Ambiguous Loss: Learning to Live with Unresolved Grief.* Cambridge, MA: Harvard University Press, 1999.

21. Ibid.

22. American Psychological Association. "Recognizing the Signs of Bipolar." Retrieved November 15, 2016. http://www.apa.org/helpcenter/recognizing-bipolar.aspx.

9. Adjusting to the Boomerang Kid

1. http://www.aarp.org/home-family/friends-family/info-2016/millennials-living-at-home-mq.html.

2. Livesey, C. M. W., and Rostain, A. L. "Involving Parents/Family in Treatment During the Transition from Late Adolescence to Young Adulthood." *Child Adolescent Psychiatric Clinic of North America* 26 (2017): 199–216.

3. https://www.law.yale.edu/amy-chua.

4. Mohapatra, D. "Expressed Emotion in Psychiatric Disorders: A Review." https://www.academia.edu/4041130/Expressed.

5. Baronet, A. M. "Factors Associated with Caregiver Burden in Mental Illness: A Critical Review of the Research Literature." *Clinical Psychology Review* 19 (1999): 819–841. http://www.sciencedirect.com/science/article/pii/S0272735898000762.

6. Martin, J., Padierna, A., van Wijngaarden, B., Aguirre, U., Anton, A., Munoz, P., and Quintana, J. "Caregivers Consequences of Care Among Patients with Eating Disorders, Depression, or Schizophrenia." *BMC Psychiatry* 15 (2015): 124. doi:10.1186/s12888-015-0507-9. https://www.ncbi.nlm.nih.gov/pmc/articles/PMC4459460/.

7. Brown, G. W. "The Discovery of Expressed Emotion: Induction or Deduction?" In *Expressed Emotion in Families,* edited by J. Leff and C. Vaugh. New York: Guilford Press, 1985. 7–25.

8. Brigid Schulte, author of *Overwhelmed,* notes that many mothers as-

sume numerous tasks unasked, compelled by stereotypic familial and cultural expectations.

9. Martin et al. "Caregivers."

10. Urbano, R. C., and Hodapp, R. M. "Divorce in Families of Children with Down Syndrome: A Population-Based Study." *American Journal on Mental Retardation* 112, no. 4 (2007): 261–274. https://www.ncbi.nlm .nih.gov/pubmed/17559293.

11. Ibid.

12. Quoted with permission.

13. Hayes, S. A., and Watson, S. "The Impact of Parenting Stress: A Meta-Analysis Comparing the Experience of Parenting Stress in Parents of Children with and without Autism Spectrum Disorder." *Journal of Autism and Developmental Disorders* 43, no. 3 (2013): 629–642. http://cds .web.unc.edu/files/2015/09/parentingstressandASD.pdf.

14. Whether in first or second marriages, couples whose adolescent or young adult has longstanding emotional problems or developmental disabilities experience a higher level and constancy of divorce risk. Instead of two divorce spikes (years 5–7 and 18–20) coinciding with the high-demand years of early childhood and adolescence, interrupted by a years-long lull, the threat of divorce remains consistently high throughout the years of childhood, adolescence, and young adulthood.

15. Esbensen, A. J., and Seltzer, M. M. "Accounting for the 'Down Syndrome Advantage.'" *American Journal on Intellectual and Developmental Disabilities* 116, no. 1 (2011)): 3–15. doi:10.1352/1944-7558-116.1.3.

16. Urbano and Hodapp. "Divorce in Families."

17. This approximate figure varies by level of education, age at marriage, length of marriage at time of divorce, religious and ethnic background, and even region of the country.

18. Ibid.

19. Gaspard, T. "Timing Is Everything When It Comes to Marriage Counseling." 2015. https://www.gottman.com/blog/timing-is-everything-when-it -comes-to-marriage-counseling/.

20. Pinker, Susan. "The Perilous Aftermath of a Simple Concussion." *Wall Street Journal*, April 6, 2016. http://www.wsj.com/articles/the-perilous -aftermath-of-a-simple-concussion-1459963724.

21. Fralick, M., Thiruchelvam, D., Tien, H. C., and Redelmeier, D. "Risk of Suicide After a Concussion." *Canadian Medical Association Journal* 188, no. 7 (2016): 497–504. doi:10.1503/cmaj.150790.

22. Though the Roca vignette is a composite, with all identifiers changed to protect confidentiality, "Lou's" statement is cited with permission from a particular individual.

23. "Sue's" excerpt is shared with permission from a particular individual.

24. Korb, Alex. *The Upward Spiral.* Oakland, CA: New Harbinger Publications, 2015.

25. Lopez, Shane J. *Making Hope Happen.* New York: Simon & Schuster, 2013.

26. Bernstein, Elizabeth. "An Emotion We All Need More of." *Wall Street Journal,* March 21, 2016. http://www.wsj.com/articles/an-emotion-we-all-need-more-of-1458581680.

27. Scioli, Anthony, and Biller, Henry. *The Power of Hope.* Deerfield Beach, FL: Health Communications Inc., 2010.

28. Stathopoulou, G., Powers, M. B., Berry, A. C., Jasper, A. J., and Otto, M. W. "Exercise Interventions for Mental Health: A Quantitative and Qualitative Review." *Clinical Psychology Science and Practice* 13, no. 2 (2006). http://dx.doi.org/10.1111/j.1468-2850.2006.00021.x.

29. Roberts, L. R., and Neece, C. I. "Feasibility of Mindfulness-Based Stress Reduction Intervention for Parents of Children with Developmental Delays." *Issues in Mental Health Nursing* 36 (2015): 592–602. http://dx.doi.org/10.3109/01612840.2015.1017063.

30. Denial, anger, bargaining, depression, and acceptance are classic stages of grief as conceptualized by Elisabeth Kübler-Ross.

31. Allison, Marcella. "Sisyphus and the Seed." http://www.nami.org/Blogs/NAMI-Blog/May-2016/Sisyphus-and-the-Seed.

32. Quoted with permission, and use of a pseudonym to protect confidentiality.

10. From Recovery to Relaunch

1. Lebowitz, Eli R., Leckman, J., Silverman, W., and Feldman, R. "Cross-Generational Influences on Childhood Anxiety Disorders: Pathways and Mechanisms." *Journal of Neural Transmission* 123, no. 9 (2016): 1053–1067.

2. Malagon, A. "Hikkikomori: A New Diagnosis or a Syndrome Associated with a Psychiatric Diagnosis?" *International Journal of Social Psychiatry* 56, no. 5 (2010): 558–559.

3. Yarrow, A. L. "Millennial Men's Failure to Launch Is a Problem for Us All." *San Francisco Chronicle,* June 5, 2015. http://www.sfchronicle.com/opinion/article/Millennial-men-s-fail ure-to-launch-is-a-problem-6305817.php.

4. Ibid.

5. Lebowitz, E. R. "Failure to Launch: Shaping Interventions for Highly Dependent Adult Children." *Journal of Child & Adolescent Psychiatry* 55, no. 2 (2016): 89–90.

6. Lebowitz, E., Dolberger, D., Nortov, E., and Omer, H. "Parent Training in Nonviolent Resistance for Adult Entitled Dependence." *Family Process* 51, no. 1 (2012): 90–106. doi:10.1111/j.1545-5300.2012.01382.x.

https://www.researchgate.net/publication/221721416_Parent_Training
_in_Nonviolent_Resistance_for_Adult_Entitled_Dependence.

7. Dell'Atonia, K. J. "The Families That Can't Afford Summer." *New York Times,* June 5, 2016, 4. http://www.nytimes.com/2016/06/05/sunday -review/the-families-that-cant-afford-summer.html.

8. Lebowitz, E. http://podcasts.elsevierhealth.com/jaac/jaac_pc_55_2.mp3.

9. Granic, I., Lobel, A., and Engels, R. C. "The Benefits of Playing Video Games." *American Psychologist* 69, no. 1 (2014): 66–78.

10. Pinker, Susan. "To Beat the Blues, Visits Must Be Real, Not Virtual," *Wall Street Journal,* June 2, 2016. http://www.wsj.com/articles/to-beat -the-blues-visits-must-be-real-not-virtual-1464899707.

11. Van Orden, K. A., Lynam, M. E., Hollar, D., and Joiner, T. E., Jr. "Perceived Burdensomeness as an Indicator of Suicidal Symptoms." *Cognitive Therapy and Research* 30 (2006): 457–467.

12. These few examples are excerpted from: *School Interventions to Prevent Youth Suicide* (Los Angeles: Center for Mental Health in Schools, 2000), 23–28.

13. Veale, David. "Behavioral Activation for Depression." *Advances in Psychiatric Treatment* 14, no.1 (2008): 29–36. http://apt.rcpsych.org/content /14/1/29.

14. Ferster, C. B. "A Functional Analysis of Depression." *American Psychologist* 28 (1973): 857–870.

15. Martell, C. R., Addis, M. E., and Jacobson, N. S. *Depression in Context: Strategies for Guided Action.* New York: Norton, 2001. Image reprinted with permission from Rachel C Leonard, Ph.D., published by Medscape Drugs & Diseases (https://emedicine.medscape.com/), Cognitive Behavioral Therapy for Depression, 2017, available at https://emedicine.medscape .com/article/2094696-overview.

16. Though a composite vignette, the Ulysses pact is quoted with permission, from a particular individual and family.

17. Quoted with the student's permission.

18. "Tobacco Use Among Adults with Mental Illness and Substance Use Disorders." CDC. http://www.cdc.gov/tobacco/disparities/mental-illness -substance-use/index.htm.

11. Recasting the Safety Net

1. http://www.thecampusprogram.org/learn-about-campusprogram.

2. http://www.thecampusprogram.org/framework-for-success.

3. Task Force Report, University of Pennsylvania Almanac Supplement. February 17, 2015. http://www.upenn.edu/almanac.

4. Zimmerman, J. "High Anxiety: How Can We Save Our Students from Themselves?" *Chronicle of Higher Education,* November 3, 2017.

5. Field, K. "Stretched to Capacity: What Campus Counseling Centers Are Doing to Meet Rising Demand." *Chronicle of Higher Education,* November 6, 2016.

6. Kadison, R., and DiGeronimo, T. F. *College of the Overwhelmed: The Campus Mental Health Crisis and What to Do About It.* San Francisco: Jossey-Bass, 2004.

7. https://www.paloaltoonline.com/news/2018/05/18/lawsuit-stanford -violated-students-rights-in-mental-health-response.

8. Bower, K., and Schwartz, V. "Legal and Ethical Issues in College Mental Health." In *Mental Health Care in the College Community,* edited by Jerald Kay and Victor Schwartz. New York: John Wiley & Sons, 2010. 129–132.

9. Ibid., 132–133.

Index

academic accommodations, 196–97, 282

academic preparation, 24

acceptance:
culture of, 283
of mental illness, 230–31
of self, 33, 47–49, 61, 259–60

accountability, 258–59

Active Minds, 57, 276–77

Adams, Abigail, 14

Adams, John, 14, 20

Adderall, 132

addiction, 134–36, 191
nonchemical, 243–44
see also substance use and abuse

Advanced Placement (AP) courses, 15, 16

aggression, 239–41

alcohol, 12, 27, 46, 125–29, 132, 135, 136, 141, 265
binge drinking, 9, 46, 125, 129
blackouts from, 128
death from, 23, 131, 141
poisoning from, 23, 75, 131, 280
sexual assault and, 130, 131, 141
see also substance use and abuse

Alexander, William, 272, 274

American Academy of Child and Adolescent Psychiatry, 151

American College Health Association, 8

American Psychiatric Association, 150

American Psychological Association, 6

Americans with Disabilities Act (ADA), 106, 264

amphetamines, 132

anxiety, 7, 8, 9, 12, 56, 61, 81, 149–61, 191
parents' responses to, 152–53
productive vs. debilitating, 150–51
signs of, 151–52
social, 38, 67, 69

anxiety disorders, 12, 67, 124, 149–52
generalized anxiety disorder (GAD), 151–52, 157, 180, 185–86
signs of, 151–52

Apollo 13 lunar mission, 178

Aristotle, 14

Arnett, Jeffrey, 18, 19

Asperger's syndrome, 38, 185

Association for University and College Counseling Center Directors (AUCCCD), 271–72

ASU (alcohol and substance use), *see* alcohol; substance use and abuse

attention deficit hyperactivity disorder (ADHD), 38, 103–4, 124, 186
executive functioning problems and, 104–16
medications for, 132, 133

autism spectrum disorder (ASD), 38, 67, 124, 185–87
Asperger's syndrome, 38, 185
executive functioning problems and, 105, 106

baby boomers, 19
bad habits, 256–58
Baldwin, James, 72
Barkley, Russell, 104–5
barriers, mental, *see* mindset barriers
Baumrind, Diana, 87
Beck Depression Inventory (BDI), 170
bedtime routine, 255
behavioral activation treatment for
        depression, 241–43
behavioral strategies for better
        mental health, 255
belonging, 52, 53, 54–59
bias, 56
*Binge: What Your College Student
        Won't Tell You* (Seaman), 119
bipolar disorder, signs and
        symptoms of, 206
Black Swan, 88
blame, 80
boomerang kids, 19, 20, 208–32
    emotional expression and, 212–16
    helping your child bounce back,
        209–11
    over-parenting and, 233
    parent-child deal and, 238–39
    and parents as mental health
        caregivers, 210–12, 217–19, 229
    parents' mental health and,
        217–25
    relaunch from, *see* recovery and
        relaunch
    social support net and, 228–29
    and trap of family
        accommodations, 236–38, 251
    and trap of protection, 235–36
    well child and, 225–26
boomer generation, 19
boredom, purpose out of, 253–54
Bower, Karen, 282
Brach, Tara, 48–49
brain, 11, 23, 46, 80, 84, 105, 114, 222
    depression and, 164, 165, 167
    executive functioning in, 104–16,
        122, 125

nonchemical addiction and, 243–44
    rewiring of, 122
    risky behavior and, 119, 121–24
    substance use and, 133–34
bright-siding, 229
Brown, George, 212–13
Buber, Martin, 247
bullying, 56, 57, 183
bupropion, 171, 175
Bureau of Labor Statistics, 234

campus counseling, *see* college
        counseling services
Campus Sexual Violence
        Elimination Act, 130
cannabis, *see* marijuana
Carrick, Ashton, 128–29
Chambliss, Daniel, 54, 55, 126–27
Chronicle of Higher Education, 7, 127,
        271, 272
cigarettes, 132, 239, 256–57
cognitive behavioral therapy (CBT),
        63, 107
cognitive distortions, 113
cognitive readiness, 25
college(s), 14
    academic accommodations at,
        196–97, 282
    admissions, 10, 15
    campus security, 279
    College for All movement, 14–15
    conflict situations at, 280–81
    costs of, 59, 64–66
    crisis handling at, 277–79, 280
    deferring attendance, 70, 101
    disciplinary proceedings at,
        281–82
    dormitories in, 55, 281
    dropping out from, 12, 52–54, 59,
        61, 63, 65, 67, 101, 265
    freshman year of, 193
    leave of absence from, 282–83
    questions to raise with student
        affairs personnel, 273

responses to mental health
    problems, 10–11
safety net and, 195, 262–84
search for, 57
student-affairs divisions of,
    263–64, 273
weekly visits and, 193
college counseling services, 7, 10,
    67–68, 76, 86, 263, 267,
    270–74
    questions to raise regarding, 275
    what to do if child is seeking out,
        274–76
comparisons, invidious, 113
confidentiality, *see* privacy concerns
    and laws
conscientiousness, 33–34
coping skills, 165–66, 176, 236, 254,
    255
counseling:
    campus services for, *see* college
        counseling services
    therapists, 76–77
Crenshaw, Kimberlé Williams, 56
crises, 178–207
    colleges' handling of, 277–79, 280
    denial and, 194–95
    levels of, 201
    warning signs and, 192–98
critical comments, 214, 215
culture of acceptance, 283

danger, 22–24
death, 23
    from alcohol, 23, 131, 141
    suicide, *see* suicide
decisions, two-person rule for, 211
denial, 194–95
depression, 7, 9, 12, 27, 56, 61, 67–68,
    124, 149, 161–76
    Beck Depression Inventory, 170
    behavioral activation treatment
        for, 241–43
    in bipolar disorder, 206

brain and, 164, 165, 167
    coping skills and, 165–66
    irritability and aggression as
        symptoms of, 239–41
    sadness vs., 161–62
    signs of, 162–64
    suicide and, 190, 191, 241; *see also*
        suicide
    triggering loss and, 198
depression treatment, 166–67
    medications, 165, 171–72, 175
*Diagnostic and Statistical Manual of
    Mental Disorders-5 (DSM-5),*
    135, 149–50
dialectical behavior therapy (DBT),
    157–58
disciplinary proceedings, 281–82
distress-tolerance skills, 44
Disturbing the Peace (Havel), 227
Down syndrome, 217, 218
drugs, 136
    see also substance use and abuse
Duckworth, Angela, 44

eating disorders, 9, 27
Edge Foundation, 110
emerging adulthood, 18–19
emotional coach, 90
emotional expression (EE), 212–16,
    222
    harmful, 213–15
    helpful, 215–16
emotional intelligence, 27
Emotional Intelligence (Goleman), 3
emotionally focused parenting, 89–90
emotional overinvolvement of
    parents, 214, 215
emotional problems, *see* mental
    health issues
emotional reactions of parents,
    98–100
emotional readiness, 25, 26–27
    see also social/emotional maturity
emotional reasoning, 113

emotions, negative, tips to reduce, 99–100

empathy, blending structure with, 250–53

environment, in brain development, 105–6

executive functioning (EF), 104–16, 122, 125

exercise, 229

Facebook, 17, 38, 40, 166

Facing Addiction in America, 132, 134, 136

failure deprivation, 60–61

failure inoculation, 61, 63, 66

failure to launch (FTL), 233–34

faltering launch, 234

family mental health history, 84–86

fear, 48–49

Fear of Missing Out (FOMO), 17

Fear Of Not Making It (FONMI), 52, 53, 59–67

Fellowship of the Ring, The (Tolkien), 70

Fences, 88

FERPA (Family Educational Rights and Privacy Act), 11, 75, 177, 195, 264

Ferster, Charles, 243

fight-or-flight, 23

financial crisis and recession of 2008, 18, 59, 64, 208

Fischer, Karin, 127

FOMO (Fear of Missing Out), 17

FONMI (Fear Of Not Making It), 52, 53, 59–67

Food and Drug Administration (FDA), 184

fraternities, 128–30, 132, 133

Freud, Anna, 22

friendships, 52, 53, 54–59, 197–98
  interpersonal skills and, 33, 37–41

Furda, Eric, 35, 47–48

gap years, 70, 101

gender, 12

generalized anxiety disorder (GAD), 151–52, 157, 180, 185–86
  see also anxiety disorders

Generation Gap, 19

Generation X, 19, 64

Generation Z (iGen), 7, 18, 197, 234

genetics, 105–6, 135, 151, 165

goals, setting new, 231–32

Goldfarb, Michele, 129, 131, 281–82

Goleman, Daniel, 3

Gottman, John, 89–90

Great Recession of 2008, 18, 59, 208

grit, 33, 43–46, 62

Gutmann, Amy, 268

habits, bad, 256–58

Havel, Václav, 227

help, openness to seeking, 33, 49–51

Hibbs, Janet, 5

HIPAA (Health Insurance Portability and Accountability Act), 11, 73, 74–75, 177, 180, 194, 195, 264, 274, 280

Hoover, Eric, 127

hope, 227–28, 249–50, 283–84

hostility, 213–15

How College Works (Chambliss and Takacs), 54, 126–27

Hugo, Victor, 208

identity groups, 56

iGen (Generation Z), 7, 18, 197, 234

implementation intention strategies (IIS), 108, 114–15

impression management, 17

IMPROVE method, 45

Inside Higher Ed, 23

insomnia, 12

Instagram, 38, 40

International Association of
    Counseling Services, 11
intersectionality, 56
irritability, 239–41
irritable bowel syndrome, 12
isolation and loneliness, 55–56, 86,
    190, 197, 239, 265

Jed Foundation (JED), 57, 266–68,
    269, 272, 277, 282
jobs, 14, 15, 18–19

Krislov, Marvin, 10

lamotrigine, 254
learning difficulties, 38, 106, 282
leave of absence, 282–83
Lebowitz, Eli, 234
Lehmann, Chris, 65–66
Leonard, Rachel, 243
Lezak, Muriel, 104
LGBTQ youth, 56
loneliness and isolation, 55–56, 86,
    190, 197, 239, 265
Lovell, James A., 178

magical thinking, 113
magnification/minimization,
    113
Malmon, Alison, 276–77
marijuana (cannabis), 46, 125, 126,
    132, 135
    decriminalization of, 142
    talking about, 140–42
Marshmallow Test, 41–42
masculine norms, 169–70
maturity, see social/emotional
    maturity
medical records, 187
    privacy and, see privacy concerns
        and laws

medications, 211, 254–56, 271
    for ADHD, 132, 133
    for depression, 165, 171–72,
        175
    side effects of, 184, 254–56
    withdrawal from, 183–85, 211
meditation, 229
mental health issues:
    acceptance and, 230–31
    behavioral strategies for, 255
    colleges' response to, 10–11
    co-morbidity and, 179–80
    crises in, see crises
    family history and, 84–86
    masculine norms and, 169–70
    medications for, see medications
    and mood phases vs. disorders,
        78
    negative biases and, 52, 67–71,
        79–80
    not seeking help for, 52, 67–71
    parent-child deal and, 238–39
    peer support for, 57
    positive biases and, 74, 79–80
    privacy concerns and, see privacy
        concerns and laws
    recovery from, see recovery and
        relaunch
    and setting new goals, 231–32
    statistics on, 8–9
    stigma of, 10, 28, 68, 79–81, 176,
        265, 277
    stress and, 11–13
    violence and, 79
    warning signs of, 79
    well child and, 225–26
mentation, 158
migraine, 12
Millennials, 7, 18, 197, 234
mindfulness, 114, 283
mindset barriers, 52–71
    belonging, 52, 53, 54–59
    emotional problems, 52, 67–71
    FONMI (Fear Of Not Making It),
        52, 53, 59–67

minimization/magnification, 113
minorities, 56
   and Fear Of Not Making It, 62–63
Mintz, Steven, 13, 14
Misérables, Les (Hugo), 208
monoamine oxidase inhibitors
    (MAOs), 165
mood:
   phases of, disorders vs., 78
   tips to improve, 255

NASA, 178
National Alliance on Mental Illness
    (NAMI), 57, 76, 80, 179, 2228
National Institute of Mental Health,
    150, 192
National Institute on Alcohol Abuse
    and Alcoholism (NIAA), 125,
    137
National Institute on Drug Abuse, 142
National Sexual Violence Resource
    Center, 131
New Yorker, 133
New York Times, 6, 133

On Speed (Rasmussen), 132
open mindset/help-seeking, 33,
    49–51
optimism, 227
ownership of one's actions
    (conscientiousness), 33–34

pain, 158–59
panic, 12
parent bouncer events, 23
*Parent Handbook for Talking with
    College Students About
    Alcohol, A* (Turrisi), 137, 141
parenting, 21
   authoritarian, 87–88
   authoritative, 87
   changing style of, 88–91

differing styles between partners,
    219–22
disengaged, 88
emotionally focused, 89–90
golden rules of, 242
helicopter, 24
historical trends in, 13–14
over-parenting, 24
permissive, 87–89
responsive, 174
styles of, 87–88, 174
parents, 22–30
acceptance and, 230–31
as mental health caregivers,
    210–12, 217–19, 229; *see also*
    boomerang kids
emotional overinvolvement of,
    214, 215
emotional reactions of, 98–100
investment in child, 19–22, 24–25
negativity and, 90–91
and parent-child deal, 238–39
readiness of, 74
safe spaces and, 57, 86
self-care for, 229
social support net for, 228–29
steps for repairing relationship
    between, 223–24
stress between, 219–25
suggestions for helping your child,
    176
Ulysses contract between child
    and, 234, 243–46
and young adults returning home,
    see boomerang kids
Pediatrics, 187
perfectionism, 111, 113
   destructive, 16, 22, 24, 47–48,
    153–54, 176
persona management, 17, 40–41
Pew Research Center, 20
phobia, 152
Piltch, Steve, 42
positive remarks and regard, 215
Power of Hope, The (Scioli), 227

Prevatt, Frances, 108–9
Price, Vincent, 268
privacy concerns and laws, 74–76, 274–76, 279–80
    FERPA, 11, 75, 177, 195, 264
    HIPAA, 11, 73, 74–75, 177, 180, 194, 195, 264, 274, 280
privileged backgrounds, 60–61
procrastination, 110–14
Procrastination Equation, The (Steel), 110
procrastivity, 112
PTSD, 12
purpose, from boredom, 253–54

racism, 56
Radical Acceptance (Brach), 48–49
Ramsay, Russ, 112
rape and sexual assault, 130, 131, 141, 264
Rasmussen, Nicolas, 132
readiness, 25–27, 31
    parental, 74
    see also social/emotional maturity
Recession of 2008, 18, 59, 208
recovery and relaunch, 233–61
    accountability and, 258–59
    bad habits and, 256–58
    and boredom leading to purpose, 253–54
    coping skills and, 238, 254
    empathy and structure in, 250–53
    hope in, 249–50
    medications in, *see* medications
    self-acceptance and, 259–60
    and trap of family accommodations, 236–38, 251
    and trap of protection, 235–36
    Ulysses contract and, 234, 243–46
resilience, 31, 44, 283
risky behavior, 22, 24, 27, 33, 46, 166
    brain and, 119, 121–24
Ritalin, 105
Robinson, Marilynne, 20

Rostain, Anthony, 5, 61–62
Rush, Maureen, 278–79

safe spaces, 56–57
    in the family, 57, 86
safety net, 195, 262–84
Satow, Donna and Phil, 266
Schwartz, Victor, 267–68, 282
Science Leadership Academy (SLA), 65
Scioli, Anthony, 227
Seaman, Barrett, 119
selective serotonin reuptake inhibitors (SSRIs), 157, 165
self:
    branding of, 16–18
    theoretical, 234
self-acceptance, 33, 47–49, 61, 259–60
self-awareness, 26
self-care for parents, 229
self-control, 33, 41–43, 44
self-esteem, 47, 61
self-help for students, 177
self-management, 33, 35–37
self-regulation, 26–27, 105
Selingo, Jeffrey, 70
sexism, 56
sexual assault, 130, 131, 141, 264
Shakespeare, William, 14
Shapiro, Doug, 59
Shipley School, 42, 44
Slavin, Stuart, 16
sleep, 202
    bedtime routine, 255
smartphones, 17, 25, 38
    ways to overhaul use of, 39
Snapchat, 38
social anxiety, 38, 67, 69
    signs of, 152
social/emotional maturity, 31–51
    conscientiousness, 33–34
    grit, 33, 43–46, 62
    interpersonal skills, 33, 37–41
    open mindset/help-seeking, 33, 49–51

social/emotional maturity
(*continued*)
  risk management, 33, 46
  self-acceptance, 33, 47–49
  self-control, 33, 41–43, 44
  self-management, 33, 35–37
social identities, 56
social-interactional difficulties, 38
social isolation and loneliness,
    55–56, 86, 190, 197, 239, 265
social media, 17, 25, 38, 40–41, 166
social readiness, 25–26
social relationships, 52, 53, 54–59,
    197–98
  interpersonal skills and, 33, 37–41
socioeconomic strata (SES), 60–61,
    63, 64
sororities, 128, 129
Steel, Piers, 110
Steinberg, Laurence, 123–24
Stevens–Johnson syndrome, 254–56
stimulant drugs, 132–33, 135
stress, 6–7, 149, 283
  educational institutions as cause
    of, 15–16
  financial, 64–66
  mental health and, 11–13
stress-related disorders, occurrence
    by gender, 12
structure, blending empathy with,
    250–53
study habits, 255–56
substance use and abuse (substance
    use disorder; SUD), 9, 12, 27,
    46, 121, 122, 125–48, 265
  addiction, 134–36, 191
  brain and, 133–34
  DSM-5 criteria for, 135
  prescription drugs, 125, 132–33
  prevention of, 136–42
  Stages of Change Model and, 145–46
  talking to child about, 137–42
  warning signs of, 136
  see also alcohol; marijuana

support network, 197, 228–29
success, 26
suicide, 23, 27, 47, 56, 61, 67, 268, 271,
    280
  rates of, 191
  risk factors for, 190–93, 241
  social media and, 17
  statistics on, 8
support groups, 81, 86

Takacs, Christopher, 126–27
Task Force on Student Psychological
    Health and Welfare, 47,
    268–70
therapists, 76–77
There Is Life After College (Selingo), 70
THRIVE, 61, 66
Time, 132
Tolkien, J. R. R., 70
transfer students, 59, 166
Turrisi, Robert, 137, 141
Twitter, 38
two-person rule for decisions, 211

Ulysses contract, 234, 243–46
University of Pennsylvania, 47–48,
    268–70, 272, 278–79, 281–82

venlafaxine, 183–85, 254
violence, and mental illness, 79

warmth, 215
well child, 225–26
Winter's Tale, The (Shakespeare), 14

Yeager, David, 57, 63

Zimmerman, Jonathan, 31, 270